ZEN IN AMERICA

ROBERT AITKEN

JAKUSHO KWONG

BERNARD GLASSMAN

MAURINE STUART

RICHARD BAKER

ZEN IN AMERICA

Five Teachers and the Search
for an American Buddhism

by Helen Tworkov

KODANSHA INTERNATIONAL
New York • Tokyo • London

Kodansha America, Inc.
114 Fifth Avenue, New York, New York 10011, U.S.A.

Kodansha International Ltd.
17-14 Otowa 1-chome, Bunkyo-ku, Tokyo 112, Japan

Published in 1994 by Kodansha America, Inc.
This is a Kodansha Globe book.

Printed in the United States of America

94 95 96 97 98 99 7 6 5 4 3 2 1

Library of Congress Cataloging-in-Publication Data

Tworkov, Helen.
Zen in America ; five teachers and the search for an American
Buddhism / by Helen Tworkov.
p.   cm.—(Kodansha globe)
Includes index.
ISBN 1-56836-030-4
1. Priests, Zen—United States—Biography.   I. Title.
II. Series.
BQ9298.T89   1994
294.3'927'092273—dc20
[B]   94-2488
CIP

Text design by David Bullen

The cover was printed by Phoenix Color Corporation,
Hagerstown, Maryland

Printed and bound by Arcata Graphics, Fairfield, Pennsylvania

CONTENTS

FOREWORD

I studied Zen for twelve years with a Japanese Zen master who lived in Minneapolis, Minnesota. Evidently, for a Japanese person, English can be hard to learn. Katagiri Roshi, I think, could understand it almost fluently, but he had trouble speaking it. Many times, I saw him in his study, looking up words in a big Webster's dictionary. I admired his effort and determination. He very much wanted to transmit the Buddha Dharma to his American students. In his lectures, he would have one point he really hoped to get across. He would repeat that phrase or word over and over, giving it great emphasis. Often, sitting in the zendo, listening, I was not sure what that phrase or word was— I couldn't understand his English.

I remember during one seven-day sesshin in the fall that he talked a lot about _____ . We were on silence, so I couldn't ask fellow students what the word was. I decided he was saying "beans." "You count the beans. You hold them in your hand." I had been at Minnesota Zen Center two years by that time. "Beans" didn't quite make sense, but then that's the way Zen was for me anyway—none of it quite made sense.

The day after the sesshin, I was eating breakfast with my husband. He said, "Beads, you know, prayer beads."

Oh, I nodded. Beads. I'd been imagining pinto beans.

Katagiri was also associated with the San Francisco Zen Center. He often taught there. The last time he spoke at Green Gulch (the San Francisco Zen Center farm), the word in his lecture that he kept repeating with great joy and enthusiasm was one that, again, no one was sure of. After his talk, there was a tea. Several old Zen students sitting together mused on what the word could be.

A well-known businessman, who was also a Zen student, joined the group. "Oh, I know the word. It was obvious. Roshi was saying 'economic success,'" he told his fellow Zennists triumphantly.

Everyone nodded and tried to piece the lecture together with that new information. "The whole world depends on *economic success*." Hmmm, Katagiri had certainly learned American ways.

They found out later that Roshi was not saying "economic success" but "egolessness." That was his last lecture at Green Gulch. Soon after he returned to Minnesota and found out he had cancer. After a year and a half of treatment, he died in March, 1990. This mix-up of "economic success" and "egolessness" is part of the legacy left to American Zen students. It is a very tricky business to transform Zen from one culture to another.

Zen in America is about this transformation. The five Zen teachers interviewed here all studied directly with a Japanese Zen master. Two of them—Richard Baker and Jakusho Kwong—studied with Shunryu Suzuki, the same San Francisco-based Zen master with whom Katagiri Roshi was closely associated.

I loved Katagiri Roshi very much, but he was always exotic to me—I never thought I could actually be like him. No matter how hard I practiced, Buddha nature was across the sea. If a moment of it came over to visit in the form of my great teacher, it was still all too wonderful and foreign. Yet the Americans in this book made the transformation, turned the foreign native and accomplished the cultural transfer I thought was impossible. They are some of the first seeds of American Zen.

When I first read this book in 1989, I loved it. Reading about these Americans, these dharma heirs—Robert Aitken, Jakusho Kwong, Bernard Glassman, Maurine Stuart, and Richard Baker—opened me to the possibilities of how Americans can manifest Zen. Like our culture, their roots are widespread and varied: Bernard Glassman is a New Yorker, Maurine Stuart a woman and a concert pianist, Jakusho Kwong a Chinese-

American. If it was possible for these Americans, couldn't it be possible for me too? Of course! I can be who I am. We don't become better; we become ourselves.

I have an image. It is in Medford, Massachusetts, a small town right outside of Boston, with rows of duplex houses lined up next to each other. It is predominantly an Italian-American neighborhood, with lots of good pizzerias. They even sell it by the slice.

I visited a friend there in the fall and sat on her cement stoop in early evening, watching a woman walk by, her black small dog on a chain. In the yard were two rose bushes like none I had ever seen before. They were each at least nine feet tall, standing on their own and full of large pink roses. Those roses were the most beautiful I had ever seen. Fat and multipetaled, they were a pink that moved over into lavender and violet, and at the stem the petal was a bright yellow. And the most amazing thing of all, the flower did not merely open, each petal *curled* out from itself to give the whole bloom a feeling of exquisite lushness.

These holy, glorious flowers were growing on a street called College Avenue. If you followed the street all the way down, it led to Tufts University. Coincidentally, Tufts was the school Katagiri's youngest son, Eyjo, went to after he graduated from high school. Katagiri had even visited him there. I realized my Zen teacher had passed through these same streets.

I woke early the next morning, clipped at least a dozen of those roses and brought them to the altar at the Cambridge Buddhist Association. Maurine Stuart, the former teacher there, had died of cancer in 1990, five days before Katagiri. I was just beginning sesshin with another American Zen teacher. I settled on my zafu and all the way across the room I could smell the perfume of those fat, unfolding American blossoms. It hit me that the dharma is everywhere.

I admire each of the teachers in this book. It has taken dedication, discipline, great heart, and a wild longing for each of them to become who they are. Reading this book encourages me that Zen can become American and that even I—feminist, writer, Jew from Brooklyn—can attain its terrific taste.

I also applaud Helen Tworkov, the author, for her research and her clear, thorough, and generous writing. It is obvious that her deep commitment enabled her to integrate this material into one rich volume.

I invite readers of this book to witness the unfolding of five unique Zen teachers rooted in America.

—NATALIE GOLDBERG

ACKNOWLEDGMENTS

When I started off I knew little about how much help I would need and even less about how much help would be forthcoming. In my travels to various Zen centers I was assisted by teachers, guestmasters, cooks, librarians, secretaries, by students who wanted to talk and those who preferred not to. There have been few encounters these past years that have not in ways great and small contributed to this book. My gratitude extends to friends, family, and neighbors in New York and Nova Scotia, and in particular to Anne Aitken, Gary Clevidence, Rick Fields, Norman and Kathy Fischer, Laura Kwong, Lou Nordstrom, Toinette Lippe, to Wally Tworkov for early encouragement, to Pema Chödren for silent blessings, and to the staff of North Point Press for their support and assistance. I owe special thanks to Nancy Baker, Sheila LaFarge, Larry Shainberg, and Rudy Wurlitzer. More valuable than their editorial help was a persistent faith in this book that held me to it during those times when my own was strained.

In each case the teachers I have written about were completely generous with their time and patience, and their cooperation extended far beyond the requirements of this book. Their understanding of the personal questioning that beleaguered my attempts at objectivity has given me far more than I can return in these pages. In both obvious and subtle ways I owe this book to them. I have done my best to tell their stories, but inevitably they have become my stories. Where discrepancies exist, the responsibility is mine alone.

Much of this work went on at the Zen Community of New York where I have been studying with Bernard Glassman. I am indebted to the membership of this community for standing by my efforts while bearing the brunt of my preoccupations. Once I started this book, Glassman Sensei thoroughly encouraged its completion. But when I first discussed the idea with him, he listened and said nothing. I wish to express my gratitude to him for his guidance in Zen studies and for the wisdom and compassion of that very active response.

ZEN IN
AMERICA

INTRODUCTION

"The land of the white barbarians is beneath the dignity of a Zen master," argued Soyen Shaku's monks when Soyen was invited to the World's Parliament of Religions in Chicago in 1893. But the Japanese abbot already had high expectations for the New World. Disregarding the objections of his monks, Soyen Shaku (1859–1919) became the first Zen priest to visit the United States. In Chicago he represented Zen Buddhism with diplomatic discretion. Privately, however, Soyen felt that Zen in Japan had grown impoverished, sapped of true spiritual inquiry. On Soyen's horizon, the future of Zen rested with the barbarians in the West.

In less than a hundred years the United States produced its own generation of Zen teachers, attesting to Soyen's foresight. But the contradictions suggested by Soyen's monks still had to be overcome. Japanese Zen first struck many Americans as indeed too dignified. Compared with casual American behavior, it appeared mannered in the style of aesthetes. From ceremonial tea parties to rigid class hierarchies, things Japanese appeared too close to the old British order that Americans had once rejected. Zen might appeal, as it in fact did, to the intelligentsia, to artists, and to refined New Englanders influenced by the Transcendentalists, but the precise formalities of ancient Japanese customs, all of which are reflected in Japanese Zen, inhibited the possibilities for establishing Zen roots in the United States.

Despite these obstacles, the relative emptiness of the American cultural landscape continued to attract Japanese Zen masters. By the early 1960s Japanese teachers began developing Zen centers in the United States. Although none of these urban centers resembled the mountain monasteries of Japan, their archetype for Zen training—from the environment to interior design, utensils, dress, and personal demeanor—remained firmly rooted on the other side of the Pacific. Then in just one generation, with the passing of Zen from Japanese to American teachers, there was a dramatic change in the accepted look of Zen. By the mid-1970s, converted barns were legitimate meditation halls, scrambled eggs were more common than pickled seaweed for breakfast and most important, Zen teachers spoke English. Only with these obvious transitions did the more profound differences emerge. With the Americanization of Zen, the authority of Japanese tradition began losing ground to the American insistence on questioning tradition. Zen may have made itself at home in the United States, but the process of adaptation has not been easy. At the same time, these abrasions have sparked an inquisitive approach to the ancient teachings that has infused Zen in America with a vitality that has all but been lost in Japan.

When Japanese Zen first came to the United States it was not, as it first appeared, in a tidy package that accurately reflected the larger historical picture of established ideals. It was introduced to the United States by mystical pragmatists and creative abbots who had challenged and changed the Zen system as it was known in Japan. Like that of virtually all the Japanese masters who influenced the course of Zen in the United States, Soyen Shaku's religious training incorporated elements contrary to the monastic conventions of his day. Soyen received his training as a young monk at Engakuji, a prestigious monastery in Kamakura which he later served as abbot. His teacher, Kosen, was the first in Japanese history to combine academic studies with monastic training, thus releasing Zen from its hermetic heritage and paving the way for its move to the West.

Kosen arranged for Soyen's modern education at Keio University, established in 1866 for the study of Western culture—and then sent him to India to study the ancient language of Sanskrit. From there Soyen traveled south to Sri Lanka, where the Theravadin Buddhist monks still followed the mendicant life of the historical Buddha, Gautama Siddhartha Shakyamuni, and his disciples. Soyen wrote to Kosen: "The main purpose for coming to Ceylon is to hide myself from the world of name and fame. Throughout the history of Zen, there have been many teachers who have mingled with beggars, laborers, farmers for the same reason—to hide themselves. I am simply trying to follow their examples in a way that is appropriate to life in the nineteenth century."

By the time Soyen had received his training from Kosen toward the end of the nineteenth century, Zen monasteries had become increasingly co-opted by a wealthy and influential priesthood. While this fortified the religious bureaucracy, the proliferation of temples turned the monasteries into schools for careerists. The quest for temple property and a complaisant life within the priesthood corroded spiritual aspiration. To counter this, Kosen, in addition to providing a secular education for his more astute monks, opened the temple gates to lay students. With their career interests elsewhere, they came to study Zen with no professional investment. This heretical move extended beyond the monastery. In Tokyo, Kosen started a meditation group for lay students called *Ryomokyo Kai*—the Association for the Abandonment of the Concepts of Objectivity and Subjectivity.

Kosen's innovations paid more attention to the spirit of Zen than to the accepted conventions of monasticism, and no one's vision was more instrumental for Zen's transmission to the West than his. For the first half of the twentieth century, Zen activity in the United States was carried out by his lineage alone. Its influence continued through Soyen Shaku's two messengers to the West: the world-famous D. T. Suzuki (1869–1966), who became the popularized voice of Zen, and the little-known Zen saint and monk Nyogen Senzaki (1876–1958).

By orthodox standards neither Senzaki nor Suzuki qualified as a "lineage holder," since neither received formal "dharma transmission," the master's seal of approval to transmit the Zen teachings. This seal authorizes one to be a Zen teacher of the dharma, the Buddhist teachings. "Teaching" and "transmitting" have been used interchangeably, but a distinction is sometimes made between the two terms in an attempt to separate the Western concept of teacher as one who passes information and knowledge from the Zen concept of one who *embodies* the teachings and "transmits" nothing more or less than his own quality of being. In dharma transmission, a master acknowledges a disciple's capacity to "succeed" him in terms of spiritual understanding. The student becomes the teacher's embodiment of Buddhism. In addition, since each dharma heir has theoretically attained his master's understanding, an intimate exchange between master and disciple brings the disciple into direct contact with the realization of Shakyamuni Buddha. Technically, Senzaki and Suzuki represent a break rather than a continuity in Kosen's lineage. They have no place on Zen lineage charts, which list each successive generation of dharma heirs from Shakyamuni Buddha to the present. But whether the transmission of Zen teachings is formally acknowledged, as it was between Kosen and Soyen Shaku, or passed on with no legal seals, as it was from Soyen Shaku to Senzaki and Suzuki, the essence of the transmission system is face-to-face intimacy between master and disciple. Ironically, their lack of pedigree made Senzaki and Suzuki perfect first emissaries to the United States, itself a product of disrupted lineages.

Availing himself of Kosen's program for lay students, D. T. Suzuki lived at Engakuji while attending university. Because he had studied English, he was asked to write the abbot's acceptance letter to the 1893 conference in Chicago. Suzuki, the word-magician of Zen, used language to point the way of no language; to audiences in New York and London he talked about the futility of talk and explained the inadequacy of explanation. For readers, he was the archphilosopher of Zen. For those who knew him, however, his presence authenticated his message. Embodying Zen in the manner of masters, he eliminated the gap between preaching and practicing, and the common failure to achieve this in the West, among clergy or intellectuals, made his presence all the more remarkable. A prolific writer, he attracted some of the most creative thinkers of this century—John Cage, Erich Fromm, Karen Horney, Aldous Huxley, C. G. Jung, Thomas Merton, Arnold Toynbee— and it was mainly through their interest, as well as through the impressions of poets and writers like Allen Ginsberg, Jack Kerouac, and Alan Watts that Zen entered the American landscape. Gary Snyder, the best known of the American poets associated with Zen, also came under Suzuki's influence, and in 1955 he left San Francisco's Beat scene for Daitokuji, a Rinzai monastery in Kyoto.

Through his books, Suzuki set the stage for Zen training in the United States. He suggested possibilities for self-realization that lay beyond the psychological investigations familiar to Westerners, but he did not dishearten his enthusiastic audience with alien rituals and strenuous meditation postures. Missing from his work are comprehensive descriptions of Zen's precise methodology. These methods have been standardized by Japanese customs, whereas Suzuki's concern was to alleviate cultural impositions for his Western readers.

What he emphasized most was the capacity of the mind to attain enlightenment. His own dharma name, Diasetsu, or "Great Stupidity," implies a mind emptied of preconceptions and free, therefore, to experience life "as it is." Emptying the discursive mind is the focus of *zazen*, or "sitting meditation," the foundation of Zen training. The basic radicalism of Zen lies in its insistence on the individual experience of emptying the mind of all personal and cultural descriptions. Dissolving discursive thoughts and stilling the habitual chatter of what Buddhists call "the monkey mind" offer therapeutic benefits. But as a spiritual discipline, zazen not only tames the monkey mind, it channels the religious impulse to surrender the discrete ego-bound mind to the infinity of "skylike" mind.

Suzuki translated the Chinese characters for "skylike" into English as "emptiness." Skylike emptiness implies a boundless state of unity through time and space in which the concepts of objectivity and subjectivity are abandoned. Skylike is so empty, it can receive absolutely everything; it is—to use another translation—"all-encompassing mind." Emptiness is now thoroughly integrated into the English terminology of Zen, but it has generated misconceptions of Zen as a philosophy of nihilism. Yet one empties the small mind not to extinguish one's humanity but to uncover its deepest levels. Releasing what already exists is the process of Zen practice, and it explicitly primes spiritual awakening.

Between the philosophical inquiries spawned by Suzuki and the formal Zen training that soon followed, Suzuki's recurrent references to enlightenment and emptiness led to an unusual chapter in the history of Zen. From the 1930s to the 1950s, Zen traveled a fairly narrow channel in the United States from a recognizable intelligentsia to the avant-garde underground. With the emergence of the Beat generation in the fifties, the emptiness of Zen became a critical reference for a new social iconography. Formal Zen practice was correctly identified with traditional monasticism. But in Beat Zen, form was "square." Only the romance of emptiness was hip. For the Beats all institutions, including those of religion, were rejected for categorically assaulting one's spirituality. The Beats championed the emptiness of Zen as they had American space, an unexplored territory where the past wasn't acknowledged and the future was always in the present. The freedom of mind taught by the Buddhists was confused with freedom from social convention. Life beyond reality, as it was known, was suddenly the only life worth living. Forays into drug-induced enlightenment states did not resemble traditional Zen; but they were often called Zen, and their effect changed America. Zen practice centers eventually transformed much of this fashionable intoxication, but the popularization of Zen lunacy has continued to evoke a faddist curiosity that the practice itself contradicts.

With its focus elsewhere, Suzuki's presentation of Zen delayed the question of how much the methodology should be Japanese—or could be. Japanese monasticism has reflected the same respect for authority, hierarchy, ritual, and circumscribed social behavior that informs all of Japanese life—the very qualities Americans are apt to mistrust most. To what extent the traditions of Zen training are culture-bound and to what extent they uphold the integrity of Zen remains an open question.

Suzuki's dharma brother, Nyogen Senzaki, was the first Zen teacher to suggest to Americans that in addition to dissolving habitual patterns of identification in terms of kinship, status, occupation, sex, religion, age, and so on, ultimately the Zen adept has to let go of ideas of Zen, too. In Buddhist teachings, this dissolution of form into emptiness reawakens the state of original enlightenment. Zen teachings can be used for guidance, but Senzaki made it clear that as concepts, they too have no intrinsic value. The first Zen teacher to take up permanent residence in the United States, Senzaki, like Suzuki, was careful not to introduce too much too soon.

Born in Siberia in 1876, the infant Senzaki was found by a Japanese monk at the side of his mother's frozen body. He came under the care of a Soto priest but was schooled as well in the Shingon faith of his foster father, who also taught him the Chinese classics. Eventually, ill with tuberculosis, he arrived at Engaku Temple to study with Soyen Shaku; during this five-year period of Zen training he also educated himself in Western philosophy. Then, in a move as divergent as his master's journey to Sri Lanka, Senzaki left the temple to start a nursery school in Hokkaido, Japan's desolate northern island. Inspired by the German philosopher Friedrich Froebel, he named the school *Mentogarten*—a place free of any systematized dogma, where everyone could be both mentor and disciple.

In 1905, twelve years after the World's Parliament conference in Chicago, Soyen returned to the United States at the invitation of Mr. and Mrs. Alexander Russell of San Francisco, a wealthy and adventurous couple who had met the abbot in Japan. Senzaki joined Soyen, theoretically to raise funds for his school. But Senzaki had been disgusted with the Japanese Zen establishment and its complicity with the Imperial rule. He had compared Buddhist priests to businessmen, their temples to chain stores, and reviled their common pursuit of money, power, and women. Shortly before arriving in California, Senzaki had spoken out against the militant nationalism that had fomented the Russo-Japanese War and that the Zen monasteries had supported with as much patriotic fervor as the public sector. Exactly what happened between Senzaki and Soyen no one knows. Robert Aitken Roshi, the American Zen teacher who studied with Senzaki in Los Angeles in the 1950s, suspects that although Soyen would never sever ties with a disciple over political attitudes, he did nonetheless disapprove of Senzaki's denouncements. It may be that Soyen asked Senzaki to come to the United States. If this is so, whether it was an act of punishment or protection remains one of several mysteries surrounding Senzaki's relationship with his master.

After working as a houseboy for the Russells, Senzaki made his way alone in California with strict instructions from Soyen not to teach for twenty years. Neither of them ever publicly discussed the intent of this twenty-year ban. Most likely Senzaki had not completed his studies, and Aitken suggests that this stiff sentencing to silence was Soyen's means of instilling, in his own absence, the personal discipline necessary for teaching. As he saw Senzaki off to a Japanese hotel, Soyen told him: "This may be better for you than being my attendant monk. Just face the great city and see whether it conquers you or you conquer it." This was their last meeting.

But whereas Sri Lanka had provided Soyen Shaku with a well-worn path closest to the bones of Buddha, California in 1905 was a Zen monk's tabula rasa, and it tested Senzaki's capacity to invent form from nothingness. He wrote of his isolation and loneliness, of hours spent in public libraries, and of solitary zazen in city parks. For Senzaki the United States was always "this strange land." With little command of English and no professional skills, he worked as a dishwasher, houseboy, laundryman, clerk, manager, and, briefly, part owner of a Japanese hotel. In 1925, the prescribed twenty years over, he began renting public halls in San Francisco with money saved from his scanty wages. In these "floating zendos," as he called them, he talked alternately in English and Japanese. In 1931 Senzaki moved to Los Angeles and opened his Mentogarten Zendo in the modest rooms of his hotel residence in Little Tokyo. There he and his students did zazen on metal folding chairs that he had purchased secondhand from a funeral parlor; sitting cross-legged on the floor in the customary meditation posture struck him as a most un-American activity.

With Senzaki's help, Americans began to learn that although Zen training may tame the mind, it does not necessarily lead to mystical awakening;

but that if the mind can get quiet enough, something sacred will be revealed. The experienced Zen master makes this possibility known by the quality of his own presence. Senzaki assured Americans new to Zen that allowing the unknown to consume the habitual descriptions of reality is the ultimate act of sanity, not a psychotic plunge. Compared to his monastic education under Soyen Shaku, Senzaki's methods were limited. But the ability to let go of self-centered descriptions does not depend on methodology. Senzaki conveyed that while letting go approximates dying, Zen has to do with living. He said of himself that he was "like a mushroom," with no roots, no seeds, no flowers. He wished, at the end, to be blown away like dust. He had none of the quixotic flash of Jack Kerouac or Alan Watts, who by the time of Senzaki's death in Los Angeles in 1958 were generating the Zen boom in San Francisco. He offered Zen training, however rudimentary, when there was little interest in it. He was too "square" for Beat Zen and the Beats had no use for him. "I have neither an aggressive spirit of propaganda," he said, "nor an attractive personality to draw crowds." Purity of heart was his special legacy; with time, it has grown more important.

His isolated and inconspicuous life as a passionate Zen monk in a spiritual wilderness has endeared Senzaki to a subsequent generation of American Zen students. A man of no rank, he disregarded robes and religious titles and wanted only to be, as he put it, "a happy Jap in the streets." Yet despite his mushroom metaphor and the fact that he left no dharma heirs, Senzaki transmitted his realization through two pivotal teachers: Nakagawa Soen (1907–1984), who came to the United States through Senzaki, and Haku'un Yasutani (1885–1973), who came through Nakagawa Soen. These two teachers were trained in the two main schools of Japanese Zen: Rinzai and Soto.

The Rinzai school developed from the teaching style of Rinzai Gigen, of ninth-century China. In his efforts to rid his disciples of their pious idolatry and futile wanderings, he lashed out with nonrational words and gestures and asked questions that stumped the intellect. These encounters evolved into *koan* study. Koans such as "What is the sound of one hand clapping?" and "What was your original face before you were born?" have entered the American vernacular as caricatured examples of Zen at its most enigmatic. Yet while koans are popularly known as "paradoxical questions," they are used to push the logical mind into a realm where no paradox exists.

The Soto school in Japan derived from Eihei Dogen Zenji (1200–1253). Dogen's radical conclusion undercut the rewards of materialistic piety. Zen practice, he said, was not a vehicle for enlightenment but was itself an expression of enlightenment. Undermining the prevalent concept of stages of practice leading to the great liberation, Dogen spoke of the activity of "practice-enlightenment." For him the deliberate striving toward a future goal diffused into the contemplative quality of concentrated stillness in the midst of everyday activity. The Soto way of "gradual awakening" contrasts with the Rinzai emphasis on "sudden enlightenment." According to Soto teachings, one takes a long, slow walk through the morning dew to realize the Buddhist ideal of getting thoroughly soaked by the rains of wisdom. The atmospheric conditions of Rinzai come closer to those of a flash flood.

The Rinzai master Nakagawa Soen's contact with the United States began in 1934 when Senzaki read his poems in a Japanese magazine and initiated a correspondence that lasted for fifteen years before the two men met. Soen completed his university studies in Western and Japanese literature prior to becoming a monk on his twenty-fourth birthday. But like Senzaki, he resisted monastic confinement and divided his time between his temple at the base of Dai Bosatsu mountain and a hermitage on top of the mountain that faced Mount Fuji. When he was at the hermitage, he rose each morning to make prostrations to the sun, then scavenged for berries and edible plants, wrote haiku, and sat full-lotus in the moonlight.

Senzaki collected donations from his students to bring Nakagawa Soen to America. In July 1941 he wrote to the United States consulate general in Tokyo: "Please visa the passport of my Brother monk, Soen Nakagawa." Five months later, the Japanese bombed Pearl Harbor. At the time, Soen was at Ryutaku Temple at the base of Mount Fuji. He remained there throughout the war while Senzaki was interned in Wyoming at the Heart Mountain relocation camp for Japanese-Americans. Since Buddhism had spread east from India to China, and east again to Japan, and then to the United States, Senzaki wondered if the wartime roundup of Japanese-Americans from the Pacific Coast to inland camps was not, in fact, supporting the "eastbound tendency of the teachings." Making the most of adverse circumstances, he called Heart Mountain "The Mountain of Compassion" and named the zendo he started "The Meditation Hall of the Eastbound Teaching." Throughout the war, on the twenty-first day of each month, called Dai Bosatsu Day in Japan, Nyogen Senzaki and Nakagawa Soen, with palms together in the traditional gesture of greeting and respect, bowed to each other, dissolving the Pacific Ocean between them.

Nakagawa Soen Roshi's first visit to the United States was in 1949. He arrived in San Francisco on April 8th, Shakyamuni Buddha's birthday by Japanese calculations. At a reception at the Theosophical Society library he told the story of Nangaku, the Chinese Zen master, who was asked by the Sixth Patriarch, Hui Nêng, "Who are you?" According to Soen Roshi, "Nangaku was dumbfounded and could not answer. Nowadays, there is no one capable of being dumbfounded like Nangaku. Everyone knows everything and can answer any question."

His audience was not dumbfounded like Nangaku. Still, they were amazed by this tiny Japanese monk, who then reminded them that it was the two hundredth birthday of Wolfgang von Goethe. He went on to quote Faust, who lamented that his studies of philosophy, medicine, jurisprudence, and theology had made him "no wiser than before," and who concluded, "that we in truth can nothing know."

"This 'we in truth can nothing know,' or 'I don't know anything,'" explained Soen Roshi, "is exactly the point of Zen. We monks apply ourselves day after day, year after year, to the study of the 'Unthinkable.'"

Soen Roshi had acquired a reputation in Japan for tolerating the casual interest in Zen of Western students. Gentle and mischievous, he also acquired a more lasting reputation for eccentric behavior. Under his direction, retreats in New York ended with Beethoven symphonies. Occasionally he appeared wearing women's jewelry or masks. Once he arranged to have students bow at the doorway of his interview room before they could see that a pumpkin had been placed on the master's cushion.

In 1962 Soen Roshi canceled an American tour because of his mother's illness and arranged for Haku'un Yasutani to replace him. Three years later, Yasutani Roshi became widely known to Americans through *The Three Pillars of Zen*, compiled and edited by Philip Kapleau Roshi. The first Western publication to concentrate on Zen training, the book opens with Yasutani Roshi's lectures to beginning students. These were derived from Yasutani's master, Dai'un Harada Roshi (1871–1961), long considered the regenerative force of Soto Zen in this century.

In an attempt to revitalize Zen in an age of degeneration, Harada Roshi devised introductory talks to inspire the modern mind. Students in the West take this format for granted, but it was heterodox in Japan, and Harada was sharply criticized by his conservative peers. There the traditional training of a novice monk was deliberately devoid of verbal instruction. Paying attention, listening, and what Zen calls "being mindful" were both methods and targets of practice. Even more disturbing to Soto officials was Harada's incorporation of Rinzai koan study, effectively used to shake out the complacency that can creep into the Soto way of "just sitting."

Yasutani studied with Harada on the rugged coast of Japan's inland sea for twenty years, receiving at the age of fifty-eight his master's approval to teach. Shunning the Zen establishment, Yasutani then removed himself to a small rural temple, Taiheiji, in the outskirts of Tokyo, where students lived in their own residences and continued their regular employment. At Taiheiji he founded the *Sanbo Kyodan*—the Order of the Three Treasures—an organization that attributed to lay students the kind of worthy intention Zen orthodoxy had reserved for monastics.

Yasutani used combative tactics in the zendo that reflected the Rinzai methods incorporated by Harada into Soto training and were further intensified by the limited time allocated for lay practice. He made no concessions to Americans new to Zen, running his zendo in the militaristic style associated with Japanese samurai. Exhorting retreatants to break the barriers of conceptual thought, Yasutani projected a battlefield that pitted the forces of ignorance against the forces of enlightenment and urged his troops to "attack the enemy." When testing students individually, however, he probed, questioned, and analyzed every nuance of an answer, disabusing anyone of the notion that a Zen master could not hold his own in Western dialectics.

In Japan the association of Zen with the samurai tradition sanctioned it as a masculine ideal, but in the United States in the early sixties the nonaggressive activity of zazen initially attracted mostly women. While intellectuals, both male and female, approved of reading about Zen, for the time being American men were not to be found sitting still on a cushion apparently doing nothing. What appealed to many women was the affiliation between Zen and the refined arts of calligraphy, ceramics, tea ceremony, and flower arranging. And the style of Zen training did nothing to dispel this. There is nothing gaudy about Zen meditation halls. Notoriously neat and clean, they feature simple altars with few images; the incense is not overpowering and the flower offerings are limited to one or two elegant arrangements. Of all the Asian disciplines to come to the United States, Zen alone augmented the Anglo-Protestant legacy of aesthetic classicism and suggested a gentility and aristocratic grace that affirmed ancestral tastes. This aesthetic validation was more apparent on the East Coast, which remained largely unfamiliar with the racial prejudice that had plagued Oriental laborers in California. New England had long enjoyed an influx of Oriental art objects imported through the Boston-based East India Trade industry; and influenced by the Transcendentalists as well as the Unitarians, educated people in the Northeast were generally familiar with numerous Oriental texts in translation.

For a segment of New England's sophisticated upper class, and particularly for women, Zen aesthetics legitimized an attraction to Zen practice. Not only did this influential elite gain approval for Zen on a larger scale, but by the mid-1960s it was providing solid financial patronage for some teachers. Yet in the process of stimulating a favorable climate for Zen in the United States, the meeting between the puritan legacy and Japanese Zen aesthetics also kindled some tenacious misunderstandings. Puritan simplicity evolved from moral, not artistic, discrimination. The association between refinement and moral rectitude is American, not Japanese. Aesthetic austerity has differed widely in these two cultures. In Japan it was cultivated for sensual pleasure; in the United States it was intended to retard sensuality and, specifically, sexual response, the asceticism of the Shakers being an extreme example. Japan is not a puritanical culture, and so it is ironic that the first patrons of Japanese Zen in the United States were the direct heirs of puritan values.

When American definitions of morality are applied to Zen training as measures of approval or censure, a kind of cultural gridlock occurs in which the integrity of both systems remains obscured. This conflict, which has yet to be resolved, was not addressed directly until 1983, when at Zen centers in Los Angeles and San Francisco the moral behavior of the teachers was openly questioned by students and publicly documented. The public charges, similar to private allegations leveled at other Zen teachers, American and Japanese, included drinking and sexual misconduct. Underlying these denunciations was the fundamental question of the spiritual authority of the Zen teacher. Rooted in Zen history, this line of inquiry ultimately confronts the enigmatic domain of the Zen adept.

Zen evolved in China in the seventh century in defiance of the scriptural authority established by the existing Buddhist schools. The try-it-and-see-for-yourself method advocated by Shakyamuni Buddha had degenerated into memorization and repetition of holy texts. Repudiating mimicry and idolatry, Zen masters said things like: "Buddha is a shit stick!" "If you meet the Buddha, kill the Buddha!" "Don't look to me to get enlightened!" Responses like these have continued throughout Zen history, contributing to its eccentric reputation. But for all its apparent iconoclasm, knocking Buddha-images off their pedestals was meant to restore faith in personal experience. "Look within," said Shakyamuni. "You are the Buddha," Buddha meaning "awakened one."

When Zen developed in China, the Confucians were the arbitrators of moral probity. The specialty of Zen masters resided in guiding the disciple beyond mental realities, beyond cultural and moral biases. Their domain was, as Nakagawa Soen said, "the Unthinkable." To forge a discipline for the attainment of the unthinkable called for revisions within religious structures; but behavior allied with the unthinkable did not threaten social cohesion, nor was it provoked by social disintegration.

In the United States the attraction to Zen training was prompted by a decade of moral confusion. The election of President John F. Kennedy promised a cultural reawakening that came about only with the violence of the Vietnam War. With the help of consciousness-expanding drugs and Eastern religions, members of the counterculture pursued personal transformation with a vengeance. Zen studies combined the individual quest for spiritual guidance with a need for a new social morality, and Zen teachers were delegated the moral roles of American clergy. Yet American moral codes and the traditional authority of the Zen teacher are not always compatible. Trying to bring them into alignment has, thus far, proven a stumbling block to acculturation. For the jurisdiction of the Zen teacher finally to come under scrutiny indicates just how far Zen has dug its roots into the grit of American habits. The mystique of Zen, which initially inhibited the investigation of traditional practice, was subsequently used to protect an idealized version of Zen training and Zen teachers. With the recent questioning of spiritual authority, the romantic era of Zen in America has come to an abrupt close.

Challenging this spiritual authority could not begin until there were American teachers and students matured in their practice. Japanese Zen masters had arrived from a culture long considered exotic, spoke little or no

English, and were reputed to embody spiritual wisdom—to be living masters—a phenomenon for which white America has no indigenous reference. Glamorized, the authority of the Zen master went unquestioned. To examine its exact nature was inadvertently to admit that no remarkable experience had occurred that was profound enough to silence all the unaskable questions. In the heady ambience of Zen circles, this was tantamount to personal failure on the part of the novice. To embrace the authority of the master with blind devotion, on the other hand, was just as often considered an indication of spiritual insight. The result was a perverted glorification of Zen. In addition, Americans simply did not know how to think about living masters or their spiritual traditions in human terms. Only with the appearance of American teachers did the mystique of Zen become sufficiently neutralized to allow basic questions to emerge. What does it mean to call someone a fully realized Zen master? What is enlightened behavior? Who is enlightened and how does one know? What, if anything, can the unenlightened mind use for measurement and assurance? Is there any view that is not culturally biased? There are no absolute answers, but it took a quarter of a century of Zen practice before Americans could even begin asking the questions.

For the teacher, spiritual autonomy is rooted in Zen orthodoxy and validated through the system of dharma transmission. The Zen lineages now in the United States trace their descent through eighty to ninety sequential generations of Buddhist patriarchs back to Shakyamuni Buddha.* According to texts written after the Buddha's death, the first transmission occurred when Shakyamuni, sitting before his assembly, twirled a flower. In response, his disciple Makashapa smiled. On the lineage charts, the first six names are mythological Buddhas who represent beginningless time. Shakyamuni Buddha is the seventh and Makashapa the eighth. No seals, signatures, or papers verified Makashapa's understanding. Presumably Makashapa's smile conveyed the same quality of skylike mind as Shakyamuni's. At that point, the boundaries of dualistic perception abandoned, there was no teacher or dis-

---

*There is a recent tendency in the United States to replace the word "patriarch" with the ungendered "ancestor" when referring to Zen. The change reflects the participation of American women in Zen and accurately communicates that Zen is not for men only. But the elimination of the term "patriarch," particularly with regard to lineage, denies the masculine dominance of the tradition and the fact that none of the teachers listed prior to the current generation has been female.

ciple, no object or subject, nothing taught, nothing to teach. This unified state of skylike mind remains the ideal archetype for Zen transmissions.

Makashapa's is the simplest transmission story ever told. In Japan, as Zen developed an extensive religious structure, transmission became increasingly shrouded in the kind of mysterious religiosity that Shakyamuni Buddha and the Chinese Zen masters had originally rejected. Dharma transmission in Japan became confirmed in a secret week-long ceremony culminating in a midnight ritual and witnessed by a few select clergy. What happened between Shakyamuni and Makashapa, however, is never openly revealed either. Truly mysterious by nature, dharma transmission remains self-secret, unknowable however public it may be. This dimension of transmission is indicated in a famous Zen quote attributed to Bodhidharma, the first Zen patriarch of China:

> A special transmission outside the scripture
> No dependency on words and letters,
> Pointing directly to the mind of men,
> Seeing into one's nature and attaining Buddhahood.

Bodhidharma's direct teaching was a blasphemous affront to scriptural authority. The ruling priesthood in turn attacked his heretical claim, but what evolved as the Zen school legitimized itself by asserting that its "special transmission" descended directly from the historical Buddha. Historians now suggest that this direct descent is somewhat fictional, that the lineage charts list consecutive names of masters who lived hundreds of years apart. Zen protectors may have resorted to a kind of written validation similar to the scriptural authority they attacked. Perhaps the claim for an unbroken lineage enabled Zen to attract some of the Imperial patronage enjoyed by the prevailing Buddhist schools. Perhaps claiming direct descent from Shakyamuni was a skillful attempt to establish the viability of these radical teachings in a conservative and antagonistic climate.

In any event, the system of transmission became increasingly corrupt as Zen became more institutionalized. Dedicated masters from the time of Dogen Zenji ranted against the self-serving abuses of dharma transmission. But appeal to personal probity still remains the only recourse for protecting true transmission, since the self-secret aspect of the system allows for every possible pitfall. Whether transmission is between Shakyamuni and Makashapa or between some scurrilous father and son scheming to keep temple property in the family, the paradoxical integrity of the system is that there are no external references, no objective tests or measurements. It is a kind of Zen honor system which, by human law, will inevitably be defiled.

When defiled, transmission became something "to get," "to have," "to possess," a kind of religious credit card that proclaimed authority and guaranteed respectability. Transmission certificates were obtained through bribery and forgery and given liberally by abbots to their eldest sons to assure family ownership of temple property. During the nineteenth century, the abuses of transmission accelerated the decline of Zen in Japan.

When Yasutani Roshi and Soen Roshi traveled around the United States in the 1960s, no one knew or asked about dharma transmission. Shunryu Suzuki Roshi (not to be confused with D. T. Suzuki), who founded the San Francisco Zen Center in 1962, never mentioned it. But by the early seventies, while many Americans were already studying with Asian teachers, many more were facing a perplexing array of guides and gurus. The "guru circuit" was derisively compared to a spiritual marketplace, but where aspiration outlasted curiosity, there was genuine concern for what defines a legitimate teacher. Centers for disseminating Asian religious teachings were sprouting up all over the country, and competition for students and financial support was considerable. For some new spiritualists, implicit trust in a teacher made "proof" of authenticity irrelevant. Others, however, felt inadequately qualified to assess spiritual attainment. Within this confusing proliferation of New Age alternatives, Zen offered dharma transmission as a system of certification by which authenticity was not sanctioned by personal opinion but screened and confirmed by one experienced in spiritual matters. That only the ideal version of transmission was presented to students new to Zen was not a promotional falsehood. Until recently, it was the only version available.

The Japanese Zen teachers may have underestimated how their idealistic American students would respond to the dilemmas of dharma transmission. In Japan, the so-called impurities of Zen culture came with the territory, and deviations from the ideal did not diminish or threaten the pursuit of Zen for dedicated aspirants. But open-hearted American students of Zen have been altogether a little naive about spiritual matters.

One common misconception in the West is that spiritual realization diminishes—if not altogether eradicates—the personality, a view that assumes similarities and reduces differences between dharma teachers. Yet throughout Zen history the individuality of the great masters suggests that long after the layers of ego-protection have dissolved, the attributes of personality will flourish and particularize the teachings. For this reason, masters themselves speak of "Dogen's Zen," "Rinzai's Zen," "Ikkyu's Zen," and so on. Zen teachers have singular personalities and individuated teaching styles, and they present their understanding of Zen in very different ways. Shakyamuni Buddha's enlightenment remains the model of an awakened mind, but in Zen history there is no one behavioral ideal against which lesser gods are measured. Without objective measurements, one person's genuine master is another person's spiritual fake. There is no system, no gauge, no test that will change this—nothing to relieve the personal pursuit of what is real, what is true. Yet the Japanese system of dharma transmission continues to provide useful guidelines from which to explore possibilities of Zen studies.

When I first conceived of this book in 1984, there were seven Americans whose qualifications for transmitting Zen had been acknowledged by their Japanese masters and who were independently teaching Zen at their own centers. Five agreed to be interviewed for this book. Since then, this first generation of American teachers has doubled in size. In addition to the Zen derived from Japan, Zen is being conveyed to Americans by Chinese, Vietnamese, and Korean masters, and in some cases by their American successors. There are also American teachers of Buddhist traditions other than Zen. Concentrating on Americans within the Japanese Zen tradition, however, makes it possible to trace patterns of cultural adaptation. Americans were involved with Japanese Zen earlier and more extensively than with other forms of Buddhism, and it is now evident that the difficulties of assimilation go beyond individual teachers, centers, and lineages and are generic to acculturation itself.

These five American Zen teachers present their own understanding of Zen—not American Zen, not Japanese Zen. The transformation into a truly American version of Zen will evolve with successive generations of practitioners, teachers, and students. As a Buddhist expression puts it, "When the student is ready, the teacher appears." Yet it is incumbent on the teacher to manifest spiritual insight in a form that is recognizable to the student. These first

American teachers have appeared under unique circumstances. Their historical position requires considered distinctions between the traditional styles of Japanese Zen and the essential spirit of Zen teachings. At once bearers of the old and pioneers of the new, they must withstand the fragmentation of tradition and the reinvention of form and arbitrate the possibilities for continuity through trial and error. Each of these teachers is currently engaged in new directions, experiments, or major ventures. All their choices are themselves the transmission of Zen and contribute to the ongoing translation of Zen into an American vocabulary. And while their individual teaching styles are distinct voices engaged in a common search, at this time there is nothing that can properly be called "American Zen."

Master Sekiso said, "How will you step forward from the top of a hundred-foot pole?" Another eminent master of old said, "Even though one who is sitting on the top of a hundred-foot pole has entered realization, it is not yet real. He must step forward from the top of the pole and manifest his whole body throughout the world in ten directions."

What does "the top of a hundred-foot pole" mean? Figuratively, it is the stage of complete emptiness. When you attain self-realization, your eye will open first to the state of consciousness where there is absolutely nothing. That stage is called the "great death." It is a stage where there is no dualistic opposition such as subject and object, good and bad, saints and ordinary people, and so on. There is neither one who sees, nor anything seen. Zen usually expresses this stage with the words, "There is not a speck of cloud in the spacious sky."

Anyone who wants to attain the true Zen experience must pass through this stage once. If you remain there, however, you will be unable to attain true emancipation from deep attachment to this emptiness. This stage is often referred to as the pitfall of emptiness. It becomes a kind of Zen sickness.

When we attain kensho, we come to the top of the high pole where most of us are seized with this malady. It is said that even Shakyamuni succumbed to it for two or three weeks after his great enlightenment. The Zen master in this koan warns us not to linger at this point when he says, "Take a step forward from this stage, and you will be able to manifest your whole body throughout the world in ten directions." That means that you must become completely free from all kinds of attachments.

Yamada Koun

ROBERT
AITKEN

Koko An Zendo occupies a large white house in the hills above Honolulu. Over sloping vistas of coconut and banana trees lies the crater Koko Head, close to where Robert Aitken grew up, not far from Pearl Harbor. On the main altar inside the zendo, looking grumpy as ever with his sagging fleshy jowls and fierce scowl, sits the unmistakable Bodhidharma. Aitken bought this statue in Japan in 1951 after studying Zen there for a year. A few days before returning to Hawaii, as he meandered through the back streets of To-kyo with Nakagawa Soen, Bob Aitken confided his misgivings about his ac-complishments, if any. Passing a Buddhist bookshop, they spotted the Bo-dhidharma image in the window. Dismissing the self-preoccupied doubts of an American beginner, Soen urged Aitken to purchase the statue, telling him that someday it would be the central figure in a temple that he would estab-lish in the United States. At that time, recalls Aitken, "such a thing was be-yond my dreams." Slow in coming, Soen Roshi's prophecy took a course that Aitken would later describe as "Willy-Nilly Zen."

Zen master, scholar, author, and radical pacifist, Aitken Roshi is the un-official American dean of Zen, a respected elder to Zen Buddhists across the United States. Born in Philadelphia on June 19, 1917, he came to Hawaii at age five and was educated with children who were to become prominent state leaders. But since his early childhood, conventional values had so eluded Aitken that his contribution to society, however willy-nilly, seemed destined for another direction.

In 1959 he and his wife, Anne Aitken, opened their living room in Hono-lulu two evenings a week to anyone interested in zazen. The meditation pe-riods were opened and closed by the rap of a wooden spoon hitting a Pyrex mixing bowl. At first these meetings were attended by only one other couple, but they marked the beginning of the Diamond Sangha. Ten years later the Aitkens moved to the Hawaiian island of Maui, settling in an area propitiously named Haiku. There they started a Maui extension of the Diamond Sangha, and it was from this remote tropical paradise that Aitken emerged as leader of American Zen Buddhism. For fourteen years he traveled frequently to Honolulu, and in 1983, with the energy of the sangha as a whole stabilized in Honolulu, the Aitkens moved back to the capital city.

Sitting barefoot in the living room of their rented house near Koko An, wearing blue jeans and a faded work shirt, Aitken conveys the dignity of a gentleman farmer, while his gray hair has the slightly disheveled look of professorial abandon. His current reading selection, scattered on the nearby coffee table, includes *The Tales of Genji*, *The Selected Poetry of Rainer Maria Rilke*, *Childhood, Youth and Exile* by Alexander Herzen, and a photographic study of Hawaiian birds. Reflecting on his relocation back to Honolulu and all the years of self-doubt that followed that first year of Zen training, he says, "What with all the problems we had in establishing the Maui zendo and the turnover of people and all the problems with having two centers and going back and forth between Maui and Honolulu—I don't think I've ever gone through a crisis of faith at anytime. But I'm always on the edge of doubting method, questioning method. Are we doing it the right way?"

Aitken, a lay roshi, has been described as a teacher who asks a lot of questions and doesn't pretend to know all the answers. His qualifications were certified in 1974 when he received dharma transmission from the eminent Japanese roshi Yamada Koun. The only Westerner who is a documented successor of Yamada Roshi at this time, Aitken is also the only American member of the recently established Zen sect *Sanbo Kyodan*, the Order of the Three Treasures. While this sect retains orthodox methodology, its founder, Haku'un Yasutani Roshi, departed from the Zen monastic convention by starting a temple for nonordained, nonresidential students.

With the Sanbo Kyodan lineage invested in Aitken Roshi and the American expression of Zen still evolving, Aitken has unintentionally become the authority on lay practice. Removing a pair of thick glasses, he rubs his eyes and repeats wearily, " 'What's lay practice?' That's like asking a fish, 'Hey, how's the water?' " But his life doesn't beg the question. He demonstrated against nuclear testing in the fifties, for unilateral disarmament in the sixties, and against the Trident submarines in the eighties; he counseled draftees during the Vietnam War and cofounded the Buddhist Peace Fellowship in 1978. He has called himself a feminist, performed ceremonies for aborted babies, and advocated sexual equality within a Buddhist community where historically none has existed. In 1982 he and Anne crossed the legal line for the first time by withholding from the Internal Revenue Service that portion of their federal income taxes slated for military expenditures, a stand they have continued to take each year. This action alone departs radically from the Japanese Zen tradition in which opposition to political authority has been negligible and civil disobedience unknown.

Aitken's political convictions developed long before the Diamond Sangha existed, so that his involvement with politics—however contrary it may be in terms of Japanese Zen—has never aroused controversy in his own community. As a lay roshi, he cannot ordain students; he has never taken monastic vows nor advocated traditional monkhood as a model. Yet he has continued to invest in the traditional practices of his spiritual discipline. His radical divergence from the cultural expression of Eastern Zen, combined with his adherence to orthodox Zen training, represents a direction that has far-reaching implications for Zen in the West.

By the age of twenty-two, Bob Aitken had quit college once, flunked out once, and was working with a construction crew on Midway Island where he had risen from messman to timekeeper. In July 1941, after a one-year contract on Midway, he returned home to Honolulu. His father, a first lieutenant in the reserves, had just been called into active duty; his younger brother was also in uniform. Everyone was talking about the war. Two years earlier, Aitken's patriotic father had persuaded him to join the National Guard. To Robert Aitken Senior the sight of an American flag unfurled past sundown was so blasphemous that he felt morally obliged to rebuke whoever was responsible for the violation. In Honolulu the inescapable signs of the coming war were so oppressive to Aitken that he stayed drunk for several days in a row. When he sobered up, he made his way to the construction employment office again. He registered for the draft, which had just come into effect, and after one week in Honolulu shipped out for his new construction job as timekeeper again—this time in Guam, the farthest U.S. possession in the western Pacific.

From the moment he arrived on Guam, he felt caught behind enemy lines. Many men could see the war coming; they could predict the consequences, but inertia and fear kept them from taking action. A superintendent assigned to Aitken's construction crew arrived two days after Aitken and left immediately. "He knew," Aitken recalls. "I knew. But he acted on what he knew and none of the rest of us had the guts to do it. We just waited it out."

Some forty-five years later, Aitken's hoarse, searching voice recaptures waiting it out on Guam: "The war began on December 7th here and December 8th there, across the date line. There were something like fifty-seven marines on the island and a couple of hundred sailors. There was no way we could defend the island at all. The second morning we climbed to the highest peak, where we could see the whole island ringed with Japanese ships. So we knew that we had to give ourselves up."

After being imprisoned on Guam for a month, Aitken was taken by steamer to the Japanese port of Kobe. For the next three years and nine months he was held under the classification of "Military Civilian Prisoners of War." The enforced labor of the military camps was not required here, but the men were more restricted than civilian prisoners. "We never had barbed wire; we never had to work. There was only one brief phase where we were intimidated and threatened with execution if Japan lost the war, but otherwise we had a good relationship with the guards." For the first nine months he was interned with seventy-five other men in the British Seaman's Mission, which contained an extensive nineteenth-century library that nourished Aitken more than his meager meals. After this he was moved to Marks House, the five-room former home of a British banker in the foreign district of Kobe, where he was kept until the spring of 1944. The men were permitted to take books from the mission library to their new camp, and Aitken's sustaining immersion in literature continued uninterrupted.

Toward the end of the war, the diet of both prisoners and their captors was reduced to scanty rations of soybeans, contributing to the death of some of the older men and leaving many others critically malnourished. At the best of times Aitken's health had not been robust; he had suffered from psychosomatic illnesses, starting with extreme eczema in his infancy and then asthma in his childhood. The dampness and lack of heating in Japan further exacerbated an already weakened respiratory system. But the brutality inflicted systematically by the Japanese on their prisoners throughout Southeast Asia was not, according to Aitken, evident in their home camps. The prisoners were allowed, for example, to leave camp for visits to the dentist that included stops at the foreign bookstores. To supplement the Western

classics offered by the mission library, Aitken used his stipend to buy translations of Oriental poetry. He was already familiar with Arthur Waley's
translations of Chinese and Japanese poetry, which he had read along with
the poetry of A. E. Housman and Walt Whitman during his erratic attendance at the University of Hawaii.

Aitken's reliance on books did not originate in the prison camp. At the
start of each school term he had devoured all the materials distributed for the
entire course and remained bored and alienated for the rest of the semester.
"In a lot of ways I was a mess. As an adolescent I was totally lost, confused,
unable to find an acceptable way of relating to the world around me. I think
that, really, from the very beginning I was a kind of marginal person. Even as
a baby. I grew up feeling completely outside all the social and athletic and academic work of my peers."

Against all odds, an internment camp was the fortuitous circumstance
that allowed Aitken's marginality to become his best ally. As an internee he
stayed remarkably detached from the pervasive ennui that enveloped the
prison-striped psyche of the average inmate. Surrounded by men who were
spending their days dividing an intense fantasy life between the past and the
future, he methodically proceeded to capitalize on the present: "I didn't feel
any desperation at all. I just woke up each morning thinking, what am I
going to do today? We had complete freedom. We didn't have any responsibilities except to keep our camp clean, and so I would sort of map out my
project for the day and do it: 'Today I am going to work on my Spanish or
today I'm going to finish *As You Like It*."

One evening during his stay at Marks House a drunken guard entered his
room waving a book in the air and announced in English, "This book, my
English teacher." The guard had been a student of R. H. Blyth's, and the book
was *Zen in English Literature and Oriental Classics*, then recently published
in Tokyo. Without suspecting that Blyth himself would soon become a fellow inmate, Aitken read that book ten times straight through. It was his "first
book," the way *Walden* was for many of his friends. Blyth had learned Italian
to read Dante, Spanish to read *Don Quixote*, German to read Goethe, Russian to read Dostoyevski, and Japanese to read Basho—to list just some of
the languages he had mastered. He then used classical works to elucidate for
the Western reader the treasures of Zen, which, according to his singular insight, had been buried undetected within their own traditions. By this stan-

dard, Don Quixote merited a chapter all to himself, being for Blyth "the purest example, in the whole of Zen literature, of the man who lives by Zen." Also noted for their exceptional expressions of "Zen attitude" were Shakespeare, Wordsworth, Dickens, and Robert Louis Stevenson.

Born a British subject, Blyth became a conscientious objector during the First World War and was summarily imprisoned. Following his release, he left England for his long curious odyssey through Asia. In 1940 he accompanied his Japanese wife from Korea, where he had been teaching at the Seoul Imperial University, back to the Japanese port town of Kanazawa, where he taught at the local high school. When Japan entered the Second World War, he was interned in a camp for civilian enemies.

In May 1944 all the camps around Kobe were combined, and Blyth and Aitken found themselves housed together at Futatabai Koen, in the hills above Kobe, in a complex of three interconnected buildings that had previously been a reform school. Blyth was initially put off by Aitken's adulation, but succumbed to not only his interest in Zen but his capacity to convert a prison cell into a seminary, to use his days for self-transformation. Indeed Blyth, whose internment interfered little with his furious work habits, was the only inmate whose study program could compare with Aitken's. At Futatabai Koen, he spent his days reading Japanese texts and translating haiku poetry. After a cautious introduction, the intellectually flamboyant Englishman became an unofficial tutor to the malleable young American. He lent Aitken D. T. Suzuki's *Essays in Zen Buddhism* and translations of Chinese Buddhist texts. They agreed that Aitken would learn Japanese, and Blyth secured an elementary text through his wife.

In the evenings Aitken joined Blyth in the room the Englishman shared with five other men. More evenings than not, the smoke-filled room became crowded with seasoned residents of the Orient arguing about the virtues of East and West, politics and religion. "Mr. B.," as Blyth was affectionately called, was considered pro-Japanese by the Americans and a Johnny-come-lately by the part-Japanese internees. The discussions were often heated, accusatory, even wild; for Aitken they were far more challenging than anything he had ever known. In his determination to contradict his father, Aitken had pitted political philosophies against each other, assessing comparative merits without investigating their internal strategies. Blyth, however, had absolutely nothing good to say about any philosophy or system that legitimized a nation-state. His brand of free thinking offered an imaginative, eagle-eyed watch on cultural and political shifts, and his analysis of international power-plays remained detached from the sentimental patriotism that provided most of the homesick captives with whatever little hope they had left.

Blyth had started the application procedures for Japanese citizenship before the war began but then allowed the process to lapse, vowing to renew his application only if Japan lost the war. In an essay on Blyth, Aitken later explained that "somehow he sensed how badly the Japanese were handling their responsibilities as occupation forces in Southeast Asia, and he knew that a national defeat would be the salutary experience the country needed for true maturity." While this kind of creative logic infuriated other inmates, Aitken learned from it something of the wisdom of paradox.

When the Japanese surrendered, the American occupation forces offered the internees the option of remaining in Japan. Aitken did not want to stay. He left Japan knowing that he would study Zen, a decision not influenced by Blyth, who had little use for formal Zen training. He also knew that he did not want to be Japanese, making a distinction between Zen and Japanese culture that often escaped Western enthusiasts of Japanese Zen, especially at that time. He did not realize, however, that the war had altered the collective consciousness of the United States. In the midst of a national community celebrating its victory, his inglorious exile from military duty left him isolated, ashamed, and more cut off from the mainstream than he had been in Japan. Even his knowledge of the atomic bomb had been delayed. The Japanese-English newspapers had reported "a new type of molecular bomb," and engineers detained in the camp had figured out that the new bomb had been achieved by splitting the atom. "But the implications of it didn't hit me until I got back to the United States," Aitken says. The dampness and poor diet had aggravated his bronchial ailments, moreover, and he returned to Honolulu gaunt and infirm. The immediate effect of coming home after the war was a crippling disorientation that lasted for several months.

Then, determined to overcome past academic failures, Aitken reapplied to the University of Hawaii and was accepted on probation. Confident and content in school for the first time, he easily earned his B.A. in English Literature. He continued to explore political ideologies but, influenced by Blyth, did so with new-found discrimination. He also attended meetings at the university to discuss peace and labor issues. In the cold-war climate of the times, these activities, however innocuous, were enough to get him investigated by the FBI.

In 1947 Aitken married for the first time and with his wife, Mary, left for Berkeley, California, where he enrolled in a Japanese studies program at the University of California School of Far Eastern and Russian Studies. During the Christmas recess, he traveled to Ojai, a town north of Los Angeles, to meet the Indian teacher J. Krishnamurti at Happy Valley, a school established to disseminate his teachings. Krishnamurti, however, was in India, so Aitken went on to Los Angeles, where he visited P. D. and Ione Perkins' Oriental Bookshop. Richard Gard, now a distinguished Buddhist scholar, was then the clerk at the bookstore and had been a prewar friend of Aitken's at the University of Hawaii. He told Aitken about Zen teacher Nyogen Senzaki, who was then living at the Miyako Hotel. Aitken learned that while he was interned in Japan, Senzaki had waited out the war in Wyoming at the Heart Mountain camp for Japanese-Americans.

Aitken left the bookstore and went directly to Senzaki's hotel, where he found the squat, elderly master, his white hair fastidiously parted on one side, sitting alone in his small library. By then Senzaki was seventy-seven years old and had already spent half a century in California. Over tea, Aitken engaged Senzaki in a conversation about haiku and Zen. It was the first of many erudite discussions; Senzaki was well educated in Western philosophy, and their subjects ranged from Basho to Kant. (He once told Aitken, "I like Immanuel Kant. He's very good, but he just needs one good kick in the pants.") Senzaki was eventually to give Aitken the Buddhist name Chotan, which means "Deep Pool." A few months later the Aitkens moved to Pasadena to be near Senzaki.

Aitken has described his first Zen teacher as "a marginal Zen monk," Senzaki's rejection of conventional monasticism, political criticisms of Japan, and subsequent residence in the United States all earning him that title. While the early American practitioners of Zen were turning to Japan for orthodox directives, Senzaki's investigations of the Buddhadharma in America were isolated and intuitive. He tried his best, moreover, to be an American gentleman, as he said, going so far as to take lessons in social dancing. Having once watched mischievous boys sneak up to rub Soyen Shaku's shaved head on a streetcar in San Francisco, Senzaki let his own hair grow— one of his many ways of protecting the dharma from ridicule. His hotel rooms were furnished Western-style, and he conducted his meditations sitting on chairs rather than cross-legged on black cushions, which he considered un-American. Aitken laughingly recalls that "by the time I met him, he had trouble sitting on a cushion because he was so very stout."

Although Senzaki was the first Zen teacher to live in the United States and to advocate Zen practice, he gave his students relatively little instruction. According to Aitken, students were inspired mostly by his kindness, modesty, patience, and humor. He was an unassuming monk who did not dress like a monk because he so valued his anonymity. Nor were his spiritual merits marked by official seals and titles. Aitken respectfully refers to him, as he does to Blyth, as *sensei*, the Japanese word for teacher. Although among American students the term sensei has become associated with formal teaching credentials, Aitken's usage is correct. Senzaki, for his part, outspokenly disdained the titles of Japanese Zen clergy and criticized the monks, abbots, and bishops for straying from what he believed was the true monk's path of celibacy and utmost simplicity. He claimed that for true Buddhists titles were mere business labels, and he abhorred the corrupt practice of selling government-issued Buddhist teaching licenses. He called himself a "kindergarten nurse," a "mushroom monk," "a nameless and homeless monk," embodying the very transience he had known from his start in life as an orphan. "You may laugh," he wrote, "but I am really a mushroom without a very deep root, no branches, no flowers, and probably no seeds." And indeed, having never received formal dharma transmission, he left no dharma heirs. His given name, Nyogen, means "like a phantasm," and his Buddhist name, Choro, means "Morning Dew." Both images appear in the final part of the *Diamond Sutra*:

> All composite things are like a dream,
> A phantasm, a bubble and a shadow;
> Like a dewdrop and a flash of lightning—
> They are thus to be regarded.

Although the Aitkens were progressing in their studies with Senzaki in Los Angeles, Mary grew homesick for Hawaii, so they returned to Honolulu in 1949. At the same time that he worked with second- and third-generation Japanese at the Moliili Community Organization, Aitken completed his master's degree in Japanese studies at the University of Hawaii with a dissertation on Basho. In his book, *Zen Wave: Basho's Haiku and Zen* (1976), Aitken writes that his dissertation drew a sharp admonition from one member of his thesis committee: "He said that just because its subject is everywhere, I must be careful not to claim universal manifestation for Zen Buddhism." Aitken concludes that Zen Buddhism "does not pervade the cosmos. It presents essential nature—universal mind—but it does so as a particular teaching. Confusing the specific teaching with its vast and undifferentiated subject is a trap that has caught many tigers."

One of these tigers, Aitken realized, was Blyth, whose attempt to illuminate the universal truth of Zen through world literature made him a ready victim of this trap. Like D. T. Suzuki, he stressed the amorphous, ecumenical Zen spirit; for Western readers this spirit contributed to Zen's influence on the life of the intellect, but it obscured the practical efforts of Zen training. "I used to think afterward," writes Aitken, "that both Suzuki and Blyth were presenting Zen the way a florist presents flowers, minus the dirt and the roots. And you just presume that—boom!—there are the flowers." So Aitken resolved to study formal Zen. In 1950, with the help of D. T. Suzuki, who had been in residence at the University of Hawaii the previous year, he received a $1,000 fellowship to study Zen in Japan. That same year his son Thomas was born, and Aitken returned to Japan alone.

In November 1950 Aitken sat his first sesshin—a week-long intensive meditation practice—at Engaku Temple in Kamakura, where both Senzaki and D. T. Suzuki had trained together almost fifty years earlier. Senzaki had never held formal sesshins, but in a dharma talk to his American students he had explained that "sesshin has two meanings—since there are two Chinese characters, both having the same pronunciation. One meaning is concentration of mind, the other, unification of mind. In the first sense, mind has a psychological meaning. For example, when one reads a book and forgets his surroundings, he is concentrating his mind on that book. This is sesshin in the first sense. In the second sense, mind means the essence of mind. It is *this* sort of sesshin we are concerned with. In Zen meditation we think non-thinking—that is, we think nothing. What this means is that our whole psychological mind ceases to function, and as a result, our whole being becomes united with the essence of mind, which we signify by Mind. You call this essence the God within you, absoluteness, Ultimate Reason—it doesn't matter. No matter what you call it, to unite with this essence is the very reason we are gathered here to meditate together."

On that first morning of sesshin at Engakuji, Aitken at long last took his assigned seat in the meditation hall of a Japanese monastery. The heady smell of incense and the staunch resolve of the black-robed monks were just as inspiring as he had always imagined. Unsmiling and self-contained, Asahina Roshi, the abbot, fulfilled Aitken's image of a Zen master. The boom of the wooden fish drum accompanied the recitation of the monosyllabic sutras, the Buddhist scriptures. Then Asahina Roshi made nine formal bows before the altar. Suddenly Aitken realized that he, too, would have to make nine formal bows. And just as suddenly, Zen practice appalled him.

Until that very moment, Aitken's studies had not included any aspect of traditional Buddhist services. From Senzaki he had learned only the Four Great Vows: to save all creations ("sentient beings") without restriction, to put an end to ever-arising delusions, to perceive reality, and to embody the enlightened way. Now he was expected to perform the Japanese full bow, which requires standing with palms flat together at the chest, then kneeling and placing the top of the head on the floor between opened and upraised hands in a gesture of supplication, vulnerability, and surrender. "Not just three bows, you know, but nine bows, before and after service," remembers Aitken. "And I was thinking, what is this bowing? What am I doing? It was as though all the beliefs that I had about the righteous importance of the individual were suddenly just snatched. And I thought, my God, what am I doing?"

It wasn't until after Aitken started studying with Yamada Roshi in 1971 that he began to internalize bowing practice. In *Taking the Path of Zen* (1982), a detailed manual for Zen practice, Aitken explains that when bowing, "we are lifting the Buddha's feet over our heads. It is a sign of throwing everything away, or as one of my students described it, the act of pouring everything out from the top of the head. All our self-concern, all our preoccupations are thrown away completely. There is just that bow." But for his very first sesshin, Aitken persevered by telling himself, "This is your sitting-up exercise." And as he pressed his swollen knees into the wooden floor, perhaps he was beginning to learn that, as another of his students put it thirty-five years later, "the wonderful thing about Zen practice is that you get to do it whether you like it or not."

Aitken got to do Zen practice, but without the kind of guidance that his own *Taking the Path* provides. Newcomers to a monastery traditionally received no prior instruction in form, ritual, or sitting practice. As a Westerner in a Japanese monastery in 1950, Aitken was quite an oddity, and the monk seated next to him was assigned to help him along. But while this big brother system offered some comfort, he still left Engakuji to seek out Nakagawa Soen, the English-speaking friend of Senzaki's.

Soen invited Aitken to come to Ryutakuji in Mishima at the base of Mount Fuji and do sesshin with the abbot, Yamamoto Gempo. Aitken recalls that, "The first time I met Gempo Roshi, he was already in his mid-eighties. It was winter and he sat bundled up against the cold he felt keenly in his old age, sipping sake, and munching toasted mochi (a glutenous rice cake). He exuded warmth and love and was a great teacher for a young Westerner uptight with aesthetic preoccupations."

For the next seven months Aitken remained at Ryutakuji. While he studied under Gempo Roshi he became friendly with Nakagawa Soen, whose appetite for all forms of art was rare for a Zen monk. "The artistic talents of the roshi," explains Aitken, "are pretty much limited to calligraphy and tea ceremony. They tend to be uninformed and somewhat philistine when it comes to art and when it comes to music and poetry, even within the Japanese tradition—not to have a real sense of what haiku is, not to have a real sense of Noh drama and so on." In addition to writing haiku and studying Western literature, Soen had obtained a standard museum slide set of the history of Western art. "I remember him looking at this Venus on the half-shell," says Aitken, "and then passing it to a monk who said, 'Oh pretty, isn't it?'" Soen also had recordings of Gregorian chants, which he explained to the other monks "as the way Western monks chant their sutras." The monks were always respectfully amused by Soen but thought he was just about as odd as Aitken.

Soen had been warned by Gempo Roshi that "poetry is a loss of virtue." But that didn't stop him from writing, and years later Gary Snyder called him Japan's greatest haiku poet of this century. Nor did it diminish his reverence for Master Gempo. With Soen's example before him, Aitken learned to see no conflict between Zen practice and making art, nor much point in attaching significance to the aesthetic limitations of Japanese teachers. "I think it's just that most people are philistines when it comes to art and music."

Aitken's notions about the discipline of surrender and spirited creativity, however, were once again challenged by bowing practice at Ryutakuji. Particularly galling were the avid devotions of his friend. "I would see Soen

Roshi bowing his head off before Kannon, the Bodhisattva of compassion, invisible behind a screen. And my reaction was that he was my beloved friend, a free-minded poet, and what was he doing bowing away like that!" But Aitken vowed to suspend judgment, to maintain "beginner's mind," to be a student, and to concentrate on zazen. The pain in his knees was unremitting. Only years later would he repeat Yamada Roshi's claim that "pain in the knees is the taste of zazen." His respiratory system was again troublesome. The steady diet of rice gruel and pickles did not help his declining health. Yet Aitken still had no hesitation about what he was doing. "It wasn't that I was so determined, it was the only thing I could do. I can't explain that."

During a spring sesshin, Aitken accompanied the monks on a begging trip to Namazu City, where he caught dysentery; with this new affliction, he stoically suffered through the subsequent June sesshin. After that Soen took him to a local doctor, but it was not until he went to Tokyo and got antibiotics through Blyth that his symptoms were relieved. Shortly afterward he returned to Hawaii. For the second time he left Japan set back in his tiresome struggle to maintain his health; once again he arrived home emaciated.

The next five years were dismal. In Honolulu he faced a dissolving marriage and soon moved on to Los Angeles. Flat broke, he stayed at a YMCA and worked at a bookstore. But his respiratory ailments, aggravated by his year in Japan, along with the emotional strain of a divorce, culminated in a critical bronchial illness for which he had to be hospitalized. Friends helped him through a tedious recuperation, and then an unexpected mid-term request for an English teacher landed him a job at the Happy Valley School.

Aitken arrived in Ojai in 1956, and there he met Anne Hopkins, then assistant director of Happy Valley. They married the following year. Born in Chicago on February 8, 1911, Anne was raised in a well-to-do family that fostered the Christian ethics of charity and social responsibility. As a young woman she had worked in a settlement house in one of Chicago's grim immigrant neighborhoods and served as a professional Red Cross hospital worker during the Second World War. In an autobiographical sketch, Anne wrote that her parents' commitment to Christianity "was belied—enriched—by the fact that they were religious seekers. Christian Science, seances with mediums, Christian mysticism, astrology, graphology, theosophy, spirit guides, Krishnamurti's lectures—all these were, at one time or another, a part of our lives as we were growing up, and, with varying degrees of tolerance among the four children, taken for granted along with music lessons and summer camps on Wisconsin lakes."

The liberal spiritual investigations of her family did not predispose her toward the rigors of Zen training. Her romance with Aitken did little to dispel the cautions of a neophyte, and she approached Zen practice very warily. Years later she was startled to discover a letter she had written to her father at the age of eighteen; having just read a book on Zen, she wrote that she had now found her spiritual path.

In the summer of 1957 the Aitkens traveled to Japan on a wedding holiday. They arrived at Ryutakuji, where Aitken had trained seven years earlier, one day before sesshin began. Anne had tried zazen in Ojai and had no intention of doing it for seven days. Soen Roshi, now the abbot, had arranged for her to stay in a guest room that looked out over a small pond and garden, and he sent her gifts of fruit and cake along with whatever books he had in English. "One of these books provided me with a fine pitfall," wrote Anne. "It was a nineteenth-century translation of some sutras and precepts, and I happened upon a section that was enumerating the various ways in which one accumulated merit. Somehow that word 'merit' set off a strong reaction. Accumulating merit! What was this anyway? Was Zen a kind of superior Boy Scout hierarchy with little gold stars and an Eagle badge on a flapping black robe as a goal? With no one to talk to who might provide some sensible frame of reference against which my indignations could bounce back at me, I indulged in finding increasing causes for irritation, never stopping to consider that there might be some mistake in my perceptions."

After an isolated week of such disturbing ruminations on Zen, Anne found herself traveling with her husband and Soen Roshi to yet another sesshin, a very special one she was told. It would be led by Yasutani Roshi, the independent, fiery Zen master who had removed himself to a rural outpost of Tokyo. In the community of Tokorozawa, in a temple not much bigger than a house, Yasutani worked with nonresidential lay students. What made this sesshin so special was not only the singular attributes of Yasutani himself, but also that Soen Roshi, abbot of a prestigious Rinzai monastery, was traveling to Yasutani's humble environs to be his attendant. Soen's teacher, Gempo Roshi, had been the spiritual adviser to the emperor, so it was said, and now his successor, the current abbot and most famous haiku poet in Japan, was leaving his monastery to attend a Soto Zen renegade. In Japanese social hierarchies, all of which are reflected in Japanese Zen, this behavior turned the tables upside down. It was, explains Anne, "unheard of, even for one always doing the unexpected."

Once the Aitkens arrived at the small country temple, Soen Roshi failed to locate the inn that he had chosen for Anne while her husband did sesshin. So he arranged for her to stay with a doctor-friend and share a room with the doctor's aged mother, herself a devout practitioner. By the second morning Anne was accompanying the old lady down the dark path to the zendo, where Yasutani provided her with a stiff high-backed Western chair upholstered in bright blue plush and invited her to attend *dokusan*, the face-to-face encounter between master and student that takes place during zazen. "I sat the sesshin looking past the shoji panels to the green bushes on the other side of a public path, watching the passers-by watch me," recalls Anne. "I didn't care. I didn't want to do zazen. I had no idea really how to do zazen and—at least half the time—I kept telling myself, I wasn't going to try. And yet when I would go to dokusan with that wonderful old man with the burning vitality, it was impossible not to be moved; and so at intervals, I did begin to try."

In the fall of 1957 the Aitkens left Japan and went back to Ojai for their final year at the Happy Valley School. They had planned to return to Honolulu the following summer so that Aitken could spend more time with his young son. In May 1958 Nyogen Senzaki died. Soen Roshi came from Japan to lead two memorial sesshins with Senzaki's students. The Aitkens attended the first one before leaving for Hawaii. The sesshin was conducted in Senzaki's ground-floor apartment on Second Street in Boyle Heights, East Los Angeles. Soen Roshi, always inventive, swept out the garage behind the apartment for his dokusan room and brought in a folding chair, a portable card table, and a candle. Each morning everyone rose at 4 A.M., and under the cloak of darkness Soen Roshi led the fifteen retreatants on a quick-paced, single-file walk to Hollenbeck Park. During the day students left the apartment for walking meditation, crossing the enclosed laundry yard where Soen Roshi led them through a forest of hanging wash.

Senzaki's memorial sesshin was the first full, seven-day traditional sesshin to be held in the United States. While Senzaki wished to be as ephemeral as a mushroom, with his help Zen had taken root, and he has emerged as the most widely shared Zen ancestor of American students. As for Soen Roshi, lines of hanging laundry barely hinted at the mazes through which he would lead his American students.

Back in Hawaii the Aitkens opened a second-hand bookstore in Honolulu's Chinatown, a raunchy and dissolute section of town. The store specialized in Asian literature and featured the best selection of Buddhist books in the city. The Aitkens kept the names of all those interested in Buddhism, and when they started the sitting group in 1959 they sent invitations to these people. Soen Roshi's prophecy that Aitken would someday have a Zen Buddhist temple was beginning to unfold. In January 1959 Soen came to Honolulu to lead sesshin at the Koko An Zendo. The Aitkens chose the name Koko An because at that time they were living close to the crater Koko Head and because in Japanese it means "the hermitage right here." And they named their group the Diamond Sangha to reflect the Buddhist text *The Diamond Sutra* as well as the Waikiki landmark Diamond Head.

Soen Roshi returned to Hawaii in 1961 and held two sesshins. In his autobiographical portrait, "Willy-Nilly Zen," Aitken writes:

> At that first spring sesshin, I felt particularly determined. I sat up for a portion of several nights and found myself in rather a deep condition. I experienced a makyo [mysterious vision occurring within zazen] in which I was seated on the floor of a huge old stone temple, with enormous pillars extending to a lofty ceiling. Very tall monks dressed in black walked slowly around me in a circle reciting sutras in deep voices. The total experience had the flavor of something from the ancient past.
>
> On the afternoon of the fifth day, Nakagawa Roshi gave a great "*Katsu!*" [shout] in the zendo, and I found my voice uniting with his, "Aaaah!" In the dokusan, he asked me what I now know was a checking question. I could not answer, and he simply terminated the interview. In a later dokusan, he said that I had experienced a little bit of light and that I should be very careful.
>
> In his closing talk after sesshin, the Roshi said, "Someone got a little bit of light." I knew he was referring to my experience, but I did not treat it very seriously. However, I found the ceiling of my mind to be infinitely spacious. Everything was bright and new. I felt that I had had a good sesshin.

Following Soen Roshi's visit to Hawaii, the Aitkens started the *Diamond Sangha Newsletter*, which now serves as an invaluable compendium of Zen activity in the United States during the years 1961 through 1971. At its most personal, it addressed the extended family of practitioners, recording the American itineraries of Japanese roshis, the passing away of Soen Roshi's mother, a book in progress by Philip Kapleau, a new temple construction at Tassajara; it also listed contacts for the sitting groups that had begun all over the United States. The newsletter also served Aitken's scholastic and inquiring mind. He reviewed books on Japanese Zen, Chinese Buddhism, Zen Catholicism, haiku, and Basho. He often referred to Blyth, and his articles combined the same eclectic scholarship, personal search, and literary attention that he admired in Blyth's work. The newsletter contained articles by "R. A."—as his byline read—on "Zen and Marriage" and "Zen and LSD and Hippies." An editorial on "Zen and the Art of Merchandizing" turned into a lengthy and defiant campaign against the Shiseido Cosmetic Company of Tokyo for exporting a line of "Zen Cosmetics." And in a new look at Beckett's *Waiting for Godot*, Aitken concluded that "waiting not religion becomes the opiate of the people."

In the fall of 1961 the Aitkens returned to Japan for seven months of study with Yasutani Roshi, who then joined them the following year in Honolulu to hold a sesshin that attracted about fifteen middle-aged, conventional-looking adults. The New Age progeny of Beat Zen had not yet joined the Diamond Sangha. "The first sesshins in Hawaii," explains Aitken, "saw the tag end of widespread interest in theosophy and general occult things. There were folks who had studied Blavatsky and her successors and who had gone through all kinds of spirit-writing episodes and astrology. The young people didn't start to come in until the dope revolution."

Within a few years, however, the Vietnam War caused such painful ruptures within families that for the younger generation the only attractive direction was any which way but home. The urgent need to deny the past revitalized the singularly American belief in the possibility of starting life over. With disdain for both political power and materialism running high, nothing promised to turn that belief into a reality more than spiritual practice.

From 1962 to 1969 Aitken worked for the University of Hawaii in various administrative positions, most of them connected with the university's East-West Center. From Hawaii's most prestigious campus he delivered the kind of anti-Vietnam War warnings that would soon disrupt universities across the mainland. In 1963 he became a member of the Hawaii Committee to End the War; at the time, most Americans, their vision still distorted by Kennedy charisma, did not even see that a war was already on. During these years, Aitken continued to participate in the letter-writing campaigns of the

American Friends' Service Committee (AFSC), which he had joined during those difficult years in the early fifties.

The Aitkens always announced their ongoing political activities to the Diamond Sangha in hopes that some members would join them, but these announcements were usually to no avail. For the most part the sangha took the view that, as Aitken puts it, "If you are a Buddhist then you're not political."

In 1965, with both the "dope revolution," as Aitken calls it, and the Vietnam War well under way, Yasutani Roshi came to Honolulu to hold sesshin. By then the composition of the Diamond Sangha had shifted from older theosophists to younger dropouts. One evening a man with his hair in a pony tail asked Yasutani Roshi, "What should I do if I'm drafted into this unfair bloody war in Vietnam?" "If your country calls you," replied the venerable master, "you must go." In the days that followed, Aitken, in the role of senior student, tried to explain that Yasutani Roshi, like anyone else, was subject to the time and place of his own karma, and that he had come of age during the Russo-Japanese War, which had evoked jingoistic fervor in Japan. Most students were troubled by Yasutani Roshi's answer but tended to suspend judgment; a few could not fathom it, however, and dropped out of the Diamond Sangha right then. For those students, Zen Buddhism seemed to be as allied with right-wing patriotism now as it had been with the Japanese military a generation earlier. And although some could accept Zen's association with a warrior code that exalted the loyal samurai, no one could abide the war in Vietnam.

Unlike the young man who had asked Yasutani Roshi about being drafted, Aitken had a firm grasp on the distinctions between Zen practice and Japanese culture. He also had learned from the Japanese something of the diplomacy of discretion; familiar with the political allegiances of most Japanese teachers, he had long ago concluded that certain activities were simply not discussed.

By the time of Yasutani's visit, Aitken was counseling draft resisters. Following the guidelines established by the AFSC, he presented to the draft inductees all their options and what consequences they could expect from their decisions. If an inductee decided to plea for conscientious objection, then Aitken made an all-out effort to help arrange his papers.

The pressure of leading the Diamond Sangha in the ambiguous role of senior student had become exhausting for Aitken, for it required taking responsibility without having authority. In June 1965, however, Katsuki Sekida, a lay student from Soen Roshi's monastery, joined the Diamond Sangha, bringing with him a simple, impersonal version of the way Zen was practiced in Japan. Endless, steady, and undramatic, Sekida-san's version was dubbed "Applied Zen" by a student who explained that "Zen was so unfamiliar to us, it was hard to just get past its newness. Sekida-san showed us a way of doing this practice and not making such a big deal out of it. It began looking less like some quixotic American fad."

In 1967, with Sekida-san in residence at Koko An, the Aitkens vacationed in Haiku, an area of Maui rich in pineapple plantations. There they came across a former plantation house for sale—a small wooden house shaded by banana trees and approached from the road by a path lined with mango-colored day lilies—and they spontaneously purchased it as a future retirement home. Aitken was then fifty and Anne six years older. They returned to Honolulu after arranging for the current tenants—"some very unusual young people"—to pay twenty-five dollars a month in rent as well as cut the grass. "Finally," recalls Aitken, "we just said, 'Forget about the twenty-five dollars, just keep the grass cut.' Well, they didn't do that either. They were very interesting people who were experimenting with many different substances."

Maui was one of the many beautiful havens discovered in the late sixties by New Age nomads in need of refuge from mainstream America. The island offered a variety of rent-free shelters, isolated from the towns and public beaches. "The New Age people"—as Aitken respectfully calls them—could live in the open, wash in the sea, and stumble stoned and naked upon bananas, pineapples, and guavas that had fallen onto public ground or could be unobtrusively "liberated" from private gardens. Everything about the island offered a welcome contrast to segregated housing, restrictive clothing, chemical food, and parents who confused the reality of who their children were with who they wanted them to be.

While the 1968 Democratic Convention galvanized the political components of the counterculture, Maui attracted hard-core hedonists from flower children to jock surfers. Though the surfers may have taken adolescence way past its limit, they did not challenge middle-class values and were able to claim free and easy domination of the public beaches. In a reenactment of the larger cultural panorama, the New Age people were consigned to the untended peripheries, where the pursuit of life, liberty, and happiness took a peculiarly Dionysian twist.

McKena's Beach, at the end of a long, bumpy dirt road, was home to almost two hundred people; the Banana Patch, an area formed by the floor and sides of a valley, accommodated another fifty to one hundred. The only shelters were lean-tos constructed from found materials and covered with scraps of corrugated metal. The Aitkens visited Maui frequently from 1967 to 1969 and discovered that their new house was one of the most popular crash pads for residents of McKena's Beach and the Banana Patch. Its tranquil setting, indiscriminate hospitality, and loving vibrations had already earned it the nickname "the House of God."

The Aitkens stayed with their young tenants and their transitory friends. With each visit, Aitken felt more compelled to help the children in the House of God—and each time he mowed his own lawn. "No one was working with these New Age people at all except a Christian program called Teen Challenge—and the Maui police department." As lost or laid-back as these New Age people appeared, their refusal to be a part of what they regarded as a disintegrating and corrupt society indicated to Aitken some degree of moral awareness and spiritual vitality. "A lot of them were really searching, and we felt we could be of some use here."

Aitken retired from the University of Hawaii in 1969 and moved to Haiku with Anne and Sekida-san to start the Maui Zendo. On leaving Koko An, they rented the house to tenants, who though not affiliated with the zendo, agreed to open the house for the scheduled zazen meetings. After a year, however, Diamond Sangha members took over the lease, and soon a daily zazen schedule was maintained by the students in residence. The membership at Koko An continued to grow, and Aitken soon began returning to Honolulu each month to participate in the sitting group. After 1974, when Aitken was authorized to lead sesshin, serious students from both Maui and Honolulu routinely traveled between the two locations.

Maui provided Aitken a chance to become fully involved in a community. He attracted—and responded to—people who were as disoriented as he had once been. Whereas at their age, Aitken, reserved and isolated, had turned to his books and kept his dreams private, this generation had a tribal support system; collective disorientation was converted into social rituals that could be as fragile and appealing as they could be destructive. What Aitken had kept guarded, the Maui hippies expressed not only in alienated behavior and despair but also in a quest for joy, free love, and sanctified union with nature and each other. What attracted Aitken was the acting out of these needs, not their fulfillment, for he clearly understood that most often his new friends could not transcend their inhibitions any more than he had. What also drew Aitken to these people was that like Zen followers they trusted experience over speculative thought and strove to grasp reality from within rather than have it imposed on them. Having lost their bearings in the ideological bogs of the sixties, they had been brought to the edge of Zen; they had not been prepared for a disciplined path of realization, but they had less to lose for trying it than their conventional counterparts. In the process of zazen, one's external identifications begin to fall away, the social face dissolves, and the mask cracks. With the Vietnam debacle, the mask of the whole culture began to crack. "When Big Daddy LBJ betrayed us as he did," says Aitken, "we lost everything. And so we needed to find our way."

When they first moved to Maui, the Aitkens found themselves sleeping on the floor of their retirement home next to half-dressed adventurers with dilated pupils and names like Squeak, Flower, Blue, and Cloud. In the process of converting their home into a residential Zen center, the Aitkens counseled and consoled, cooked and provided sleeping mats. Financial arrangements were loose. Anne's graciousness and warmth made her "mother to us all," recalls a woman who now studies at Koko An. "The early days were truly pioneering days," Anne says. "The walls leaked, there were never enough beds, there were never enough pots or zabutons; there was usually enough food because we grew it ourselves, but everything was makeshift. And everybody accepted this."

The new zendo might have received the entire population of both McKena's Beach and the Banana Patch but for one factor: the schedule. For all of their leniency and support, the Aitkens strictly enforced a traditional monastic schedule. Payments, clothing, sexual conduct, and food preferences were subject to personal need and whim. The schedule was not. Grueling and rigid, it quickly screened out students who were not committed to Zen practice. Marine boot camp is the only American experience that has ever been compared to life in a Zen monastery. For Maui's new population boot camp was the last hell, and few could sustain this daily routine:

5 :00 A.M.	rise and wash
5 :10	zazen
5 :50	study period
6 :30	breakfast
7 :00	work meeting, cleanup, work period
9 :30	refreshment break
10:30	work period ends
11 :10	zazen
11 :50	zazen ends
Noon	dinner, short rest
1 :00 P.M.	work period
3 :00	work period ends, refreshment, rest
4 :30	zazen
5 :10	zazen ends
5 :20	supper, silent rest
7 :10	zazen (talks twice a week)
9 :00	lights out

The designated work periods, or *samu*, involved household and gardening chores. For many students new to Zen, the emphasis on work was associated with bad memories of a detested Protestant value. In "A Note on Samu," Aitken writes: "Terms in Zen Buddhism often point to both the world of practice and the world of essence . . . [samu] refers to the work necessary for the upkeep of the monastery, and on the other hand to the act itself; just the sweeping, just the hammering." Samu lacked the exoticism that glamorized Zen and it contradicted preconceived ideas of spiritual practice. "Getting high" on drugs had been an invitation to "space out"—not to take care of business, cook, or wash dishes. When the spaciousness induced by zazen became as seductive as the spaciousness induced by drugs, then work practice became the equivalent of "coming down." "We used to think," recalls an early member of the Maui Zendo, "what a terrible waste to apply this wonderful meditative quality of infinite mind to washing the dishes! We just didn't get it."

Another student remembers that it wasn't just the rigidity of the schedule that challenged a nebulous sense of freedom: "Roshi himself seemed very rigid to us. He was kindly, but formal, like a minister. But some of us, like myself, were so tired of floating around. And suddenly, like a mirage, this good man appears and says, 'Here, my child, why don't you sit down on this black cushion.' You could call it meditation. You could call it Zen. I didn't care. I just needed to stop."

Some people floated briefly through the Maui Zendo but have identified their experience there as a turning point in their lives. Whereas in cities and on campuses across the mainland the ideals of the counterculture had gained respectable adult support, Maui was divided by segregated polarities, with the middle-class and middle-age residency at odds with nomadic and younger members of the counterculture. There the Aitkens were a rare crossbreed: adults who could be trusted. For some wanderers, this alone was a welcoming road sign. Anne calculated that at one point as many as seventeen people were living in their house, and that over two hundred people had passed through in one year: "People came for a night, three nights, or a week or as long as they could stand our program, and we tried to do our best for all of them—not realizing at the time that you can't do everything for everybody. You have to define your objectives and limit them in order to be of the most help." In general, very few of these people had the will, stamina, discipline, or interest to pursue Zen studies.

Then there was the man who arrived at the Maui airport, walked up to the information desk, and asked, "Can you show me the way to the monastery?" The information clerk was clearly baffled, but a man standing nearby directed the newcomer to the Maui Zendo. He was led into the house to meet Aitken, who was standing next to a beautiful young woman wearing a flimsy summer dress. Aitken recalls this man saying in a very solemn manner, " 'Greetings! I have come to enter the monastery,' one huge suitcase in each hand, all the while looking out the tail of his eye at the young woman. I said, 'I'm sorry, this isn't a monastery, but come in anyway.' He's still here."

Aitken was skilled in diplomatic relations with social agencies, having worked in several community organizations, and he arranged a meeting with the mayor of Maui to introduce himself and foster good relations between the city and the zendo. Word filtered down that a professional man, an older, conservative, well-educated gentleman, was interested in Maui's new population. Subsequently, if under the influence of hallucinogenic drugs someone ended up in the police station or the mental ward of the local hospital, Aitken was often notified. At various times extremely disturbed people were placed in his care. They were segregated in an extension of the main house, and the daily schedule continued uninterrupted. Some of these people eventually joined the practice, while others collected themselves and moved on. "Once, at the Maui Zendo, some people had a flat tire on the road in front of the temple. They came in to use the telephone and stayed six months. There is significance to each human encounter," concludes Aitken, "so you need not conjure up a deep reason for coming to Zen practice."

As it happened, virtually all of the new inquirers at both the Maui and Honolulu centers in the early seventies, according to Aitken, "learned about religious possibilities through taking dope. There were exceptions . . . but these were rather strange people." Aitken smoked marijuana several times and experimented with LSD once in 1970. He understood from the residents in his house that the spaciousness induced by drugs could lead to meditation. What he learned from his own experience was "what a limited perspective one got from marijuana." He spent a day on acid at the top of a mountain, watching Roman soldiers float in and out of the clouds and musing over his inability to remember even the first syllables of the *Heart Sutra*. It had been, for the most part, "a wonderful day, but what a waste of time! A whole day shot."

"We've always had a No Dope rule at Maui Zendo and at Koko An Zendo," says Aitken. "I once told some people that what they did on their own time was their business. But soon I began telling them that they shouldn't smoke ever, because I find that people who are off marijuana for a while, and then smoke again, go through a period of having to get back into practice. It's not really worth it. And besides they're putting themselves in a stratum of society that is really nasty. We have former members who haven't been able to break the habit. I'm as cordial to them as I can be, but you see, they just can't come around."

Aitken encourages "right livelihood," and drug dealing has not been the only occupation he finds problematic. "I told a girl who was a barmaid, 'I can visualize over the course of time that either you would stop being a barmaid or stop coming to the zendo.' That's as close to directive counseling as I've come with a student. A person is a barmaid for a deep reason, you know, like everything else. There is some very deep need that is being satisfied with that kind of life. So it's very difficult to change. I also worked with a masseuse, one of those marginal masseuses—I have other students who do massage and they're professional but they're straight. This gal wasn't straight. And I told her the same thing. But she was fascinated by zazen."

Aitken may have seen himself as the adviser, older brother, senior student, and *tanto* (zendo monitor); but surrounded by students thirty years his junior, he was cast into a parental role, as an authority figure, with all the convoluted emotional ambivalence that attends that projection. When the Maui Zendo first started, he himself still harbored a political and psychological mistrust toward authority figures. He was an anarchist by preference, a leader who wanted to guide without goading, direct without enforcing, be patient and permissive; but he could not readily abandon his own rigidities and judgments. His facial gestures and finger tapping gave away his disappointment when discussions didn't go his way. And to students young enough to be his children, disappointment was generally experienced as disapproval. Students now recall that his style in the beginning was tentative, hesitant, groping, and that he compensated with a carefully ordered environment. When it came to ethical codes of behavior and the daily schedule, he was inflexible. A therapist, after studying for fifteen years with Aitken on Maui, said: "People came here looking for this nonhuman and what they found was this guy in his sixties wrestling with the integration of his character through Zen practice."

Aitken's ideals were sometimes at odds with his personality. He encouraged democracy but inclined toward paternalism. He encouraged openness and direct expression, but he was hard to get to know. "Roshi's desire to be open," said the therapist, "did not automatically make him open, but his commitment to the process was always in evidence. He made every effort to reveal his personality, to show us his 'imperfections.' Students who wanted a demigod were disillusioned by his humanity; students who wanted a hero were abused by his humility."

"I came to practice wanting to idealize a teacher," said a woman in her early forties. "And so anything that was 'human' shook up my faith. But then I saw that if he was in any way like me, then I could attain what he had attained. His humanity inspired me. The very things that were obstacles fifteen years ago became the most valuable assets."

Not everyone around Aitken has been able to use his personality or his struggles for integration as a source of inspiration. For some students the gap between the real and ideal democratic process for community decisions became untenable. Although Aitken Roshi has strayed far from the autocracy granted the Japanese roshi, for some American students it will never be far enough.

In an essay entitled "The Vocation of Zen," Aitken outlines the basic differences between Japanese and American notions of authority:

> In our Western society we don't have a built-in support system for cleaning up the residues of self-centered compulsions. In the East, an authority figure stands forth and says, *you* clean the toilets and *you* ring the bells. The students know that cleaning the toilets and ringing the bells are both part of the practice and that the likes and dislikes of particular tasks are vain and ultimately empty. So they just do what they are told. I am sure that often it is difficult to accept orders in the Asian monastery, but the precedent is there in the Confucian ideal of loyalty to the superior. So the students stick it out, obey orders, and gradually their rough edges are worn smooth, and character change does occur in conjunction with their zazen and their koan study. They are able to face their selfishness and overcome it and to give their experience of empty oneness a good chance to expand and fill the universe.
>
> Thus the monastery works in the East, but in our own Western egalitarian society there is no authority figure to set forth a program of change, and indeed, if some such figure does emerge and is the ultimate boss of everything, then by our heritage, naturally we feel a lot of discomfort, a lot of questioning, a lot of doubt, a lot of dissatisfaction.
>
> So really for us the responsibility of change lies with ourselves, individually and as a community. We are faced with resolving the uniqueness of the individual and with the unity of the Sangha, entirely on our own.

Although never able to shed the vestiges of authority entirely, Aitken has steered clear of formal teaching modes that reinforce the autocracy of the Japanese roshi. To attend the roshi is, by Japanese standards, a privileged position that allows for an intimate relationship between the master and an exceptional disciple. For Aitken this is not only antithetical to American ideology but reflects the complex investment that Japan places in social hierarchies, religious or secular. And as far as he is concerned, this is not intrinsic to Zen. The Aitkens employ students to help with household and office work, and they pay them the going hourly wage. In restaurants Aitken insists on paying his share and discourages gifts. "When it comes to money matters," explains one student, "Roshi is like a fanatically honest cop. Hardly a free cup of coffee."

Throughout the late sixties, while Aitken was leading the Diamond Sangha, he and Anne made lengthy trips to Japan to continue their studies. They worked with Yasutani Roshi, as well as with his principal disciple, Yamada Roshi. After conferring with both Nakagawa Soen and Yasutani, the Aitkens invited Yamada Roshi to lead the Diamond Sangha. Yamada arrived in Hawaii in 1971, just as the county decided finally to close down McKena's Beach and the Banana Patch. An inordinate number of the dispossessed landed on the lawn of the Maui Zendo. "Very strange, very unusual," Yamada Roshi kept murmuring. As for the Zen students, their style too was perplexing, and Yamada Roshi was alternately amused and offended by their informality but consistently impressed by their sincerity.

Aitken's studies with Yamada during this visit were critical, and in "Willy-Nilly Zen" he writes: "Looking back, I understand my 'dark night' from 1961 to 1971 much better than I did a decade ago. My experience with Nakagawa [Soen] Roshi in the first 1961 sesshin was not deep enough to give me significant insight and it took several more years of zazen to prepare me to really begin Zen practice. This kind of chronology is not usual but I do occasionally meet others with similar histories."

During each spring from 1972 to 1974, the Aitkens returned to Japan and engaged in intense koan study with Yamada Roshi. When Aitken received dharma transmission in 1974, it was a point of maturation for the entire community, at once a public recognition from teacher to student as well as a confirmation of the faith that the Diamond Sangha had already placed in Aitken. Yamada Roshi's acknowledgment did not put an end to all the questions that Aitken or his students had about the authority of the teacher in general or about Aitken's authority in particular. According to sangha members, however, it did spur a sense of confidence in the practice and in the development of the community. Not coincidentally, it was now time for the Maui Zendo to move out of the Aitkens' home.

The new zendo was relocated a mile down the road in a secluded hilltop lodge that had been built during the First World War. After the war it was purchased from its Japanese-American owners by the Baptist Church and used as a retreat for overseas Baptist missionaries. Surrounded by gardenia bushes, birds of paradise, banana and guava trees, the house was sold to the

Maui Zendo by a New Age idealist who had failed to establish his utopian commune. The purchase was initially financed mostly by Anne Aitken, who had used her inheritance to buy the first Maui Zendo as well as Koko An. Sangha members labored over roof repairs, the meditation hall, the grounds, and the vegetable garden.

By the mid-seventies the membership of the Maui Zendo showed signs of the postwar lull that befell most social activists of the sixties. But Aitken remained convinced that the role of a contemporary Bodhisattva—one who has vowed to save "all creations without restriction"—is effectively served by social action, specifically by radical pacifism. In 1967 he had become associated with the Fellowship of Reconciliation, an organization devoted to world peace that was founded in England in 1916 and spread to this country shortly after the end of the First World War. Then in 1976 Aitken and two students, Nelson Foster and Stephen Cockley, decided to form their own chapter of the fellowship on Maui. "We attracted members of our group, and also some from outside the Buddhist community, and we tried to get something started in prison visitation. We also began to investigate what was going on at Haleakala Summit where there are observatories connected to satellite tracking and space warfare. As we talked, it gradually became clear to us that what we really wanted to do was form a Buddhist Peace Fellowship and so we just switched it."

The nonsectarian Buddhist Peace Fellowship (BPF) is still an affiliate of the Fellowship of Reconciliation; its newsletter functions as a critical networking guide for the political activities of what the Vietnamese monk Thich Nhat Hanh has called "engaged Buddhism." The most active Buddhist organization to promote world peace, the BPF cosponsored an interreligious delegation to Honduras and Nicaragua in 1987 for the purpose of gathering firsthand information on the crisis in Central America.

In his effort to confront global greed with the politics of compassion, Aitken has had to leave behind the biases of the Japanese Buddhist establishment, which historically has been too dependent on political approval to function as a moral witness. "The Buddha," Aitken has written, "did not live in a time like ours, when dangerous competition between nations threatens to blow up the world. He was not faced with the probability of biological holocaust. . . . I wonder what he would say today." But given the threatened state of the world, the Buddhist way of "being peace" for the sake of peace has taken on a political urgency previously unknown in Buddhist societies. In *Blind Donkey*, a journal published by the Diamond Sangha, Aitken writes:

> In the West we have a clear sense of personal and group responsibility for the government and welfare of everyone, set forth by Locke, Rousseau, and others in the late eighteenth century and developed for the next two hundred years in the democratic societies in Europe and the Americas. As Western Buddhists, we are building on one tradition of social responsibility that has been developing from Moses, Jesus, and Plato, and on another tradition that has been cultivated in monastic settings by yogis, Taoists, and Buddhists, as well as in the institutes of Confucianism, where highest probity was sought. With such a synthesis of traditions, Buddhism in the West is sure to apply the Precepts in a new way.

Aitken himself applies the Buddhist precepts directly to the world's most pressing ecological and political problems, which historically have been ignored by the monastic Zen tradition. As he explains in *The Mind of Clover* (1984): "The experience of peace is not enough. *Samadhi* [deep concentration] on one's cushion is not enough. Unless that whole mountain is swallowed and digested and you sit with sightseers on your scalp, zazen is altogether incomplete." He reiterates that caring for oneself and others on this planet, however threatened and fouled it may be, must not be avoided—and certainly not in the name of Zen practice.

Aitken has always scrupulously ensured, however, that his own political activities neither solicit nor discourage interest in traditional Zen training. BPF events, for example, are announced to the sangha but with no pressure for members to take part in them. So far Aitken's American students have displayed little more interest in politics than Zen adherents have in Japan. "There is still not the widespread concern about planetary affairs in our sangha that I hope might appear someday," Aitken admitted in 1987. Still, discussions about Zen and politics are not uncommon in his presence. One afternoon on the porch at Koko An a woman asked if there was a difference between the state using Zen for its own purposes and the peace movement using Zen for its own purposes. Aitken answered, "I don't suppose there's any difference really. Exploitation is exploitation. But I think that Buddhism has something to say to the peace movement. That's different from exploitation. What we're coming down to here is a question of morality. What is the basis of morality? Ultimately, good is the Tao. Recently in Los Angeles, this fellow from Vietnam asked me, 'Is warfare real?' 'You bet your life it's real, if anything is real, warfare is real.' That's what I told him. We can't duck around such issues. Emptiness is form."

In Zen the tendency for spiritual seekers to cling to the mountaintop—despite the universal pleas for them to return to the lowlands—is reflected not only by traditional monasticism, but in the proclivity of monks and laymen—Japanese and American alike—of "getting stuck in emptiness," of overestimating the value of emptiness at the expense of form. "It's really hard for students to get this," Aitken says, and he repeats, "emptiness *is* form." That one cannot use an encounter with emptiness to justify staying on top of the pole has been an especially difficult lesson for students who discovered Zen in America while America was in Vietnam and who identified spiritual practice as a noble and somewhat romantic exit from the profanity of material greed and political passion.

While Aitken avoids imposing social concerns on his Zen students, his planetary-political vision reflects basic Buddhist teachings and, furthermore, elucidates that aspect of Buddhist doctrine recently complemented in the West by quantum mechanics. His teaching emphasizes a classic understanding of the Jeweled Net of Indra, the Buddhist image for "the interrelatedness of all things without restriction." Each intersection of Indra's net has a jewel that reflects every other facet of every other jewel. No thing exists outside this net, this "one body." According to quantum theory, the world can no longer be disassembled into independent entities. The isolated building blocks of the past are now perceived as a complex web of interrelations within a unified whole, and trying to maintain even the illusion that any man is an island is fast becoming impossible.

> Baby mice in their nest
> Squeak in response
> To the young sparrows.

Aitken writes on this poem by Basho: "Not only baby mice and sparrows, but all people, animals, and things are intimately interconnected. The word 'symbiotic' means the living together in mutual dependence of dissimilar organisms. That says it all. We are a symbiotic universe, a symbiotic family of nations, a symbiotic country, state of that country, island, community, family and even individual (for we have all kinds of creatures living in our insides)."

According to Zen teachings, each individual has the capacity to change his or her own consciousness, and as the one body is "all creations without restriction," it follows that changing one's consciousness *is* changing the collective whole. This reasoning has been used to advocate meditation as the supreme political act. If zazen is the molecular seed of change—the most effective, the most potent activity—then why, Aitken was asked, leave the cushion? Aitken responded, "Why did the Buddha get up from the bodhi tree? He walked the Ganges Valley afterward all his life. Turning the wheel of dharma. Never stopping. I don't think that people are ready to hear this, for one reason or another, and besides, just as there are people who are not active in my own sangha—most people are not active in my own sangha—they're not ready and that's all right." With all his political commitments, zazen is still the most important activity for Aitken. "Unless you yourself are clear," he said, "nothing you do will be clear. If you have a busy mind, you get burned out."

Aitken values the ritual of Japanese Zen and, comparing ceremony to cooking, says that "every cultural entity has its own way of cooking, and we need to develop our own way; but unless there's some configuration to the ceremony, then it's tasteless and secular." Like many American Zen centers, the Maui Zendo has served as an experimental kitchen, testing recipes and assessing the results. English translations have long since been added to the Sino-Japanese sutra recitations, for example, and a ceremony called *juhai*, which publicly acknowledges a student who has passed the koan *mu*, was dropped from the program after provoking too many complaints that it induced an uneasy and useless sense of competition.

Aitken has advocated communication workshops as a way of replacing the Japanese monastic model of submission to a well-defined authority with one that relies on consensus as a method of governing the center. Over the years he has tried to shift the decision-making operations of the sangha from a democratic voting system to a nonvoting method of group consensus. It never worked on Maui, but in his absence it met with some success in Honolulu. "People aren't used to this way of working," Aitken says, "and it has taken a long time to get used to the idea. The responsibility imbued in the voting members of the sangha shifts considerably with consensus. You have to learn to let go of fixed opinions. You have to learn that you don't come into a meeting determined to get a certain point of view across and to reach a particular decision. You don't have a zero/sum attitude at anytime. That is, zero for them and a hundred percent for me. The Quakers have been doing this for centuries, so it's possible, it just takes a long time. It takes more trust in the group and in other people. That's why I used to push for the communication workshops."

To diffuse competition in the sangha and instill an awareness of community has not been easy. Aitken hoped that the communication exercises would help "clean up the residues of self-centered compulsions," but as a social worker explained: "When we started the Maui Zendo there was this naive idea that Zen practice would take care of all our personal and social problems. But none of us was raised to consider the group over our individual needs, so it was unrealistic to expect Zen to teach us about community."

The problem of government by consensus at the Maui Zendo came to a head in 1982. Ever since the zendo moved from the Aitkens' home to its new location, it had been maintained by a resident caretaker. During the intensive three-month training periods when the center filled with residents, the zendo generated the concentrated energy that comes from daily formal practice. But in between retreats the dispersion of energy that comes naturally became excessive. Even members who lived nearby appeared only when Aitken gave interviews or talks. Only the occasional guest joined the caretaker for the daily schedule of morning and evening zazen, plus three hours a day of samu. Consequently, the caretaker, who also functioned as guestmaster, cook, zendo monitor, and sangha host, occupied a position that was too often lonely and short-lived. He had to rise at 5 A.M., ring bells, light incense, chant sutras, and fill the zendo with strong sitting. Situations like this may fire the aspirations of a youthful zealot and are not in fact uncommon in hilltop hermitages all over Asia, but it takes a rare American to stick it out without resentment and self-pity. The job, like Aitken's previous role as senior student, entailed too much responsibility with too little authority. The authority continued to be vested if not ultimately in Aitken himself, then in the voting members of the community, who were not residents and therefore had no commitments to the daily schedule. Maui members organized their employment around the retreat schedule, but daily input slowly drained out.

Some of the difficulties at the Maui Zendo have been attributed to the indulgences of island living. "People came to Maui to get something," said a student. "Space, sun, quiet, Zen. But 'getting' didn't fuse with 'giving.'" Maui's high unemployment rate, its lack of growing industry, the seduction of the sun and the beaches all combined to promote an indolent and languid life. One Koko An member who left Maui several years ago to escape an encroaching lethargy said, "You bring your whole bag of tricks with you to the zendo. If your lifestyle is indulgent and pleasure seeking, then it seems counterproductive to practice."

By 1982 the energy of the Maui Zendo had ebbed so low that in an effort to revitalize it the Aitkens drew up plans to build a residence for themselves on the zendo property. This measure was not endorsed by the membership, however. The island had stopped attracting new Zen students, while many of the older ones had moved to Honolulu. Some of the members did not share Aitken's assessment that his presence would regenerate the zendo, and others resented the possibility of feeling pressured into attendance. Still others who had arrived on Maui drugged and disillusioned at the age of twenty had grown up and married and had children to support. As the years went by it was no longer feasible to rely on young parents for daily participation and even less so when it came to the three-month intensives; not even installing the roshi in residence could change this.

The discussions about the Aitkens' residency plans intensified conflicts in the decision-making process of the Maui community. It brought to the fore questions concerning the authority of the Zen teacher and Aitken's authority in particular. The students had been getting crossed signals, which, as they saw it, reflected Aitken's confusion as to where to draw the line between the teacher's authority and the students' autonomy. No one mistook them as teaching devices, for Aitken has been openly critical of what he calls the "Gurdjieff syndrome": "I want to get away from this whole guru-image that if I disrupt a student's life it's always for his own good. Gurdjieff was an extreme violator of this sort of thing, sending a woman back from the Crimea through the battle lines between the Reds and the Whites, back to Moscow to pick up a rug that he left there in his apartment. It was an incredibly dangerous trip and she writes about it as if it were her practice! You see the same thing in early Benedictine history where they told neophytes to plant the carrots upside down. I want there to be some substance in what I tell people to do and if they ask why I want to be able to meet their challenge."

"I think that to some degree I'm always the teacher and I never lose that role," Aitken continues, "but I don't have a guru role and don't want it." In distinguishing himself from a guru, he has implied an invidious comparison between Vedanta and Tibetan traditions on the one hand and Japanese Zen on the other. In *Taking the Path of Zen* he writes:

> The guru, too, encourages falling away, but in the act of identifying with the guru. The guru is omnipotent, and though he or she may try to encourage the student to find independence, the Dharma will have a specific name and face and the student cannot truly be free.
>
> I may not be making an accurate presentation of guru-student relationships that would apply in all cases, but I want to show that the roshi wishes each person to develop to the highest potential. The roshi is not interested in being deified and will refuse to be placed in such a position.
>
> Just as one must have faith in one's own guide in order to traverse an unknown forest, so faith in the roshi is essential. This is not a matter of personal aggrandizement for the roshi, but a matter of utmost importance for the student. Without that faith, zazen becomes only a sterile practice in concentration, with no movement toward realization and beyond. The student cannot trust himself or herself truly to let go.

At the persuasive counsel of three senior students, plans for the Aitkens to relocate to the zendo grounds were abandoned. By 1983 it had become obvious that the most effective forum for Aitken's energies was no longer the Elysian fields of Maui, and he made plans to return to Honolulu. "I don't want to be like a junior high school teacher," he said, "left high and dry on the podium. I want to be in the life of the community."

The following year Yamada Roshi came to Honolulu to perform a ceremony that permitted Aitken formally to transmit the precepts and officiate at the *jukai* ceremony. During this ceremony the student receives a *rakusu*, a black halter that represents the Buddha's robe. To Aitken's displeasure, jukai has been defined in the United States as "lay ordination." According to Aitken, there is no such thing: "There are no etymological roots for that term. It certainly isn't what jukai means. You either receive the precepts or you don't." Students strongly resisted wearing a rakusu because of the way it distinguishes between sangha members and because of its particularly American association with the ordination of monastics. In defense of laypeople's Zen, Diamond Sangha members have been openly disdainful of what they perceive as the false piety of American Zen monks, with their ostentatious robes and shaved heads but secular lifestyles; for these students, the overt distinction of the American Zen monk contradicts the teachings. Aitken has made it clear, however, that offering jukai is not within the jurisdiction of the sangha, and the ceremony is held for those senior students who elect to have it. In Aitken's case, furthermore, offering jukai reflects his commitment to making the Zen precepts as personal as possible. For his students, Aitken exemplifies the application of the precepts in one's daily life and the world in which one lives rather than in some kind of moral vacuum.

In Zen, the Ten Grave Precepts are guidelines for an ever-changing present that by its nature demands both creative and appropriate response. Writing on the first precept, "No Killing," Aitken recalls "that someone once asked Alan Watts why he was a vegetarian. He said, 'Because cows scream louder than carrots.' This reply may serve as a guideline. Some people will refuse to eat red meat. Some people will not drink milk. Some people will eat what is served to them, but will limit their own purchases of animal products. You must draw your own line, considering your health and the health of other beings." Aitken, who generally maintains a vegetarian diet, has said that if he goes to a dinner party and is served meat he will eat it because "The cow is dead and the hostess is not."

Similarly, there are ways of understanding the Ten Commandments in terms of time, place, and function—not as hard-and-fast injunctions. But for those Americans who came to Zen through rejection of their own Judeo-Christian heritage, the Ten Commandments represented a rigid, blind, superstitious belief system perpetuated for the good of the nation-state. The myth about Zen and morality, partially inherited from Beat Zen anarchists, suggests that in the falling away of body and mind, in the *realization* of life, all belief systems have to go; correct behavior will then arise spontaneously, rendering ethical systems obsolete. Aitken, however, challenges students to investigate their attraction to Zen practice and reconsider their own beliefs about Zen itself. In his essay "Zen and Ethics," he writes: "I have heard some people say that since Zen says we must be grounded in the place where there is no right and wrong, it follows that Zen has no ethical application. But if there were no application of our experience of the unity and the individuality of all beings, then Zen would be only a stale exercise in seclusion, the way of death."

In Japan the precepts traditionally come at the end of formal studies, suggesting, as does Aitken himself, that without the experience of realization the precepts can be misused as dogmatic substitutes for true understanding. He often quotes his teacher, Yamada Roshi, who said that "the purpose of Zen is the perfection of character." Like the term "ethics," "perfection" and "character" have been difficult notions for American Zen students to digest. Not only does "character" imply a social archetype, but "perfection" further suggests goal-oriented, idealized behavior—the very models that Zen students have tried to abandon. In *Taking the Path of Zen*, Aitken illustrates Yamada Roshi's phrase with the story about Bird's Nest Roshi:

> He was a teacher who lived in the T'ang period and did zazen in a tree. The governor of his province, Po Chu-i, heard about Bird's Nest Roshi and went to see him. This Po Chu-i was no ordinary politician. He was one of China's greatest poets, well known for his expression of Zen Buddhism.
>
> Po Chu-i found Bird's Nest Roshi sitting in his tree, doing zazen. He called to him, saying, "Oh, Bird's Nest, you look very insecure to me up there."
>
> Bird's Nest Roshi looked down at Po Chu-i and replied, "Oh Governor, you look very insecure to me down there." All things are under the law of change and political position is the most ephemeral of all. Po Chu-i knew very well what Bird's Nest Roshi was talking about. So he took a different tack.
>
> "Tell me," he said, "what is it that all the Buddhas taught?" Bird's Nest replied by quoting from the *Dhammapada*:
>
> > Never do evil;
> > always do good;
> > keep your mind pure—
> > thus all the Buddhas taught.
>
> So Po Chu-i said, "Always do good; never do evil; keep your mind pure—I knew that when I was three years old."
>
> "Yes," said Bird's Nest Roshi. "A three-year-old child may know it, but even an eighty-year-old man cannot put it into practice."

Although he recognizes the potential for misuse, Aitken nevertheless prefers to present the precepts at an early stage of Zen studies: "Without the precepts as guidelines, Zen Buddhism tends to become a hobby, made to fit the needs of the ego. Selflessness, as taught at the Zen center, conflicts with the indulgence encouraged by society. . . . In my view, the true Zen Buddhist center is not a mere sanctuary, but a source from which ethically motivated people move outward to engage in the larger community."

The very idea that the world needs ethically motivated people departs radically from the views of Beat Zen. With Aitken's help, one aspect of maturation for American students has been to stop using Buddha's expression of his enlightenment—"How wonderful, how wonderful, everything is enlightened just as it is"—as a justification for not trying to effect social change, and again to ask why the Buddha returned to society to practice, preach, and help alleviate suffering.

During Aitken's fourteen-year residency on Maui, the Honolulu sangha became "community-centered." The membership has now grown to about one hundred, the average age is around forty, and, unlike the situation on Maui, students have not identified their practice with the presence of the teacher. Continuing to come to Koko An, they regularly sit together, and the center runs with an impressive degree of coordination. Furthermore, in Honolulu students may apply their Zen studies to social services. Training periods have included morning work periods at hospitals and prisons. In 1980, with Aitken's support, students in Honolulu started *Kahawai: A Journal of Women and Zen*, which has been supportive to women all over the United States disheartened by the masculine dominance in traditional Buddhist studies. *Kahawai*, as well as Aitken's books, has attracted widespread attention, and visitors from the mainland and Europe commonly attend sesshins. The Diamond Sangha now has affiliate centers in California, Arizona, and Australia, and Koko An often hosts students from these as well.

When Aitken left Maui, there were still plans to hold retreats at the Maui Zendo, but after Aitken's departure there was so little support for the idea that in 1986 the Maui Zendo was sold. The following year Anne and Aitken Roshi were once again embarking on a new residential project. In 1987 the Diamond Sangha purchased property in upper Palolo Valley, about four miles from Koko An. In this mountainous terrain Aitken, who had just turned seventy, envisioned a village with his own residence, a meditation hall, and a dormitory for families that would enable parents to attend sesshin. The House of God that the Aitkens had purchased twenty years earlier for their retirement has yet to be used for that purpose. With this new project retirement itself has become an outdated plan.

The Palolo Valley project may be difficult to realize, but no more so than any step of the enlightened way. "What you do in one lifetime is open the door," says Aitken Roshi. "You realize, 'yes, that's true: this very body is the

Buddha,' just as in the Christian ceremony you take the flesh and blood of Christ into yourself. But that doesn't mean that you are a saint like Jesus. You open up the way and then it's important for you to pursue that way. You could just let it close up again. Yamada Roshi uses the image of cutting a piece of mochi with a sharp knife. He said that if you just cut that piece of mochi with a sharp knife it's going to come back together again. We spend our lives actualizing what we realize. There is a saying in Zen: 'Buddha Shakyamuni is only halfway there.' "

Priest Paô-ch'e of Ma-ku shan was fanning himself. A monk approached and asked, "Sir, the nature of wind is permanent, and there is no place it does not reach. Why, then, must you still fan yourself?" "Although you understand that the nature of wind is permanent," the master replied, "you do not understand the meaning of its reaching everywhere." "What is the meaning of its reaching everywhere?" asked the monk. The master just fanned himself. The monk bowed with deep respect.

This is the enlightened experience of Buddha-dharma and the vital way of its correct transmission. Those who say we should not use a fan because wind is permanent, and so we should know the existence of wind without using a fan, know neither permanency nor the nature of wind.

Because the nature of wind is eternally present, the wind of Buddhism actualizes the gold of the earth and ripens the cheese of the long river.

From Genjo Koan, Eihei Dogen Zenji

JAKUSHO
KWONG

Jakusho Kwong is standing at the gate of a California vineyard under clear skies while half a dozen students question him about the jurisdiction of the Zen teacher. The morning work at Sonoma Mountain Zen Center has just ended, but no one is eager to leave the unseasonable January sunshine for the climb back to the Community House for lunch. While American Zen students have learned to question the teacher-student dynamic, investigating new terms for a relationship that has a long and dogmatic history has its awkward moments nevertheless. Kwong's students hesitantly probe the extent to which the authority of the Zen teacher should preside in all areas of life and how this might apply to their own situations. Putting down his pruning shears, Kwong stretches his arms out toward a grid of dormant grapevines as t-shaped and austere as the unmarked graves of a Benedictine cemetery. Responding directly to their hesitation, he shouts "Welcome Dharma USA!"

According to Kwong, the Buddhist teachings are only now beginning to enter the United States. To cultivate the American Buddha fields, he says, requires confusion, change, even deep despair. "The first two decades of Zen in America were about the meeting of Japanese and American cultures. Because we were so new to the form, we leaned on our teachers, projected everything onto them, and in some ways lost our center point. This is the beginning of a digestion period." Then laughing, he adds: "It's always *just* beginning. Everything is always *just* beginning."

Carrying tools and sweaters, Kwong and his students start up to the top ridge of the land, passing groves of scrub oak and peeling eucalyptus. "Isn't that wonderful work?" Kwong asks of no one in particular. But a fine-featured woman answers, "Hard for someone afraid of making mistakes." Every snip of the pruning shears requires choices that affect the yield of the five-acre crop. In the fall the palomino grapes will be harvested, sold to a local winery, and made into mediocre sherry. In an almost inaudible voice, Kwong says, "The vineyard is good to you."

A Chinese-American, Bill Kwong was born on November 14, 1935, in Santa Rosa, California, near Sonoma Mountain. He spent his childhood in Palo Alto and his early adulthood in San Francisco and Mill Valley. It was a sign of completion, not coincidence, another cycle revealed, when he returned to his birthplace with his wife, Laura, and their four sons to start this residential Zen center in 1973. A Soto priest, he is abbot of the community's Soto Zen Buddhist temple, Genjoji—the Way of Everyday Life Temple. The name comes originally from the writings of Dogen Zenji (1200–1253), which have influenced Kwong's own teachings, although now Genjoji commonly refers to the community as a whole.

To the American who still turns East to authenticate all things Buddhist in the West, Kwong, with his Chinese features, embodies the classic look of a Bodhisattva. Zensan Jakusho, the Buddhist name given Kwong by his teacher, Shunryu Suzuki Roshi, means "Zen Mountain Gleaming Calmness." "When I'm very old," says Kwong, "I'll be called Zen Mountain."

Although Kwong's Zen training took place entirely in the United States and mostly in downtown San Francisco, his own center evokes the legendary mountain monasteries of Far Eastern Buddhism. Located in the heart of California's wine country, the center houses fifteen to twenty lay students in rustic cabins clustered on the north slope of Sonoma Mountain overlooking the Valley of the Moon. A large zendo converted from a barn accommodates one hundred additional members who live in the surrounding area and come regularly for meditation, retreats, and classes. Sitting on a rise and partially hidden by bamboo and redwood, the zendo appears and disappears in the morning fog like the images in a Chinese landscape painting. Everything here is modest, unassuming, like Kwong himself.

In his early twenties Kwong started looking at Chinese painting and noticed that "all the ones with heart were done by Zen monks. And they were just very simple," he explains, "like the ink painting of the black and white persimmons. There are only persimmons, not quite in a row, done with the least amount of effort and the least amount of thought and with just the utmost simplicity. There's a phrase in a Zen story about the person sleeping who, in the middle of the night, gropes for the pillow. That's the metaphor. That gesture. Real ordinary. It wasn't the Sung dynasty paintings with all the flashy technique—they're beautiful—but it was the emptiness, the nakedness, that moved me."

In the Community House hangs a picture of a very different kind. It is a framed poster of the colossal thirteenth-century bronze Buddha at Kamakura, in Japan, and behind it lies the story of Kwong's first encounter with his teacher. In 1958 Shunryu Suzuki Roshi came from Japan to serve the Japanese-American congregation at Sokoji, the Soto Zen temple in San Francisco's Japantown. The Kwongs had been living in Palo Alto, reading D. T. Suzuki and listening to Alan Watts on the newly invented FM radio. The poet visionaries of San Francisco, fomenting the social revolt of the 1960s, were polarizing forces into "hipsters" and "squares." Inspired by the hipness of Zen and lured by the promise of a benevolent and radical life, the Kwongs moved to the city. Shortly afterward, with more curiosity than conviction, Kwong wandered into the Japanese Zen temple wearing dirty dark clothing and heavy boots. "I always dressed in black then," he says. Then staring down at his baggy black pants and the black work jacket worn by Japanese monks, he laughs at another cycle—from Beat black to Zen black.

At Sokoji he had expected the traditional mats and cushions used in Japanese meditation halls. Instead rows of wooden pews filled an ungainly room. "It looked like a Sunday school. Suzuki Roshi entered the room and I just stood there thinking, this is very square. He noticed me but I didn't even turn my head to acknowledge him, my ego was so big. I waited for him to get to the altar, and then I looked up and all he was doing was arranging the flowers, and I said, 'This is really square.' " On his way home, passing through the final hour of a Japantown street bazaar, he saw the Buddha poster discarded in an alleyway. He carried it home and tried to put it in the closet, but it was too large. Finally, not knowing what else to do with it, he hung it on the kitchen wall, and to this day he credits it with calling him back to Suzuki Roshi.

Kwong and his wife, Laura, attend zazen regularly, rarely leaving Sonoma Mountain. A small exuberant woman, Laura is also Chinese-American and since 1982 has been a full-time Zen student. From their house to the zendo is a ten-minute walk down the narrow Sonoma Mountain Road. Jakusho walks quickly with his torso bent slightly forward and his feet straddled far apart. For the dawn and evening zazen, they arrive in full-length robes.

In the redwood zendo there is nothing to look at, no gross distractions to entertain and amuse the mind; the message that resonates from the thirty-foot-high walls seems to be: "No looking out, go inside, go deeper, and then deeper."

It's 5:00 A.M. Outside the zendo, a wake-up attendant gently shoves a suspended log into the center of a big bronze gong to announce dawn zazen. Making their way through the woods, students silently file into the zendo through the double barn doors. They bow to their empty seats, turn, bow to their dharma brothers and sisters, and begin two forty-minute meditation periods during which a falling leaf can sound like thunder. Meditation is followed by a standard Soto Zen Buddhist morning service at which Kwong Roshi officiates. The Heart Sutra is chanted in both English and Sino-Japanese. The recitation of the lineage lists each teacher in Kwong's line back through ninety-one generations. On the altar is a photograph of Suzuki Roshi, the same well-circulated picture that is on the back of the slim volume of his only collected lectures, *Zen Mind, Beginner's Mind*. It portrays an intensely calm face with a highly arched, almost quizzical left eyebrow. Walking up to the altar to offer incense, Kwong comes eye to eye again and again with his watchful teacher.

He has not employed the customary prerogatives of the Japanese temple abbot. He has no private attendants, nor has he ordered the theatrical build-up of gongs that signal an abbot's entries and exits to and from the zendo or the drumrolls used to announce a master's talks. Greeting people informally, he makes a slight bow more as an instinctive expression of his own humility than in imitation of Asian custom. A young man from Germany recalls that on his first visit to the center he walked by Jakusho, who was sitting outside his house. "He was bald and sitting quietly. I asked if he knew where I could find Kwong Roshi. I thought he was the master's gatekeeper."

On a recent winter morning, Kwong stood near the bedded vegetable garden and watched students hurrying from the zendo into the Community House for breakfast. It had been so cold during meditation that students could see their own breath. Says Kwong: "They're hard practitioners, Zen students. And they strive toward some kind of perfection. The practice is so difficult, so severe and uncompromising. It was so cold in the zendo and everybody was sitting. And to sit for hours and be impeccably perfect. Maybe perfection is one of the sicknesses that we have to get over. And to realize that, especially in the Soto school, it takes a long, long time. And it's an attitude toward life. It doesn't come in a big flash but in very subtle ways. Zen students tend to get stuck in the perfection of the form. It took me a long time to let go of it. I'm still relaxing into it. Students become attached to the sitting form, to the perfection of form. When they are beginning to learn zazen— and even when they've been practicing for some time—they forget the spirit behind the form. When someone points a finger at the moon, something initiated the finger to point to the moon. And spirit is like that. It's behind the action, behind the form. Suzuki Roshi taught the spirit of the form. If it doesn't have spirit, it's dead. Without the spirit you don't have the authenticity. Many Americans left their Judeo-Christian heritage because they felt that the spirit behind the ritual was dead. And when they came to Zen it was a new form, so it felt alive. But if you only perfect the form without getting the spirit, Zen is just as dead. When the spirit is alive you can see changes in people's lives and this is expressed outside of the zendo."

"Zen is tough," acknowledges Kwong Roshi. "At every turn the wandering mind is thrown back on itself." And getting the spirit has sometimes been made especially difficult by Sonoma Mountain's rural isolation. Efforts to promote the assimilation of Buddhadharma into the American mainstream through businesses, restaurants, publications, and academic or social institutes are missions that Kwong has so far left to others. The smallness of this center, with its atmosphere of rural containment, has been experienced as both pure and problematic. Not many Americans attracted to Zen have been prepared to sacrifice worldly pleasures to pursue with all their might a life that is like a sleeping man groping for a pillow. And as yet Kwong has shown little inclination toward making the practice more enticing or easing the demands made on residents.

Sonoma Mountain Zen Center is run on an annual budget of about $50,000. Membership dues and contributions are subsidized by resident fees of $325 per month. To meet their financial needs, students work outside the community. The hours allocated for employment are from nine to six, Monday through Thursday, almost double what they were a few years ago. Still, residents are expected to attend the monthly retreats, which vary in length from one to seven days, as well as the one-month July intensive. Most employment is therefore limited to odd jobs that pay little, preventing members from pursuing professional careers. This sacrifice of a career or trade for Zen training has traditionally defined the role of monkhood.

The integration of monastic values and secular living has helped define Zen in the United States, but it hasn't been an untroubled marriage, either at Sonoma Mountain or elsewhere. Like other residential Zen communities, Genjoji has tried to merge the monastic and the secular by implementing the intensity of monastic practice within secular communities of men, women, and children. As in orthodox monasticism, a strict routine not only regulates and bonds the life of the community but supplies the fundamental mechanism that undercuts personal need. Adherence to an impersonal schedule offers the first roadblock to surrender. "The schedule is itself a vital and dynamic way of rounding off the edges of egocentric and selfish behavior," says Kwong. "It is not just a routine. The ego is the grist and the schedule is the active grinding stone that wears us down and uncovers our buddhanature. The schedule also implies the rules and regulations. But people get caught in a literal association of 'schedule' with sequential time slots. There is tremendous resistance to the schedule but I think it is the same as that fear of meeting God that Thomas Merton writes about in *The Desert Fathers*. The schedule is designed to invoke buddhanature, to encounter the Buddha within. That is very frightening."

Balancing financial support, school buses, and PTA meetings with this schedule has been difficult at best. Individual routines can be negotiated but always against the prime virtue of community activity. Partly because of these strictures, the residency has been almost entirely transient. It is the nonresidents, who have no formal commitment to daily zazen or the morning work period, who provide a stable constituency.

On Saturdays nonresidents come to the center for a morning of zazen, work-practice, dharma talk, and lunch. In the zendo Kwong takes his place next to the altar, which faces rows of meditation cushions placed on perfectly aligned straw mats. Addressing the assembly of practitioners, Kwong says, "In the past, when we've read about zazen practice, we've discussed the ways that the old masters would say '*shikan taza* is *just* sitting' or '*just* let your mind follow your breath.' Today I think it's okay to describe how I—or Jakusho—sits. I notice everytime I sit down, I try to make a mark, a commitment to the mind-sitting posture, and I mark this spot with my bottom as well as my knees. If you watch a hen sit on her nest, she really sits. She doesn't have to think too much, so that's perfect. Then the movement you do from left to right, nestling into your place, is marking Buddha's spot. That's *your* spot. You're sitting on it. Not my spot but your spot. *You* sit on it."

He often reminds students that "Zen is nothing but this life." From his spot his life is the Soto way, cultivated by *just* sitting, a steady, undramatic form of single-minded meditation. "Don't chase after thoughts," he explains, "and don't push them away. Just let them come in and go out like a swinging door." In *just* sitting there is no system through which one advances, no objective measures of progress, which often leaves students feeling that they are getting nowhere. Having realized the teachings of Zen, there is no place to get to, so getting nowhere is precisely where you want to go. For the goal-oriented American novice, however, this can prove too frustrating. "The heart of meditation is basically the expression of who you are," says Kwong. "This is the point: to fathom all the intricate layers of who we *think* we are until we become fully who we are."

While the common distinctions between Soto and Rinzai schools are often defied by particular teaching styles, Kwong embodies the classic attributes of his lineage and in particular the teachings of Dogen Zenji. Prior to Dogen, enlightenment was considered the fruit of practice. In Dogen's teachings practice itself expresses enlightenment, and the practice of Zen is zazen. Zazen is not confined to a black cushion, however; rather, daily activity is centered in the serenity of zazen. Dogen spoke of "practice-enlightenment," fracturing the singular quest for realization into practice as daily life. Adamantly antisectarian, he idealistically hoped for a universal Zen and would not allow his disciples to identify with any Zen school. But to challenge the preoccupation with enlightenment in thirteenth-century Japan was so radical that, ironically, his insight became the cornerstone of the Japanese Soto school.

Formal zazen occupies the essential place in Kwong's teaching. The mechanics of zazen are simple but so fundamental that Kwong stresses them continually and will get up during zazen to correct sitting posture. The ideal position is full-lotus with both feet turned up on opposite thighs. Less strenuous versions are common, but the full-lotus creates the most solid foundation and most effectively reduces back and shoulder strain. In all of the formal postures, the buttocks and knees sink firmly into the ground, the back straight and unsupported, the eyes lowered, and the head bent slightly forward. In Soto Zen the hands are placed in the cosmic mudra—left hand resting on right palm with the thumbs barely touching. "In this mudra the hands are then placed three-fingers' width below the navel," Kwong explains. "This is the tanden, considered the power spot of the body. The Chinese translation of this spot is 'the field of essence.' This hand mudra enshrines this temple area of the body."

Over and over Kwong emphasizes posture and breathing, not because they have a beneficial effect on the mind but because "In Zen the mind-body dichotomy is the ultimate delusion: to sit well is to be well," he says. "It is like the phrase about horsemanship: above the saddle no rider, below the saddle no horse. That's zazen. That's present. No subject, no object. So we can't know what's happening. Only afterward, we say, 'Oh, that was a good sitting.' Recently I looked up the word 'present' in an American dictionary and it means 'before being'; that's zazen. When the body sits well, the mind is in the body. Then there's not much thinking. And when this whole chest area is in alignment, it's like an orchestra—the heart, the lungs, the spine, the kidneys, the liver—and it makes wonderful music. And you feel this energy coming out and that's the feeling of sitting well. Not sitting well reflects the conditioned mind. When the hand mudra rises, for example, it is a sign of emotion; if it is too tight and your fingers jam, there is too much mental tension. If it is too relaxed and the mudra collapses, it means the sitter is spaced out, asleep, or in some way not present. When the trunk area breaks and you get a concave posture, there is too much mental activity, like Rodin's *The Thinker*."

"And breath sweeps mind," says Kwong, referring to the inherent capacity of breathing to cleanse the mind. "Breath will cut through thinking because you have to let go to breathe. The power of breath is beyond the discriminating mind. Numbers are primarily used when your mind is very active and you need some kind of handle for your meditation practice. Your exhalation breath is your strength breath and you count 'one' and exhale. Then 'two'—inhale, 'three'—exhale, and so forth to ten. When you get to ten, you go back to one and start again. There are variations but this is the basic way of counting. The method in breath-counting is a way of occupying the mind so that the mind doesn't occupy you. Even though we say 'one, two, three,' the sequence is really just one, one, one. It is not dependent on memory or consciousness. Even though it sounds linear, this repetition becomes mantric and in this way releases the sequential mind. Each time you exhale, the exhalation is compassion. It is the breath of giving or letting go. The inhalation is receiving. It is like birth and death. Inhaling is being reborn. It is saying I am capable of taking in life." After doing zazen for some thirty years Kwong has begun counting breaths again. "It's very difficult to count numbers, but actually you're counting your existence and something wonderful happens."

For several years Kwong has been concentrating on the quality of zazen in forms other than sitting meditation. "As the Chinese Master Sekito Kisen said, 'Anyway you do it is okay, but the most important thing is to realize your own buddhanature.' Sitting cross-legged cannot be for everybody. Even Hakuin Zenji had some students reciting mantras because they couldn't sit," he explains. "And I feel we should apply skillful means to the form and accommodate those who are sincere. So now I'm paying more attention to walking meditation, bowing practice, and mantra. Not as substitutes for zazen but in addition to zazen. Bowing practice is very good for angry people and for people who are very closed and withdrawn. Bowing practice brings their energy forward. You need energy for practice. We talk about the silent illumination of Soto Zen. But too often the silent illuminators are sleeping. They lack the energy of activity. If they are not sleeping they are thinking. But that's about the same thing. Every year there is a man who comes from Iceland to the July intensive. He has terrible arthritis and for one month he sits every zazen period in a chair. He proved to me that you can attain shikan taza in a chair."

Kwong considers group practice essential to Zen training, and the annual July retreat not only provides a month of group practice for nonresidents but also intensifies practice for the residency. "There are people who practice at home, and they do practice sincerely, but if they don't practice with a group of people their edges stay too rough. There are people who like the dharma but they don't like Buddha or the sangha. Or they like the Buddha but they don't want the dharma or the sangha. Each is one of the three refuges. And in many ways, the sangha is the hardest to cut. But the altruistic act is dependent on sangha. Compassion cannot be realized without practicing with others."

At Sonoma Mountain the week-long retreats demand fourteen hours a day of zazen. Students sit through formal meals served in the zendo, sit with mounting pain in the knees and the shoulders; they maintain silence, drink no coffee, and sleep on hard surfaces, all without the comfort of complaint. Psychically locked in the zendo, they *just* sit with the state of their own minds, however calm or turbulent, however fearful or courageous. Few survivors emerge from their first retreat without some sense of heroic achievement and often are congratulated for just sticking it out. But what happens when after the fifth or tenth time the mind is quieted but never released, even for a moment? "No problem," says Kwong Roshi. "Keep sitting." Or when the barriers of conceptual thought are broken and one is free enough to fly? "No problem. Keep sitting." Or when familiarity itself makes the hold on the practice fragile? "Zen practice can get so boring and usually nobody talks about that," Kwong says impishly, as if at last divulging one of Zen's great secrets.

Shortly after Kwong's birth his family left Santa Rosa for Palo Alto, where Bill was the fourth of five children in the only Chinese family in a white neighborhood. Barred from the United States by the Chinese Exclusion Act, his parents had come here illegally from the province of Canton. His father, Dr. Chin Kwong, had been a respected doctor there, and the move to America deprived him of his medical credentials as well as the social status that his profession enjoyed in China. In Palo Alto he prescribed ancient remedies to those adventuresome enough to try snake skins, ground bones, dried roots, and·herbal powders. Cut off from his heritage and alienated from the Chinese communities in California, Dr. Kwong became an exacting patrician in his own house, determined to inculcate his children with a Chinese education. The children grew up speaking Chinese, and every afternoon after public school they had to attend "Chinese school." Jakusho refers to Chinese school as if it were some impersonal institution organized by a local community center, when in fact it was the afternoon program devised by Dr. Kwong, carried out in his own house and for the sole purpose of educating his own children. Calligraphy, reading, spelling, and writing were the principal subjects.

"It was horrible. Two schools a day. And my father was so severe and we couldn't play and we just wanted to be like the other kids. The more Chinese culture was imposed, the more separate we felt. My father only took me through grade four because he got so fed up with me. I didn't like Chinese school because I was beaten for not doing well—it was a syndrome. Once I couldn't eat dinner and was locked in the attic. He was really harsh," says Kwong, rubbing the top of his head as if to comfort old memories. "One day my mother was cutting the head off a chicken like they did in the old days— you did it at home—and she said, 'Would you like to learn Chinese or would you like to get your head cut off?' In Chinese the expression 'head cut off' is very common. She was kidding, but instinctively I put my head on the stump even before I knew it. My body just walked right up there. She was really shocked and from then on my father stopped teaching me. Because of my father's own difficulties and his lack of confidence as an alien, life was very hard for him. Of course we didn't understand then. Being young Chinese-Americans we wanted to be like everyone else. We didn't want to be different."

Kwong speaks thoughtfully, rotating a ceramic tea bowl cupped in his large hands. His words are punctuated by pauses and characterized by the wide vowel sounds common to the Chinese-American dialect. "Going to Chinese school was a training, although it was a horrible training. My father hit me on the head with his knuckles. He liked me a lot so I got hit more. He wanted me to be stronger. I wasn't very strong. That was another thing that motivated me to study Zen."

As each of the five Kwong children turned eleven, they spent summers with their mother in the commercial aster fields that once surrounded Palo Alto. These were virtually subsidized by child labor and underpaid Chinese immigrants. The first year the Kwong children worked free as "apprentices," the second year they lied about their ages, and at thirteen they were legitimate employees, earning thirty-five cents an hour with increases up to sixty-five cents as the years went by. "We had to pick all the buds off of each stem; the buds were called suckers and we had to go through acres and acres of flowers to pick off all the buds, not once but two or three times. There were endless fields and we had to pick those suckers. It made the flowers grow taller and the blooms bigger. That was a training, too. I see that now. We had to work from six in the morning to seven at night every day through the entire summer. My mother made all the kids do this. It was a way to earn money. Very boring. Out in the fields, hot, pray for rain. Listening to the song of the passing ice-cream trucks. Talking to yourself. So what do you do with the mind all day? What does a young person do? How do you keep alive? And you have to keep working. That really was a kind of training. And staying in one place. We had to sit on these little wooden stools. You can't move that fast. You can't walk. You have to get up early and sit on your butt all day. Just like now! Sitting all day from dawn to dusk. Same thing, see what I mean? My karma didn't change that much," he says, laughing. With raised eyebrows and wide eyes, he looks, as he often does, totally surprised by what strikes him as most obvious.

Dr. Kwong had attracted a number of clients on the margins of white culture, and by the early 1940s bohemians and artists were coming to his office regularly for herbal cures. Some noticed a shy boy drawing in the corner, and unlike his family or teachers they suggested that making art was a good thing. "Confusion at home, confusion in the world, confusion everywhere," he explains. "You look for some place to hide. So it was in my art. There was no art expressed through my father. He wrote with brushes like any Chinese. But I would notice those brushes. Art was sane. It was an oasis for me. Some resting place."

While he was studying commercial art at San Jose State College, he met Laura, who was then attending San Francisco State College. "This was 1955 or so. At San Jose, there was nothing happening, but Laura began telling me about the Beats and the Upanishads." Laura's parents were also immigrants from Canton but, unlike the Kwongs, raised their six children in the protective refuge of San Francisco's Chinatown. Her father was a cook, an accountant, and a commercial artist, a combination she describes as "Chinese survival." When she was eight her family moved six blocks to the adjacent Italian neighborhood of North Beach. By the time she entered high school, North Beach and Greenwich Village were fast becoming the continental outposts for the Beat generation. She attended high school outside her home district, which was her first immersion into non-Chinese culture. She says, "I felt excluded. I felt angry and then I felt sad. I didn't want to join them if they didn't want to join me. Then I didn't want to go back to the Chinese community because Chinese people didn't prepare me for the bigger world, so I got mad at them. I felt their world was too small and I didn't know if I wanted this one. Naturally I'm wondering if anyone knows of anything different. So you can imagine I'm looking at these strange people in North Beach with beards and penetrating eyes and thinking they must be feeling like I do because they don't seem to fit either."

In the fall of 1957 Laura and Bill decided to marry. The following Memorial Day he was in a near-fatal car accident. After staying up late for several nights studying for exams, he had gone to visit Laura in San Francisco. "We stayed up late talking philosophy," he says—or as Laura's version has it, "We were talking about the philosophy of free love." In any event, on his way home Bill fell asleep at the wheel and smashed the car into a steel girder on a freeway overpass. The patrolman who finally stopped saw a completely vertical car, with Kwong hanging upside down out of the front window, his foot caught in the steering wheel. When he got to the hospital doctors found his back smashed, his crushed foot as big as an elephant's, and bits of glass stuck all over his body. "That was an awakening. That was my memorial. I wasn't the same afterward."

One immediate effect of the accident was that it unleashed his impatience with academic conventions; he became critical of the department of art education and was finally expelled for refusing to comply with the dress code required for student teaching. After that he began his own personal exploration of art, recognizing in the simplicity and emptiness of Chinese Zen paintings a sensibility that would shape the rest of his life.

Once married, the Kwongs lived in Palo Alto. Never having obtained his teaching certificate, Bill went to work as a mailman. One day as he was delivering the mail, he noticed an English story in a Japanese newspaper about the new abbot of Sokoji. He recalls that "Suzuki Roshi had given a talk about liberation, and a student had asked him, 'If you believe in that, why do you keep your bird locked up in a cage?' And Suzuki Roshi just opened the door and the bird flew out the window." The empty birdcage remains a compelling image for Kwong; but through the fifties, he typified the Zen enthusiast who was more attracted to the stories than to the formal practice, and to a lifestyle that simulated the freedom of the enlightened masters.

Bill and Laura's first son, born in July 1959, was named after Ryokan, the eccentric and beloved eighteenth-century poet-priest who called himself Daigu, "Great Fool," and left his mountain hermitage to play with the village children and pick flowers, bowing on his way to all laborers and with special veneration to farmers. Shortly after Ryokan Kwong's birth, Laura went to work part-time while Bill stayed home with the baby and painted. Together the couple engaged in the casual, experimental atmosphere of Beat living, wearing black, playing drums on their doorstep, hanging out in coffee shops, and denigrating the importance of materialism and money. When they moved to San Francisco in 1960, to an apartment on Octavia Street two blocks from Sokoji, they again enveloped themselves in Beat camaraderie. Exploring the early inklings of communal life, they shared whatever they had, fed whoever was there, and gave money to friends who needed it. Dinner guests often stayed for the night and sometimes for days. This was a celebration of "*satori* Zen"—a promise of liberation through spontaneity—and it was the only Zen they knew. In North Beach, California, 1960, the Kwongs were not alone in confusing a carefree bohemian way of life with the freedom of mind taught by the Buddhists; D. T. Suzuki's books had provided scriptural authenticity, and Alan Watts had taken up his post as Mill Valley's resident Zen avatar.

D. T. Suzuki and Alan Watts captivated their audiences with the possibility of spontaneous liberation, but their work contains little about the formal discipline of Zen that generates and grounds this experience. They have been criticized for their failure to present formal Zen by members of the first generation of practitioners, but in neither case can their influence in the United States be overestimated. It was precisely their liberal, visionary commitment to transmit Zen independent of its cultural identity that eased Zen into the intellectual life of the West and directly inspired the training that followed.

D. T. Suzuki talked a lot about satori, also called *kensho*. Shunryu Suzuki Roshi rarely mentioned it. And the shift from the earlier Suzuki to the later parallels the shift in the West from Zen philosophy to Zen practice. The word *kensho* consists of two characters: *ken*, "seeing into," and *sho*, "one's own nature." In Zen it describes the sudden moment of letting go of the individual, small, ego-bound self. Having let that self go, what is left is that self which is not, and has never been, a separate entity. "By its nature, this essential Self is inseparable from all that exists. It is not subject to the distinctions of inside and outside, of I and you, of subject and object," says Kwong. According to Buddhist doctrine, this buddhanature is the essential nature of all phenomena without exception; the dropping away of body and mind reveals this essence, considered the state of original enlightenment.

For D. T. Suzuki as for the Rinzai sect, the quest for sudden enlightenment lies at the heart of Zen. In Rinzai some "opening" experience is a prerequisite for understanding. It is the first step, without which the most devoted efforts to grasp the Zen teachings will remain superficial, the object of faith continuing to reside outside oneself. In Dogen's Zen, by contrast, no one moment is targeted as the goal of practice; Soto Zen is the way of gradual, not sudden, enlightenment. The differences between Soto and Rinzai have never held that much sway in the United States, but D. T. Suzuki's emphasis on satori initially defined Zen for Westerners. Satori provided a powerful—and romantic—attraction to Zen; as a concept of spontaneous liberation it triggered an image that Americans could grasp. In the midst of an enigmatic philosophy, emerging from an enigmatic culture, satori was something to *get*, something to *have*, something to *go for*—all of which contributed to the psychological pitfall of what the late Tibetan teacher Trungpa Rinpoche called "spiritual materialism." Disengaged from the prosaic rigors of daily practice, satori became both finite and dramatic. And with its allusions to abrupt dislocations of time and space, it provided descriptions familiar to a generation experimenting with consciousness-expanding drugs.

By the early sixties San Francisco was rapidly emerging as Planet Earth's Aquarian spa. In the midst of California's excess of New Age alternatives, Zen training outdid its reputation for paradox. The association between consciousness-expanding drugs and satori highs and no-mind mind-states had already assured its iconic status in the counterculture. Jack Kerouac's *Dharma Bums* (1958), one of the counterculture's most consecrated texts, radiated a glorious vision of the "rucksack revolution" in which Zen lunatics would sanctify the universe with prayer, dance, drugs, meditation, and free love in the floating zendos of the mountains. Ironically the dharma bum whom Kerouac used as his model was the poet Gary Snyder, who was back in Kyoto sitting rigorous seven-day sesshins in a Rinzai monastery. In sesshin the hour-by-hour discipline of precise uniform activity is nothing less than a frontal attack on "doing your own thing."

Alan Watts, who along with Kerouac was preeminently responsible for advancing Beat Zen, referred to Japanese monastic training as "Square Zen." In his 1958 essay "Beat Zen, Square Zen and Zen," Watts in fact disputed both extremes, savoring only the simplicity of the early Chinese masters, but that did nothing to diminish his tremendous influence over the Beat generation.

In the early 1960s some Zen readers in San Francisco began moving away from Beat Zen and toward the benevolence of Shunryu Suzuki Roshi. Some of the self-styled explorations of consciousness had become pretty weird, and for those who found flying through infinity on their own a little too scary, the formality of Zen training looked more and more like a resilient safety net rather than a padded cell. "Beat Zen," Kwong Roshi says in retrospect, "was a complete misunderstanding! Like saying that nothing matters. Just sit there and nothing matters. But without practice, without form, you can't get at the heart of it. The form of Beat Zen was wild spontaneity, but that didn't replenish. Too many leaks. So that was the despair of the Beats. It was completely different from formal Zen in that way. Beat Zen was high and low. Zen is even. Beat Zen was knowing that something was missing and therefore searching for something else." Somewhere in the haze of parties, bongo drums, and satori highs, Kwong recognized the need for discipline. As he explained to Laura, all the texts said a teacher was necessary for Zen studies. Laura had read the same texts but admitted that she had missed that part. It was the same part missed by a lot of Zen readers.

With familiarity rapidly slipping away from even its own natives, San Francisco in 1958 must have seemed particularly strange to a Japanese abbot who had grown up dreaming of one day coming to America. And yet legitimate high priests were just what the mecca of San Francisco needed. Born in 1904, Shunryu Suzuki Roshi was the son of a Soto priest and roshi. It had become customary in Japan for the sons of priests to follow their fathers' footsteps, becoming their disciples, and taking over their temples. But in the first of a series of divergent moves, Suzuki left home at the age of thirteen to study with his father's disciple, Gyokujun So-on Roshi, master of Zoun Temple. Although the other young novices from that time all ran away from So-on's temple to escape the harsh demands of its formidable master, Suzuki stayed until he was nineteen. So-on Roshi then sent him to the high school attached to Komozawa University, where he later did his undergraduate studies. From there Suzuki went on to become a monk at Eiheiji and then Sojiji, the two main training monasteries of the Soto sect. In the meantime So-on Roshi had become the abbot of Zoun-in, a major mother temple responsible for two hundred subtemples. Suzuki was only thirty-two when So-on died, and despite argumentative disputes among the laity and priests as to whether one so young could lead this extensive temple, he went on to succeed So-on as abbot.

Suzuki Roshi was one of very few Buddhist priests publicly to oppose the rise of militarism in Japan prior to the Second World War. Even after the militarists took control of the government, he continued to publish lectures warning against the consequences of aggressive military policies. Following Japan's defeat, the occupational government of the United States uniformly revoked the teaching licenses of all Zen Buddhist priests because of their categorical support for the war effort. Suzuki Roshi appealed, using his publications to prove his dissidence. His license to teach Zen, which had never been used, was reinstated by the United States government.

In 1958 Suzuki Roshi accepted a three-year position as the resident priest of Sokoji in San Francisco. Still standing on the corner of Laguna and Bush streets, Sokoji is a conspicuously dilapidated 1890s wooden building on a block that has been notably upgraded since Suzuki Roshi first arrived. The Star of David, set into stained-glass windows, recalls the building's original use as a synagogue, as does the Hebrew writing carved into the cornerstone, now partially hidden by a rusty drainpipe. The Japanese community bought the synagogue in 1934 and nearly lost it during the Second World War, when virtually its entire membership was interned in inland camps for Japanese-Americans. In panic and humiliation, the parishioners of Sokoji had gathered up children and aging parents, abandoned their homes, shops, and possessions, and turned themselves in for relocation to barbed-wire camps patroled by armed guards. As part of his own hurried preparations to evacuate, the head Japanese priest had judiciously entrusted Sokoji to an Indian Hindu priest and arranged for the mortgage to be maintained by payments sent by parishioners from the camps. With its crumbling black dome towers and peeling gray balustrade, Sokoji looks today like a grand abandoned bird's nest; a long time in the coming, a new temple was recently built a block away.

When Suzuki Roshi first arrived he did zazen alone each morning. Traditional Buddhist services were performed later in the day for the Japanese congregation, who showed little interest in zazen. When Americans inquired about Zen meditation, he told them that he sat at 5:40 in the morning and that anyone was welcome. Soon young Americans were showing up to sit with him. Some were barefoot and some hadn't been to bed yet.

It was these earnest Westerners showing up for dawn zazen, not his Japanese parishioners, who tapped Suzuki Roshi's immense and subtle talent for Zen training. Their openness, their naivete, their clumsy American big-hearted willingness presented a kind of beginner's mind—not at all free in the true Buddhist sense but relatively free from ideas about Zen training.

"Because I came to love Suzuki Roshi so much," Kwong says, "I stopped questioning the formal, rigid style of Zen practice. He was just very present. And ordinary. That was his special quality. The projection made him a superhuman being. But actually he was just present and just ordinary and no more and no less. And that's why I say that he was the first person I ever met. Unqualified. Just wonderful. And you came away feeling the same way. That was the dharma transmission whether we knew it or not. We were receiving something and we were being received. Many times there was resistance to the form, but I knew that the form was good. I didn't fight it externally, but I could feel the resistance in my body; it just wasn't comfortable. And you think everything takes so long. The bowing and the chanting takes so long. Gotta do nine more bows. The aggressive mind, the speedy mind, isn't used to this, so you think: we could be doing other things, like eat, or go home."

Just as he had used art as a way of withdrawing from the world, Kwong initially used zazen as a way of withdrawing from himself. "Zazen was my oasis. My misunderstanding was that I took it for a refuge, in the sense of escape. I just conked out, closed my eyes, and went away somewhere. Not into an emptiness but into a blankness. And I thought, this is it. Many people when they start sitting think the same way. In blankness you're not present. In emptiness you are dynamically present. Your body and mind are together. In the first eight years of sitting, I had a lot of sleepiness, a tremendous amount," he says, drunkenly swaying his torso in demonstration. "I didn't know how to express myself verbally, so I withdrew into a kind of stupor."

Sleepiness during zazen is in fact common. In Japanese monasteries unsolicited blows to the shoulders are still the standard antidote. Chinese monks warded off drowsiness by practicing with rocks on their heads. But sometimes, says Kwong, "sleepiness in zazen practice is necessary for a certain period of time. A lot of Zen students have a difficult time relating to other people. The form can be like a protective shell. It can make you feel like you're safely isolated from others. But as you get more grounded and confident through the practice, you can step out a little more, be less paralyzed, express your feelings, and at the same time become more present in the practice within everyday life."

Kwong sought to protect the fragile refuge he had found in zazen by perfecting the form of Zen practice. Because of its exacting style, Japanese Zen easily lends itself to a preoccupation with form. Perfecting the form can become an obsession that subsumes the practice. Kwong calls it "a Zen sickness," in which the messy emotional interior is obscured by an aura of excellence and the elasticity of a relaxed mind rigidifies into a moribund "perfection." "I used to push in a very macho way. I could sit full-lotus longer than anyone. I wanted to be 'the best sitter.' It was like a competition, which is okay for a while. The form itself is okay. But each person has his own relationship to it. Maybe someone else doesn't have to compete. I had to do that. That was my karma—the set of conditions that I came to Zen with. I found myself trying to outsit everybody until I realized—what am I doing?" Quoting a passage in the *Platform Sutra* by Hui Nêng, the Sixth Patriarch of Chinese Zen, Kwong reflects on his early quest for perfection:

> Sentient beings are immobile
> Inanimate objects are stationary
> He who trains himself by exercise
> to be motionless
> gets no benefit
> other than making himself as still
> as an inanimate object.

Facing his students in the zendo, Kwong recalls his first ten years of sitting practice: "I think I was trying to become an inanimate object. This kind of inanimate object or blankness in the Zen school is a Zen sickness. When we sit, we are not just trying to make our minds blank or trying to be motionless but we're expressing our buddhanature. The Sixth Patriarch is not belittling zazen practice but giving us some deep instruction on what can happen. It's possible to spend ten or fifteen years—or even more—becoming an inanimate object. Zazen is subtle motion. The *Platform Sutra* asks, 'How will I ever get to the platform?' But everybody's on the platform. This whole room is the platform. You don't get up to it, you don't climb it, you're it. Your body is the *Platform Sutra*. I imagine that for the teacher it is equally as hard as for the student because we're a team. I'm not over here and you're not over there. So we come here for the dharma talk and the bells ring, we make bows, light incense, and we feel like we're on some kind of platform. The idea is to lift, to erect our platform. And then I sit down and I do what I do, and some people are trying to do zazen. That's good. But people want so much. We want to be someone else. 'I want to be stronger.' 'I want to be more directed.' 'I want to be superwoman.' But it's not possible. You must accept your condition. But 'accept' is *active*. Who you are is active. Passive acceptance—that's the immobile, inanimate Zen. It's not the Zen I'm talking about. There's passion here. Spirit for the quest. This is important: the sincerity of our quest and how we go about it. It's a long path. Are you prepared? Do you want to walk on this path? Don't think about it too much. *Just* walk! C'mon, let's go! That's Zen."

Shortly after Kwong started sitting in 1960 he had jukai, the ceremony of receiving the Buddhist precepts. Suzuki Roshi performed the ceremony with no prior explanation, telling his students, "No problem. You'll learn later." Kwong says, "We didn't even know what it meant to have jukai because it was all in Japanese. And in a way that was good because it kept us pure. It was his way of protecting our 'beginner's mind.' At the time of the ceremony, you're given a square, biblike cloth called a rakusu, which represents the Buddha's robe. *Raku* means 'to hang' or 'encircle.' *Su* means 'child.' So to take the Buddhist precepts is to become Buddha's child and to live with beginner's mind." Suzuki Roshi said, "In the beginner's mind there are many possibilities; in the expert's mind there are few."

The following year, 1961, the Kwongs' second son, Cam Shunryu, was born, and a year later came Evri, who was named after *The Everyman*, a trimaran sailboat used in a peace-keeping mission in the Pacific to protest nuclear testing. Jakusho supported the family from 1960 to 1968 as a window designer and sign painter for Cost Plus Imports. Laura stayed home those years with three baby boys and wondered if Zen meditation might ease her day.

By 1964 the Kwongs had outgrown the Octavia Street apartment, and they moved across the Golden Gate Bridge to Mill Valley. Jakusho left each morning to bike over the bridge in time for 5:40 zazen. Cost Plus didn't open until nine, leaving a gap between meditation and work during which Suzuki Roshi invited him to stay for breakfast; soon he was teaching Jakusho how to cook. In Zen monasteries the position of *tenzo* or monastery cook is one of the most venerated and is given to a senior monk. Soto tenzos today still follow the detailed instructions that Dogen Zenji outlined in the thirteenth century. These include how, when, and where to clean and prepare rice, how not to waste even one grain, how to use inedible vegetable stems for broth, how to clean and place the kitchen utensils, and how to let go of one's personal likes and dislikes of certain dishes. "See the pot as your own head," advised Dogen. "See the water as your lifeblood."

"One time, I had just made some rice gruel," recalls Kwong, "and Suzuki Roshi asked me if I knew how to make rice gruel, and I said, 'Of course I do.' And he proceeded in minute detail to tell me how to make rice gruel, and I told him I already knew how to make it. It's very difficult being a student. It was only in retrospect that I thought, what a fool! I should have just listened and received."

Another time Suzuki Roshi asked, casually, if Jakusho had finished washing the sink. He assured the master that he had. Suzuki Roshi then poured a pot of tea leaves into the clean sink. Only later did Jakusho realize that washing the sink, like birth and death, has no absolute beginning and no absolute end.

One year at *rohatsu*, the Zen retreat that commemorates Shakyamuni Buddha's enlightenment on December 8th (at Genjoji it commemorates Suzuki Roshi as well, who died on December 4th, 1971), Kwong told of having had breakfast with Suzuki Roshi and Katagiri Roshi. "We were all sitting at the table, and it was not like having breakfast with a friend. It was more like a formal interview. I had hair then and it was all standing up on end. I was real uptight and I thought I was relaxed. That's how I was. When Suzuki Roshi stood up, that was my signal to wash a particular cup. And this teacup was a valuable temple treasure. So when I went to pick it up of course I used two hands, and somehow—I didn't drop it—the teacup dropped itself. You know how those things go? You're sure you didn't drop it. You're positive you didn't drop it, but somehow the teacup left the table. And it went through the back of the chair. And I missed it and it fell to the floor and broke! And I felt *so* bad. And then Katagiri Roshi went, 'Oh ooooooh.' And then Suzuki Roshi went 'oooooooh, ooooooooh, ooooh, ooh oh.' It was like an alternating chorus. I was very attached to the teacup. Then my mind started working: maybe they'll throw it away and I can keep it. I could glue it back together! Suzuki Roshi came over and we picked up all the pieces. And he took the pieces and he stuffed them into the garbage so deep that even my mind couldn't get at them."

With more and more Japanese roshis arriving in the United States, and Zen training centers developing from Hawaii to New York, the Beat Zen of Watts and Kerouac continued losing ground to Square Zen, which by the mid-sixties was rapidly becoming the one and only true Zen. More than one hundred Westerners were packing Sokoji for sesshins, and thirty to forty students were coming regularly for dawn zazen. Suzuki Roshi's zazen students had incorporated themselves into San Francisco Zen Center in 1962, and in 1966 Zen Center purchased Tassajara Hot Springs, a one-hundred-year-old resort deep in the California coastal mountains south of Monterey. This was the first Zen monastery in North America and has continued to be known by its Spanish name, Tassajara. The original summer programs were soon extended to year-round residency, and the three-hour car ride between San Francisco and Tassajara became a common run for Suzuki Roshi and his senior student and future successor, Richard Baker.

Kwong anticipated living at Tassajara but was instructed not to leave Mill Valley. "Tassajara is not for you," Suzuki Roshi told him. The timing was not right, Kwong realizes now. "Not just because of my family and my commitments in Mill Valley, but because of my own fragility, too. Of course, I would go there for practice periods, but I did not move there. From then on, I realized I had to let Suzuki Roshi go. I loved him so much. As he became busier and busier, I saw him less and less. There was a kind of weaning process going on."

In 1969 Zen Center vacated Sokoji, leaving the temple to function once again solely as a parish center for the Japanese community. A fifty-room dormitory at 300 Page Street in San Francisco, formerly a Jewish women's residence, became the new home for the center as well as for Suzuki Roshi and his wife. The following year Laura had jukai with Suzuki Roshi, receiving the name Shinko Musho, which means "Heart Fragrance Empty Nature." That same year Jakusho became a monk. "Suzuki Roshi said, 'I would like you to become a monk.' When he said that, it scared the hell out of me and, at the same time, I felt it was a great honor. I had no thoughts of becoming a monk, although I identified with Roshi very much. But stability was needed, and we were all lay students and when one becomes a monk, obviously that defines your life."

With ordination Kwong acquired the status of a "Zen professional" and was offered a teaching position in the psychology department of Sonoma State College. For its tolerance of a hip, alternative, and "flakey" curriculum, the college had already been dubbed "Granola State." A woman who has studied with Kwong for sixteen years first met him in a classroom there. Eager to explore her own Chinese-American roots, she registered for a course called Chinese Identity and ended up listening to lectures on Buddhism and learning zazen.

In the fall of 1970 Suzuki Roshi appointed Jakusho head monk for the annual three-month practice intensive at Tassajara. This was the last training period while Suzuki Roshi was alive. It was directed by Dainin Katagiri Roshi, who had come from Japan to help Suzuki Roshi and who later formed the Minnesota Zen Meditation Center. Because Jakusho had been teaching at Sonoma State, Suzuki Roshi asked him to give talks during this training, although these were not the usual responsibility of the head monk. "The head monk," explains Kwong, "is the example for the community and is empowered to lead the group in that sense. But sitting up on the altar and giving these talks, I began thinking that maybe I should try, eventually, to become a good teacher. Suzuki Roshi never mentioned 'satori' or 'enlightenment' or 'Zen teacher' or 'dharma heir.' 'Dharma heir' was a new name. It had not been in our vocabulary and it was nice that way. No one thought about it." But the vocabulary took on sudden significance when Suzuki Roshi told Jakusho, "You will be my dharma heir."

By the time Jakusho started his transmission studies, Suzuki Roshi was already suffering from liver cancer. "In the beginning of 1971, I would go to his room at Page Street where we would practice calligraphy together. Suzuki Roshi would write out a word. The first word was $d\bar{o}$, which means 'same.' I knew the character in Chinese—intellectually. But he kept saying, 'We're the same.' I had been looking at the character, but not the meaning behind it. He was trying to teach me that the student and master are the same, that we are both Buddha. But I was stuck in the literal, relative meaning, not grasping the spirit. I only got it after he died. We also wrote out the names of the patriarchs in the lineage. But they were like Iceland to me, very far away. One morning we were in his room doing calligraphy and he was so sick that his brush dropped out of his hand. From that day on, I didn't go back. I wanted to prolong his life, and I felt too unworthy to bother him. Now I realize that that was an incorrect Zen attitude. The character said 'same.' My delusion was that I was not worthy, that if I bothered him less, he would live longer. I was attached to his life, but not to the life of a Zen master. In retrospect I see that a mature Zen student would have continued to go to the lessons and to confront and accept the life given from dying."

Six months before he died Suzuki Roshi told his students, "My teacher died when I was thirty-two years old. So I was not so lucky in this point. I want to live as long as I can. I was weak. I didn't think I would live more than sixty. But now I've become greedy because of you. Ten years more. I am asking the Buddha to give me ten years more. Then you will be forty, fifty."

But Suzuki Roshi did not get his wish, and he left behind many senior students, including Richard Baker and Jakusho, still in their mid-thirties. He had lived in America for just twelve years, a complete cycle according to Chinese calculations. By the time he died, Zen practice had been stripped of its inscrutability, rescued from the hip elitism of Zen lunacy, and firmly planted on American soil. Two weeks before his death, Suzuki Roshi installed Richard Baker as abbot of San Francisco Zen Center. Jakusho never completed formal transmission with him.

Although the transmission ceremony is both the experience and the affirmation of a process that is not bound by past, present, or future, difficulties arise if a teacher dies in the midst of transmission teachings. Since the preparations and the ceremony itself are intrinsic to unifying that "sameness" between teacher and disciple, it is not easy for someone else to step in and complete the process. "To probe and test me," says Kwong, "Suzuki Roshi had confided in me that he was going to give Baker Roshi transmission. He was testing my response to receiving transmission. This was the year before he told me that I would be his dharma heir. He was slowly and subtly preparing me and others for my transmission by including me in activities and giving me more responsibilities. Before he died, he asked the board of directors to see that my transmission was taken care of, but they didn't know what to do."

Suzuki Roshi made a similar request to Hoichi, his eldest son and first dharma heir. Eventually, in 1978, Kwong did receive formal transmission from Hoichi, but at the time of his father's death, Hoichi himself was only thirty-two years old and had no idea how to interpret his father's pleas. On a visit to Genjoji in 1984, Hoichi Suzuki told students, "Many, many times my father said to me before he died, 'You must help Jakusho with dharma transmission.'" In the redwood zendo, wearing the brown robe that had been given to him by Suzuki Roshi, Jakusho sat weeping through Hoichi's talk. "Technically Jakusho received dharma transmission from me," said Hoichi. "But in heart, it was from my father through me."

In 1972, one factor that contributed to the ambiguous status of Jakusho's transmission was the absence of any handwritten document that testified to Suzuki Roshi's intentions. This option had been used in Japan to counter the false claims of careerist monks, although written documentation did not automatically allay suspicions and offered no provision in the event of sudden death. Furthermore, the term "dharma heir" was sometimes used quite casually by teachers, allowing for some genuine ambiguity as well as deception. To encourage an exceptionally talented or devoted disciple, a teacher might say, even to a relative beginner, "You will be my dharma heir." But the actuality depends on the student's maturation, and the shift needed from potential to actualization is not always similarly assessed by teacher and disciple. In Japan dharma transmission had become so corrupted by the priesthood that the claims falsely attributed to deceased teachers by disingenuous priests accounted for a relatively minor part of the spiritual disintegration. The purposeful implantation of Japanese Zen in the United States, however, offered a rare opportunity to bring the best and leave the worst behind. Well intentioned as it was, this selective effort has contributed to a false assumption of spiritual purity that illuminates every offense as if it had never before occurred in the very human history of Zen. Partly because of the corruption in Japan and the impulse to protect Zen in the United States, Suzuki Roshi's failure to provide written documentation for Jakusho was interpreted by some Japanese and American Zen clergy as a clear indication that Jakusho was not qualified for transmission. He was never suspected of self-serving abuse, but it was thought that perhaps with too much American innocence he had taken the indirect subtleties of a Japanese Zen master at face value. For two years following Suzuki Roshi's death the matter of Kwong's transmission was held in abeyance.

According to Soto custom, Kwong's failure to receive dharma transmission jeopardized his authority to teach. But he did become the priest of the Mill Valley Zendo, where his priestly functions included officiating at passage-of-life ceremonies and Buddhist services. Priestly ordination itself does not entail teaching, and at the Mill Valley Zendo Kwong continued his weekly talks in the capacity of senior student, not authorized Zen teacher.

During this time Jakusho became increasingly alienated from San Francisco Zen Center. His initial offers to share the responsibilities of the community with Baker Roshi were not acknowledged. With no one to champion his cause, the absence of written documentation from Suzuki Roshi seemed to aggravate his ambiguous status. According to Richard Baker, however, it was actually quite the reverse. By Baker's account, if Suzuki Roshi had spelled out his intentions it would have sealed Kwong's commitment to complete the transmission process with Baker himself. "Suzuki Roshi knew that Jakusho had problems with me," explains Baker Roshi, "and he didn't want to tie his hands in this way. He wanted him to be free to leave Zen Center and to choose who to work with. That had its difficulties, but Suzuki Roshi knew he wasn't doing Jakusho any favors by forcing his commitment to me." Furthermore, while Richard Baker had demonstrated a brilliant talent for administration, Kwong had not. Suzuki Roshi had kept Kwong away from the administrative side of running the center, which made it all the more problematic for Suzuki's successor to find a role for him there.

Most of Suzuki Roshi's original students had their problems with Baker. Twelve years after his installation as abbot of San Francisco Zen Center, Baker Roshi resigned under pressure from his students, ushering in an era of examination that explicitly questions the nature of dharma transmission. But as Kwong sees it, "Suzuki Roshi was a hard act to follow," and from the beginning the myths of dharma transmission did not serve Baker well. "We wanted Baker Roshi to be like Suzuki Roshi," Kwong says. "But that was not fair. Baker Roshi was an extrovert, the opposite of Suzuki Roshi; he was young, and Suzuki Roshi was the mythic old wise man; Suzuki Roshi was a subtle Japanese and very profound, and Baker Roshi was typically American, smart and cerebral. And I felt that in some way because Baker Roshi was so American, part of Suzuki Roshi's message was that if Baker Roshi could attain Bodhi Mind, any American could. But I could not relate to Baker Roshi as a teacher. We had been peers, dharma brothers. And I could not accept the distinction after Suzuki Roshi died. I tried. We all tried, including Baker Roshi. When Suzuki Roshi installed Baker Roshi as abbot of San Francisco Zen Center, he asked all of us to call him 'roshi.' And we did. We served his meals first and tried to walk out the door behind him, although often he made us go first. It was a difficult time for everyone. Very few of us shared Baker Roshi's interest in or capacity for corporate organization, and we had a kind of cultural prejudice against it and didn't appreciate its value. But for myself, I knew I had to do something. But I got no support for leaving and no support for staying.

"Suzuki Roshi always kept me out of the picture. Even when we were carrying his casket, my picture wasn't there. I was there, carrying the casket, but in the background. Or like telling me, 'You can't go to Tassajara.' So that gave me a long period to flower without pressure. The spotlight went onto Baker Roshi, and this little flower was left to grow at his own pace. In retrospect I am very grateful for this. But that gratitude came slowly, only with maturation."

Kwong moved to Sonoma in 1973 without the support of his peers. In the wake of Suzuki Roshi's death, the community became the vehicle for the propagation and support of the late master's work. For those senior students who elected to stay on, loyalty to the community and to Suzuki Roshi's dharma heir was inseparable from commitment to the late master. Dharma transmission, as it was understood at that time, confirmed a sacred unity between Suzuki Roshi and Baker Roshi that bequeathed unquestionable authority. To leave San Francisco Zen Center was tantamount to a break with the old master himself. Striking out on his own, Kwong was criticized for being self-centered and immature and for playing teacher before his time. "For eleven years I had been so closely affiliated with Zen Center that when I left there was a tremendous vacuum. But when I went back to visit it was like I had the plague. Not many people wanted to talk to me." As Kwong understands it, there was never any possibility of a break with his teacher, no matter what form his life took. And his position at San Francisco Zen Center was untenable, a conclusion shared even by his critics.

The year before he died, Suzuki Roshi had asked Jakusho to give a dharma talk to the general assembly at Page Street. He had given talks at Tassajara but Suzuki Roshi hadn't been there and, as Kwong says, "It's easy to talk when the master's not there." For this talk, he prepared all week long. As the evening approached, his nerves began to quiver. Half an hour before his talk was scheduled, Suzuki Roshi casually said to him, "I think I'll give the talk this evening." The subject was the enlightenment poem of the ninth-century Chinese master Tozan Zenji. Afterward Suzuki Roshi gave Jakusho a copy of the poem in Japanese with his own translation underneath.

> Do not try to see objective
> world
> You which is given as an
> object to see
> is quite different from you yourself.
> I am going my own way
> and I meet myself
> which include every-
> thing I meet.
> I am not something which I can
> see (as an object)
> When you understand self which include every-
> thing you have your true way.

Almost twenty years later Kwong says, "In retrospect I see that this poem, and Suzuki Roshi's giving it to me, helped me go on my way. But not 'my way' in a personal sense. That 'way' includes everything. I never felt separated from Suzuki Roshi. Because I felt that there was no invitation from Zen Center, I had to do something. To start a little sitting group."

Sonoma was a logical move. Kwong's students at Sonoma State had been rising at 4:00 A.M. every Wednesday to drive to Mill Valley for his morning talks at the Wisteria Way Zendo. At Baker Roshi's suggestion, Sterling Bunnell, an old friend of Suzuki Roshi's, offered Jakusho the eighty-acre parcel of land to start a Zen center. Laura returned to Sonoma State to start an independent career as a psychologist. Following Jakusho's Zen path suddenly felt like walking down the street ten steps behind her husband. She maintained her sitting practice, but for the first five years stayed away from the administrative and social concerns of Sonoma Mountain Zen Center.

With his move to Sonoma, Kwong relinquished all formal ties to San Francisco Zen Center. It was his conviction that his commitment to his teacher did not require him to remain loyal to his teacher's dharma heir and to a community increasingly informed by Baker's vision. "I think the fact that I had started transmission studies helped give me the confidence to leave. I felt that I had some kind of empowerment—however fragile—some edge over the others who felt that they had to stay because of Suzuki Roshi. When he was alive I couldn't go anywhere, physically, because I felt that I had to be near him. After he died others felt that they had to stay in the house that he built, in his center, near his presence."

At around the same time that the Kwongs moved to Sonoma, Japanese teachers in both the United States and Japan agreed that Jakusho should continue transmission teachings with Kobun Chino Roshi, who had come to San Francisco in 1967 to help Suzuki Roshi and was then heading a lay-people's group in Los Altos. Chino Roshi recently said from his home in Taos, New Mexico, that when he examined the calligraphy that Jakusho had been doing for his transmission studies, "There was no doubt about Suzuki Roshi's intentions." For five years Jakusho traveled two hundred miles to Los Altos one day a week. It was understood that the transmission ceremony would be performed in Japan by Suzuki Roshi's son Hoichi, who would stand in as a replacement for his father. Within that ceremony, Kwong says, "something very vital happens. And it has also been happening ever since you met your teacher. Some wisdom and knowledge and experience are being transmitted to you in a very intimate way. Subliminally. Much later you realize what he gave you, but at the time it's happening, no one knows. Then there are the bowls and robes and calligraphy that verify that transmission has happened. Studying for the transmission ceremony is itself a form of advanced practice. Studying the way you fold your bowing cloth, how one end goes over the other, or the different ways of bowing and why you bow. Learning to laugh and cry at the same time, learning what the sages said to each other, studying the Zen literature, being asked questions, being on the spot. Just the intimacy. Mind to mind and heart to heart. After that, each person's practice is to cultivate that. For the rest of our lives. The whole transmission is the tip of a lighted incense stick pointing directly at you."

At Sonoma, Kwong was Zen priest, senior student, and, since his credentials had not yet been validated, unofficial teacher. "I knew I had to continue the transmission study, but I didn't realize how much it was a study of myself. Those early years were like a foggy dream. I wasn't empowered yet. I hadn't been sanctioned by the Buddhas and the patriarchs. It was like a bardo state in between leaving San Francisco Zen Center and arriving in Sonoma; I was already here, but I hadn't arrived yet. To have a community was very difficult. It scared me half to death. I am such a lazy person, I knew I had to practice with others. But I didn't know how to plant the seeds and I didn't know how to do my role."

In other words, Kwong was left with the role of leader without the authority needed for effective functioning. His ambiguous position fueled an uneasy accord between Zen training and communal living. Attracted by Kwong's gentle nature, students availed themselves of a permissive social structure. In the absence of clear leadership, spiritual or political, the hope that strong practice would generate guidelines was undermined by divisive self-interests. From every angle—Kwong, his students, community, Zen practice, Zen in America—too much was too new.

Incapable of the patriarchal severity of his own father, Kwong passively hoped that his students would respond to a soft and reasonable style. "The way my father taught me was through unwarranted punishment. I saw it as his own anxiety being projected out to the children. It was not just. I knew I had to find another way. But because I was subjected to such punitive measures, I always gave students the benefit of the doubt. I was not mature enough to be sure of my own needs and feelings. But I did not want to project this on the students the way my father had on me. When I look back, I see how valuable a training this was. When you select your own friends they usually perpetuate your own delusions. But in a community you are stuck with each other. This is the difficulty and the richness of community."

Kwong says now that one problem in the early days was that he took Suzuki Roshi's cow-image too literally. In *Zen Mind, Beginner's Mind*, Suzuki Roshi talks about order and control in everyday life: "Even though you try to put people under control it is impossible. You cannot do it. The best way to control people is to encourage them to be mischievous. Then they will be controlled in a wider sense. To give your sheep or cow a large, spacious meadow is the way to control him. So it is with people: first let them do what they want and watch them. This is the best policy. To ignore them is no good; that is the worst policy. The second worst is trying to control them. The best one is to watch them, just to watch them, without trying to control them."

"In those days," says Kwong, "I was more focused on the exterior—what are the students doing? Now, I'm focusing more on the interior—what am I doing? And the control of these cows is *this* cow," he says, placing his palm flat against his chest. "How am I doing? How am I practicing? Now I can say to them, 'I don't think your practice is so strong. I want you to do more. I demand more of you.' That was hard for me to say."

In 1976 Kwong developed testicular seminoma, a cancer he associates with personal confusion. "The community was going," he says, "but something was not working right. I wasn't able to communicate with the people. I had let anyone come into the community. In a way that was compassionate, in a way foolish. But I thought that was my job, and our rules and regulations weren't as strict as other Zen communities because I was trying to provide for people. If I saw someone having a difficult time, I would change the rule. When I got sick, I felt that being able to express myself better would help make me well again. Also, my teacher had cancer, and there was my love for my teacher and still not knowing how to let go of him. Every good teacher is going to take a fall. Without exception. The star falls out of the sky. It's the law. It's the dharma. When it's happening, I don't wish it on anyone. It's a very painful time. And the healing process takes an equal amount of time. But it's God's grace."

By the doctors' account he had "the best cancer," and they were optimistic about its surgical removal. From his hospital bed in San Francisco he watched the Kurosawa film *Ikiru*, which just happened to come on television the night before the operation. *Ikiru* means "to live." A petty bureaucrat with no ambition, no passion, no interests—in short, no life—has stomach cancer. The film opens with an x-ray of an inoperable tumor and the words: "This is the cancer of our hero." From that grim beginning follows the story of a man who at the age of sixty is brought to life by the awareness of his death. This man was to be Kwong's personal guide through the wilderness of his disease. "The most important teaching for me was that I realized what an ass I was," says Kwong. "I could sit for a long period of time, for four hours in full-lotus, and didn't seem afraid of the unknown. I could really do that, but I felt like *I* had mastered something. As I got closer and closer to the gate of death, I felt that *I* was ready to go. I forgot about my wife, my family, my students, my friends. You see how selfish and ignorant I was? I am very much a part of this whole environment and I thought *I* was ready. That was a teaching. I had too much pride. Then with the cancer, I couldn't even sit down for zazen. The practice was completely taken away and I was just in a tailspin. Everything was out of control. No more control. So I was really lucky. '*Big* Luck!' Mrs. Suzuki said."

He was also really angry. Having identified the cancer as a growth of repression, for the first time he openly chastised students who had misused the center, who had not pulled their share of the work load, who were not practicing, who had violated the rules against drugs and liquor, or who curried favor with him while deceiving others. He was angry, too, at his own inability to say what he felt. The perfect alignment of a cushion to a tatami mat, or the perfect alignment in zazen of the back to the neck—these were the lines that Kwong knew. But the lines between himself and the students—the lines of authority—had remained hazy.

"After the cancer came," he says, referring to it as if it had been a season of hard rain, "I knew I would get better by being more expressive, more communicative." He also became less friendly. Students were asked to leave as the community underwent its first purge. Bitterness and betrayal flared up on both sides. Students were as angry with his attempts to seize control of his pasture as they had been with his failure to do so before. "That's the double bind for the teacher: the students themselves know that authority helps cut the confusion. But they resist it at the same time. There must be a benevolent or compassionate intention behind the authority—that's crucial for the teacher—although the students generally will not distinguish between this and their associations of repressive authority. There was an in-group of six or seven students who had been here for three or four years. They were not sincere Zen students. And they wanted to run the community in their own way. But it was still hard to make the decision that it was better—both for the community and for them—that they leave. This is a kind of rite of passage for every teacher. Even Shakyamuni Buddha had great difficulties with his sangha. That's why one of the five great sins in Buddhism is messing with the sangha."

Even with successful surgery, Kwong knew his life would be at risk until he remained cancer-free for six years. In the face of what he perceived as a do-or-die choice, his health and confidence strengthened rapidly, and within a year he was ready for the transmission ceremony. In December 1977 he went to Los Altos to tell Kobun Chino the news. "Five years of study," says Kwong, "and Chino was patiently waiting for me to tell him when I was ready, and the day I decided he jumped up and down and said, 'Let's call Hoichi in Japan!'"

Feeling ready is not independent from the teacher identifying the readiness, indicating, as in this case, something of the self-revealing nature of transmission. From a relative view, the ego is so disinclined to let go of itself that a teacher is necessary to help the disciple discover what already exists. Yet as nothing is "added," nothing is given. Therefore from an absolute view, one can only transmit the dharma to oneself; this is what allows for self-proclaimed recognition, however suspect it may sometimes appear.

Kwong's own recognition of readiness was affirmed by Kobun Chino, who completed studies started by Suzuki Roshi. But while no one could ever replace Suzuki Roshi as Kwong's root—or heart—teacher, the original plans for the ceremony called for Hoichi Suzuki to officiate as a vehicle for his father. But at the last minute he consulted Kojun Noiri, also known as Haku-san, "White Mountain," a renowned teacher, Dogen scholar, and respected authority on the transmission ceremony, and Noiri Roshi had told him: "You cannot be a stand-in; can you sign the signature of a dead man?"

Jakusho did not learn that Hoichi would not be able to stand in for his father until he arrived in Japan in the winter of 1978. "So my attachment to doing it the way I thought it was supposed to be done just went out the window. I just let it go. Because I loved Suzuki Roshi so much, I was being cut off again, to stand on my own without attachment. That was very interesting. I am Suzuki Roshi's dharma heir and, in a technical sense, I am Hoichi's disciple. Now, in the twentieth century, people just pay money to get their certificates, but Noiri Roshi was very pure. So instead of representing the ninetieth generation in the lineage, I represent the ninety-first. Suzuki Roshi was my teacher and one of my jobs is to establish and continue his lineage. If I had a dharma heir, I would be very happy. When I reflect on this, it is a very big burden. But it would mean that my job is complete in a sense."

With his transmission Jakusho became a *sensei*, or teacher. In June 1978, with Hoichi present at Sonoma Mountain, Kwong Sensei was installed as abbot of Genjoji, which until that time had been guided—as stated in the daily liturgy—"by the founder of this temple, Shunryu Suzuki Roshi." In the Soto school, the ascent to abbot is accompanied by the title *roshi*, which means "old teacher." Kwong waited another eight years before using it. By then he was fifty-one.

Ten years after being installed as abbot Kwong says, "Now I realize that because of the karmic conditions of a dharma heir, after the transmission ceremony his or her path has been sealed. They cannot go back in the same way. It doesn't matter if they have a temple or if they are in a hermitage or a brothel. They are stuck with that karma. How they wish to manifest it is up to them. If they don't manifest it there is tremendous suffering, for themselves and for others.

"Inner conviction has come together with the license. Things are clearer.

In a bigger way, I think of everything as the teachings. So that the difficulties I had coming into my own authority here in the community were also part of the transmission. The most important thing I see for the future is to deepen the practice. When the teacher becomes good, it makes the students good. When the students become good, they make the teacher good. They are the same."

The resolution of Kwong's status did not eliminate the difficulties faced by secular students trying to adhere to a monastic routine. Nor did it stabilize the residency. "The big difficulty is continuity," Kwong says. "I've been disappointed when people have left. I used to think it was a failure on my part. Now I'm just disappointed. I understand more that some will stay and some will leave. It can be very strange when a student leaves. You've shared something very intimate over a period of years and then it's over. Either the ending wasn't clear or there was a tizzy or your hearts are in different directions. But when they leave, they have to find something equally intimate, and until they do they will not have left."

At Sonoma Mountain some residents have left and later returned, if not to live, at least to sit regularly. Some former residents have never returned to the zendo but come to help with carpentry, electrical work, or gardening. Some have stayed away, and stayed angry, but have continued to live in the immediate area, posing a dilemma particular to the American Zen communities. In Japan monks dissatisfied with their lot in one monastery pack their eating bowls into their sacks and move on to another, unencumbered by possessions, jobs, or family. But in the United States relocation becomes problematic for parents who would prefer to remain in the area for the sake of their children, especially in rural areas, where social contact between former and current students is inevitable.

Although the Sonoma Mountain center's board of directors votes on major community decisions and a residential council governs the daily functions of the community, the abbot holds the ultimate authority and can veto decisions made at any level. In this respect Kwong has recreated Suzuki Roshi's structure for San Francisco Zen Center, which conformed to the tradition of granting power to the abbot. In Japan the Soto bureaucracy is vast, and temples and teachers under the aegis of Soto headquarters are responsible to a higher organizational authority. The Soto school even has its own tribunal court which decides ethical as well as organizational matters. Technically Sonoma Mountain, as well as other Soto centers in the United States, is part of this Soto system, but in fact distance has made Japanese jurisdiction virtually inoperative. Furthermore, in Japan teachers are guided by tradition, by lineage, by their own teachers, by their elders and peers, while in the United States, for the most part, they remain isolated, as Kwong's situation so poignantly demonstrates. This isolation, together with the attempt to tailor Japanese customs to American democratic values, has led students in the United States increasingly to delegate themselves as a kind of congressional balance to the highest authority. The question at stake—and it is a crucial one—is to what extent can Zen become integrated into the American system of democratic organization without jeopardizing the idiosyncratic intimacy of the teacher-student relationship.

The fundamental authority assigned to the Zen teacher is based on a shared agreement among students that the teacher has realized something about the nature of life that they have not, and, furthermore, that the teacher can guide them to their realization better than they can guide themselves. In small centers like Kwong's, it is almost impossible to separate spiritual from organizational authority; but where the lines between spiritual and political domains *can* be drawn, the question that keeps reappearing is: once the students grant the Zen teacher the authority of wisdom, then what, if anything, can they legitimately define as their jurisdiction, and how effectively can they operate as a witness to the functioning of a teacher? At Sonoma Mountain, while he continues to hold all the sanctioned authority, Kwong now participates more in council discussions and has made greater efforts to negotiate community policies with the council.

Kwong's administrative style has still drawn some criticism. A young man recently appeared at the center with an unusual readiness for Zen training and Kwong arranged for him to work on the grounds for a monthly stipend. A member of the council complained: "Roshi set up this council and encouraged us to make decisions. Then he comes along and does what he wants." This is a familiar complaint at Zen centers. But learning to sit on the council without getting attached to decisions is not so different from learning to sit on the cushion without getting attached to thoughts. There are other parallels as well: one releases the controls and at the same time takes full responsibility; one is fixed in a sense of groundedness and yet open and flexible. On the cushion or in the conference chair, students are encouraged to do their very best—without worrying about results. "Students are always inclined to confine Zen practice to the zendo," explains Kwong, "but organizational work is one of the simplest ways of affecting practice in everyday life."

Kwong plots the relations between students and teachers along horizontal and vertical lines. The horizontal axis represents the sangha, the community of practitioners, and the vertical axis the lineage of teachers. Kwong hopes that on the horizontal plane students will develop a greater sense of trust in each other and experiment more consciously with the applications of Buddhist teachings to social relationships. "I used to let anyone into the community," he says. "Now, another voice is coming out: 'Don't come here for social reasons, don't misuse this place. Come to realize who you are and to help all people.' The sangha must support dharmic relations. Now I think it's necessary to make a distinction between friendships and dharmic relationships." At the same time the vertical plane, the lineage of teachers, must be expressed with the authority appropriate for the role of lineage holder. "Ultimately, the vertical and the horizontal are the same. They must intersect at one point. Maybe that's where the collapse has been."

Kwong also sees great advantages to creating horizontal lines of communication among teachers as well as students—"to protect each other from going astray, because we're all so very young." He has frequently warned against dependency on external models and has urged students to internalize their practice. "If anything appears, it can disappear. This is the universal law," said Kwong Roshi in a talk delivered in 1985. "Sometimes I sit by the window and smoke cigarettes and drink coffee and think about what to say to people. I'm not much of a thinker. I don't sit and think for a long time about something. Then I read the text we've been studying. How to put it all together? I guess, maybe in one way I got pretty good at putting it all together, like a summary, and presenting it. And there's a lot to read; there's a lot to learn. But for me the most important thing is what is yours? What can you call your own? And to share that with each other. Not what Suzuki Roshi said, or Maezumi Roshi said, or Katagiri Roshi said. What you say. What it means to you. That's the only way. Zen teachers are human beings, too, and all of us struggle just like you do to know it firsthand, to have no illusion about study or about some religion doing it for you."

In residential communities, even when spiritual aspiration remains dormant, the expectation of "religion doing it for you" often goes hand in hand with the sacrifice of worldly comforts. One man in his early thirties came to Sonoma Mountain following the dissolution of his marriage. For several years he worked at odd jobs to maintain the residency fee and followed the schedule. When an opportunity came to work full time at a local school, he took it, describing it as his first "real work" in several years. Kwong insisted that he maintain the center's schedule or leave. Establishing an adult identity through income and "meaningful" work, though, suddenly looked more rewarding than the residential regime. As Kwong put more pressure on him, the student became more critical of the rules and of Kwong's refusal to compromise. As exceptions had been made in the past, he interpreted Kwong's decision as a personal assessment of his commitment to Zen practice, and Kwong did nothing to contradict this impression. The young man finally moved out of the community with the intention of being a nonresident member. Brooding as he packed his bags, he explained: "Basically, the problem is that I'm not a monk and I'm tired of living like one. Here, it's give, give, give, but you don't feel like you're getting anything back." According to Kwong, to give without investment and without reward expresses the Bodhisattva's vow and defines the rule that governs practice in and out of the zendo.

Ordaining monks has been Kwong Roshi's prerogative since his abbot installation but he has considered this step only recently. "I'm slow," he explains softly. "That's my style. And I want to make sure. We've been here more than a decade without monks. It's important to have monks, to help contain the energy. There's been too much coming and going. When someone is ordained, that puts a priority on their life. A definite direction. It is that person's livelihood. And it makes stability more possible for others. Then we could consider a more extensive livelihood project and students would not have to work outside the community. That too would stabilize and contain the energy of the practice."

Laura Kwong is one of several students considering ordination. "The feminist movement made me too self-conscious to follow my husband. And I got into some kind of competition. Then I realized with all this fight, who cares what it looks like? I am involved with Zen and it so happens that my husband is a teacher and it so happens that my situation is set, so I will use this situation to actualize my life. I used to think that I could never become a monk because I'm too small, too much of a beginner. But it would really make me feel that I'm putting myself out there, saying, 'This is my work and it is from this that I give.' I also used to think I shouldn't be Roshi's closest disciple. I thought he should have his own monk, but then that's what's happening now. I'm more trusting."

With his own shift from thinking about those cows to thinking about this cow, Kwong has come to inhabit his own authority with greater ease and has relied less on the authority of Zen form. He has been talking more about the need to be relaxed, a recognition he attributes to his friendship with the Korean Zen Master Seung Sahn, more commonly known as Soen Sa Nim. "Soen Sa Nim is very relaxed and his practice is one hundred percent. Years ago, Suzuki Roshi used to say to me, 'You should appreciate your own heritage, that you're Chinese.' In those days, I was trying to become more Japanese. Soen Sa Nim brought me back to my own roots. Korean style is much closer to Chinese than Chinese is to Japanese. Koreans are very passionate people, very human. They talk loudly; that's just how they are. The Japanese are very wonderful, too. They talk softly; they're very formal, very conservative. But Soen Sa Nim brings out that real human quality that for me is a sense of being more relaxed."

One Saturday morning Kwong urged his students, "Be friendly to yourself. I'm trying to be more friendly to myself. More relaxed. No more 'be perfect Zen.'" At the same time, he has warned that while trying to be perfect is trying too hard, "we can't afford to let go of being 'perfect' until we gain a sense of confidence. We can restructure the forms but not the actual practice of Zen. The practice is just the practice and can't be defiled. It's impeccable because each person has to do it himself, from where he or she is. The practice is perfect but we think we're not perfect. By realizing our practice in our everyday life we realize our own 'perfection,' which includes our 'imperfection.'"

Parallel to Kwong's rejection of "be perfect Zen" are his experiments with practices outside the Japanese Soto tradition. When he first started Genjoji, he imitated Suzuki Roshi whenever possible. The format for Buddhist services, the selection of liturgy, zendo procedure, and so on were all replicated from his own studies. Only in retrospect has he been able to compare that era of Genjoji to San Francisco's Chinatown, where certain customs have become rigidly fixed though in China they have evolved and changed. But re-

structuring the forms of Zen has not diminished Kwong's relationship to Suzuki Roshi, whose benevolence, according to Kwong, not only continues but
has increased with time. In fact, the latest addition to Sonoma Mountain is
a *stupa*, or shrine, that marks the ashes of Suzuki Roshi. The stupa is a two-
ton rock selected by Kwong from the Tassajara Creek, which runs through
the grounds of the monastery that Suzuki Roshi founded. Wading knee-deep
in the creek, Kwong rejected rocks laced with quartz and colored by minerals
in favor of something very ordinary. The rock was hauled out of the creek
and loaded onto the back of a rented four-ton flatbed for—as Kwong puts
it—"his" trip to Sonoma Mountain. "He had to travel with his face down,"
Kwong explains apologetically. The rock stands in a natural circle of small
oak trees on a flat ledge overlooking the Valley of the Moon and changes so
radically from every angle that it resanctifies the very act of looking. "I
wanted to make it as simple as possible," says Kwong, kneeling by its base as
he gathers small brown oak leaves and places them in a straw basket.

Suzuki Roshi's ashes were divided between Tassajara and Japan. In 1984
Hoichi Suzuki Roshi arrived at Sonoma Mountain with some of his father's
ashes from Rinso-in for a traditional "ashes ceremony." On an April Sunday
morning, hundreds of guests gathered as a bronze gong tolled 108 times to
initiate the formal procession to the stupa. After Soen Sa Nim opened the
ceremony with a Korean chant, Kwong Roshi, followed by senior students
and family members, placed the ashes in the ground, using, each in turn, a
pair of redwood chopsticks that had been made by Hoichi the day before.
Standing before the stupa Hoichi used a series of karate-like mudras to ignite
and release his father's spirit. As the wind came up some guests looked ap-
prehensively at the sky; others, including Suzuki Roshi's widow, just smiled.
Mrs. Suzuki had often said that wind was the element most characteristic of
her husband and that it manifested whenever he was present at an important
event. To the continuous accompaniment of the Heart Sutra, everyone took
turns making their offering to Suzuki Roshi, dipping a bamboo ladle in tubs
of artesian well water and pouring it over the rock. In true Zen style, the
highly ritualized ceremony opened and closed a cycle in a transmission that
has no beginning and no end.

The ceremony was all the more poignant for coming at a time of turmoil
at San Francisco Zen Center over the resignation of Baker Roshi; it offered a
respite from doubt and from the labored and often self-conscious efforts to

transmit the dharma to America. And the picnic that followed even approached Kerouac's vision of tribal Zen. More subdued than the wilder antics of Zen lunatics, East or West, it still expressed a particularly American version of celebration, with people sprawled around the grounds on colorful blankets, children running through the woods, and students playing banjos and guitars well into the night. At the end of the long day, Kwong said, "The longer you practice, the more you practice not for gain but for the sake of gratitude. Gratitude becomes the biggest treasure and practice is a way of returning it."

The next morning zazen was cancelled, and the Kwongs brought Hoichi to the Community House for a late (8:00 A.M.) breakfast. Sitting at a long table under the Kamakura Daibutsu poster, Jakusho and Hoichi contributed their own jocular commentaries on the ceremony, rating the gongs, bells, and chants for accuracy and precision. Hoichi ate his pancakes with chopsticks and, unaware of the no-smoking rule, lit up a cigarette and drank more coffee. Soon he was joined by everyone who smoked and some who usually didn't. A young woman who had recently joined Sonoma Mountain asked Hoichi if he thought that his father had made some mistakes. "A Zen master's life," answered Hoichi, "is one continuous mistake." Kwong Roshi laughed the loudest.

Three years later, Sonoma Mountain hosted a picnic for all the centers affiliated with Suzuki Roshi's lineage, and it started off with a slow-moving *gatha* walk to the stupa. "That rock is like a ballast, an anchor," says Kwong. "Buddhists say there is merit in erecting stupas and pagodas. I believe that. For me, the stupa seemed to purify the land and the community. We have problems. But they no longer seem big."

The meditative gatha walk is similar to zazen in that it is so concentrated on *just* walking that it breaks the mental expectation of going anywhere. Introduced to the community by Thich Nhat Hanh, the Vietnamese Zen master, it is one of several practices that Kwong has adopted in the past few years. "I am trying to be more experimental," he says. "I am trying to find out what works. With confidence and maturity, I was able to give up my attachment to the Soto Zen form, to doing things as close to the way Suzuki Roshi did them. What is the form? No one has the answer. I used to think that some other teachers had the 'right' answer or had the 'right' form. Now I know that we are all in the same boat, trying to keep these teachings alive in this aggressive land of confusion."

THE CASE

A monk asked Joshu in all earnestness, "Has a dog Buddha nature or not?"

Joshu said, "Mu!"

MUMON'S COMMENTARY

For the practice of Zen, you must pass the barrier set up by the ancient masters of Zen. To attain to marvelous enlightenment, you must completely extinguish all the delusive thoughts of the ordinary mind. If you have not passed the barrier and have not extinguished delusive thoughts, you are a phantom haunting the weeds and trees. Now, just tell me, what is the barrier set up by the Zen masters of old? Merely this Mu—the one barrier of our sect. It has come to be called "The Gateless Barrier of the Zen Sect."

Those who have passed the barrier are able not only to see Joshu face to face, but also to walk hand in hand with the whole descending line of Zen masters and be eyebrow to eyebrow with them. You will see with the same eye that they see with, hear with the same ear that they hear with. Wouldn't it be a wonderful joy? Isn't there anyone who wants to pass this barrier? Then concentrate your whole self, with its 360 bones and joints and 84,000 pores, into Mu making your whole body a solid lump of doubt. Day and night, without ceasing, keep digging into it, but don't take it as "nothingness" or as "being" or "non-being." It must be like a red-hot iron ball which you have gulped down and which you try to vomit up, but cannot. You must extinguish all delusive thoughts and feelings which you have cherished up to the present. After a certain period of such efforts, Mu will come to fruition, and inside and out will become one naturally. You will then be like a dumb man who has had a dream. You will know yourself and for yourself only.

Then all of a sudden, Mu will break open and astonish the heavens and shake the earth. It will be just as if you had snatched the great sword of general Kan. If you meet a Buddha, you will kill him. If you meet an ancient Zen master, you will kill him. Though you may stand on the brink of life and death, you will enjoy the great freedom. In the six realms and the four modes of birth, you will live in the samadhi of innocent play.

Now, how should you concentrate on Mu? Exhaust every ounce of energy you have in doing it. And if you do not give up on the way, you will be enlightened the way a candle in front of the Buddha is lighted by one touch of fire.

Yamada Koun

BERNARD
GLASSMAN

Greyston Seminary is the only house on Dodge Hill that is all lit up. In the cold dark of a December morning, the imposing stone mansion looks remote, grand and mysterious. Lights framed by gothic windows begin going out and the back door opens. Bundled up against the cold, twenty men and women come out and pile into two vans and one small Honda. It is 5:30 A.M., and if Zen teacher Bernard Glassman is among his students there is no way of telling.

They drive through the silent lanes of Riverdale in the Bronx, one of the most affluent neighborhoods on the East Coast, and follow the Hudson River north for three miles to a run-down section of the Yonkers industrial waterfront. Here the offices of the Zen Community of New York (ZCNY) occupy a dilapidated three-story building on Woodworth Avenue. A concrete structure connected to the first floor houses the Greyston Bakery, the wholesale business that supports this community. The vans pull into an enclosed loading dock while the car parks on the sidewalk—a common practice on this desolate block, removed as it is from the routine concerns of local police.

Minutes later a mallet striking a wooden board announces zazen in the "bakery zendo" on the third floor. Five monks enter in full-length black robes, while the lay residents wear clothing comfortable for cross-legged sitting: full skirts, blue jeans, sweaters. No longer inconspicuous, Glassman appears in the brown robe reserved for teachers of Soto Zen. A short, portly man who has grown considerably more rotund since the bakery began in 1982, he enters the zendo on the last hit of the *han*. Ninety minutes of total silence follow. Silence, save for the delivery trucks pulling up to the meat distribution plant and cargo warehouse that share Woodworth Avenue with the Zen Community.

Emerging from the zendo, two monks discuss a special order of five hundred shortbread cookies to be delivered by 4 P.M. to the World Trade Center in Lower Manhattan. The Christmas rush has already started and with it the pressing request for nonresident members to help out. The monks are joined by a large bearded man who has missed zazen in order to provide the bakers with a complete computer printout of the day's orders and deliveries. One van has already left for Manhattan. Another will leave shortly to make the Westchester deliveries. If it isn't back in time, the cookies will have to go down in private cars. The monks disappear into a changing room and come out in bakers' whites and blue hairnets. Half the residents work on the floor in the production area, the other half in the first- and second-floor offices. Glassman changes from robes into slacks and a black cotton jacket, the kind used by Japanese monks for working on the grounds, and goes downstairs to join his students for breakfast. Scrambled eggs, cooked on a stove that melts down kilos of Godiva chocolate every hour, are served with blueberry muffins, scones, and Danish—a small selection of the gourmet product line sold to the Russian Tea Room, Bloomingdales, Macy's, and Sardi's, as well as to art museums and the fanciest hotels and charcuteries in Manhattan.

While this combination of wealth, want, hi-tech, bakers' whites, and black robes has confounded visitors, for community members it is all part of "the practice." That practice is Zen Buddhism. And even though Bernard Tetsugen Glassman Sensei is the first American holder of his Soto Japanese Zen lineage, few visitors have been more surprised by this community than Japanese Zen clergy.

Ordained a Soto Zen priest in 1970, Glassman is abbot of Zenshinji, the Soto Zen Buddhist Temple of ZCNY. He is number eighty-one in a line that claims direct descent from the historical Shakyamuni Buddha. He is also the executive director of ZCNY and head of the Greyston Bakery. Against one wall of his cramped, windowless office is a small Buddhist altar. Above his desk hang photographs of Japanese Zen masters, including his own teacher, Taizan Maezumi Roshi. Aside from a chrome-framed swivel chair and an intercom phone system, the only signs of executive action are the titles of a dozen hardbacks: *Management, Strategic Management, The Changing World of the Executive, The Harvard Business Review, The Chief Executive's Handbook*, and so on.

Glassman started ZCNY in 1979 and set himself up as both spiritual director and executive administrator. After one year he was criticized by the board of directors for wearing two hats. Then when he started the Greyston Bakery two years later he was criticized for wearing two hats too many. The sole job of the spiritual director, it was argued, was to teach Zen. Glassman claimed he was doing just that. But many students had very specific ideas about Zen training, and these did not include making apple pies and chocolate cakes, driving delivery vans, or learning how to program computers for bakery production. Then again, of all the classic metaphors used to describe the job of Zen teacher, one of Glassman's favorites is that of a thief in the night who steals away preconceptions and attachments. And if he has his way, which has been the case more often than not, he will soon be the executive director of more affiliate enterprises.

Placing a pair of slippers neatly by his chair, he pulls his legs into the lotus position and explains why busy Zen is only an apparent contradiction: "Zen is *not* about nonmovement. That's a romantic idea, and a lot of students both here and in Japan have gotten caught in it. Sitting is a centered, strong position in the midst of movement. When you get a top spinning just right, even though it's going very fast, it's so stable that it doesn't even look as if it's moving. If it's slightly off balance it wobbles. It has to be centered and moving very fast in order to be stable. That's what Zen is all about."

While the Zen path has been somewhat slow for other adherents, and painfully wobbly at times, it apparently never was for Glassman. Born in Brooklyn, New York, on January 18, 1939, he began Zen practice in Los Angeles with Maezumi Roshi in 1968. At the time he was designing shuttle systems between Earth and Mars for the aerospace corporation McDonnell-Douglas. In 1970, while McDonnell-Douglas was sponsoring his doctoral work in mathematics at the University of California, Los Angeles, he became a monk and was given the name Tetsugen. *Tetsu* means "to penetrate" and *gen* is sometimes translated as "mysteries," although Tetsugen himself prefers "subtleties." "Gen," he explains, "is the stuff that's right in front of you that you can't see." In 1971 he moved into Maezumi Roshi's residential center with his wife, Helen, and their two young children, Alisa and Marc. For the next five years he lived and studied at Zen Center Los Angeles (ZCLA) and was its chief administrator while holding down his full-time job at McDonnell-Douglas. After finishing koan practice in 1976 and acquiring the status of teacher, he quit the aerospace industry to work full time at ZCLA. He did not wait until he had his own center to initiate a very fast-moving Zen practice. As executive director of the Los Angeles center, he accumulated an entire quadrangle of city real estate, led demolition crews, renovated old buildings, started a publishing company, helped establish a clinic for the largely Mexican-American neighborhood, led the monthly week-long retreats, and administered a staff of sixty resident trainees.

"I'm a fan of Tetsugen's," said a monk at the Los Angeles center, "but he runs a community like a juggernaut. The biggest problem around him is always going to be burnout. Nobody can keep up with him." His students in New York agree, but for those committed to a long tenure the trick is to stop trying. Glassman has advised his students to pace themselves, to eat when they're hungry, sleep when they're tired, and assess their needs with the same discernment that monks apply to filling their eating bowls. But the pressure to work as hard as he does pervades. Usually called "sensei" ("teacher" in Japanese), he is also called "the boss"—more often than not behind his back—which indicates just how extensive the business of ZCNY is. At this center the question of what Zen is all about has focused on hard work and work-practice. For those who have studied with traditional Japanese teachers or have visited Japanese monasteries or have read D. T. Suzuki, Glassman offers a version of Zen so different that to believe it is Zen at all requires an implicit trust in this teacher's understanding and in his capacity to reinvent authentic expressions of Zen Buddhism.

Japanese monasticism has historically been supported by patronage. In Shakyamuni's time monks begged for their keep, and even today the Theravadin monks of Southeast Asia are not allowed to handle money. The original founders of the Zen School in China, however, developed self-sufficient communities, partly because their teachings were too new and radical to secure patronage. Self-sufficiency is not new to Western monasticism, either, but neither this nor Chinese Zen has had much effect on legitimizing the Greyston Bakery for ZCNY's members. Their attitude seems to be "Yes, but is it Zen?"

ZCNY's bakery was modeled after the successful Tassajara Bread Bakery run by San Francisco Zen Center. Students there, however, have alternated between urban livelihood projects and intensive practice periods at that center's rural monastery; the very existence of a monastic center, moreover, figures prominently in the overall structure of that organization. Many urban Zen centers in the United States now maintain mountain centers that, reminiscent of secluded Asian monasteries, remain the archetypal training mode for Zen practice. Of all the various projects Glassman foresees, however, a mountain center, or anything vaguely resembling the isolation of traditional monasticism, is not one of them.

In May 1987 Glassman initiated the Greyston Family Inn, taking a holistic approach to the crises of homelessness. Not just another shelter, the inn directly addresses issues that perpetuate homelessness: lack of affordable housing, unemployment, and drug and alcohol abuse. An abandoned public school, still under the jurisdiction of the Yonkers School Board, has been proposed for a residence that would both house ZCNY members and homeless families and offer job-training programs and therapeutic counseling. While members of the Yonkers business and political consortium, familiar with Glassman and ZCNY through the bakery, have been instrumental in helping the inn get started, it has met with opposition from real-estate developers as well as neighbors fearful of both homeless shelters and religious communities, and so far no location has been approved.

Glassman had always said he would move into social action as soon as the bakery stabilized ZCNY's finances. The bakery has supplied soup kitchens with day-old baked goods and delivered a weekly order of bread for the hunger program at the Cathedral of St. John the Divine, but it has attempted nothing on the order of the projected Greyston Family Inn. Since 1982 at least a dozen students who have objected to the emphasis on business have left the community. For some dissidents, Bernie Glassman, Brooklyn Jewish businessman, had finally found his true vocation in commercial baking. As social concerns move into the forefront of ZCNY's programs, some of those students have contacted Glassman to see how they can participate. "Social action," he said wryly, "looks so much more glamorous than the bakery."

The Greyston Family Inn is Glassman's most ambitious project to date, but until it moves off the drawing boards ZCNY is a community that will continue to be defined by the Greyston Bakery. Social action may look more glamorous, it may be ingeniously timely, and it may capture the imagination of the membership in ways that the bakery has not. But in terms of work-practice, hard work, and Glassman's willful determination to make his dreams come true, there are already indications that social action at ZCNY will provoke as many questions about Glassman's teaching as the bakery has.

At ZCNY Glassman has reapportioned the values traditionally assigned to the basic components of Zen training—samu, or work-practice, zazen, and face-to-face study with the teacher. In the Japanese monastic regime, daily samu entails working on the grounds, in the kitchen, or in the office. Samu is the time to practice Zen in action, to maintain the internal stillness of zazen in the midst of motion. It is rarely pursued with the same intensity as zazen and is often appreciated as a respite from the physical rigors of cross-legged meditation. But when taken seriously, it may prove to be the tougher test of concentrated awareness.

Zazen is still considered the core practice at ZCNY, even though work-practice has dominated the concerns of the community. "You cannot have Zen training without zazen," Glassman says. "If we didn't have work-practice, we could still be a Zen community. If we didn't have zazen, we could not." The ZCNY schedule offers daily formal zazen, but Glassman warns against associating zazen with an activity performed only in the zendo. "Wherever you are, you are in the zendo. We think the zendo is that special place, which it is, and we are going to try to do something special there, try to be concentrated or quiet, and when we leave we can start screaming again. We don't see the whole world as a zendo. Of course, it's too much and we need breaks. And so we need 'a special place' and 'special training periods.' But really, every day is a special day, every place is a special place *as it is*."

While Glassman's broad view of Zen training confronts the attachment to neatly codified modes, it also jeopardizes a clear definition of a Zen community, creating an ambiguity that has been particularly challenging to students with previous Zen training. Some of these students had come from Maezumi Roshi's center in Los Angeles or East Coast centers, none of which had engaged in extensive businesses. And the more exposure students already had to Zen, the more they resisted Glassman's restless experiments to discover the American form of these Eastern teachings. Only two students remain of the original twelve who accompanied him from Los Angeles to New York, and one of those is Helen Glassman, also a Soto Zen priest. "You have to find out what works," Glassman says. "Before Dogen Zenji's time, they didn't even have sesshin. Then things changed and it became helpful. It worked. In the old days in China the students and the teacher worked alongside each other in the fields or in the gardens. The teacher didn't just sit on the 'high seat' and talk about Zen. The teachings were embodied by the teacher. He taught by being who he was."

Glassman not only gambles on the model of Chinese Zen working in America but has no trouble identifying himself as the teachings, the embodiment of Buddhist dharma. With disarming confidence in his own attainment, he takes the liberty of experimenting freely. He has retained some of the most un-American aspects of hierarchical Japanese monasticism, such as having personal attendants and commanding the drumroll for the abbot's dharma talks. Yet he will also wash dishes and drive the delivery van; he will place meditation cushions in a circle "like the Indians"; he will have a nondenominational zendo adjacent to an interfaith service hall. To his fans these experiments are liberating and creative; to his critics they are irritating and irreverent.

Glassman has been described as both too radical and too conservative. His natural comfort with Japanese Buddhist ritual as well as Japanese social custom is considered unusual for a Westerner. Indeed several other American teachers have thought his use of personal attendants as a training mode and of Japanese dharma names within the community inappropriate for their own culture. And whereas the life of his monks bears little resemblance to the life of the traditional monk, he still considers the full-time commitment of monkhood as a model for spiritual aspiration. He has simultaneously displaced the traditional emphasis on zazen and koan study by intensifying work-practice.

Advocates of classical Japanese training argue that American students, unlike Chinese Zen monks, need the restrictive methodology of Japanese Zen to attain some inkling of the nature of their own minds before they can avail themselves of a more active practice. They argue that without this foundation students have no personal experience from which to assess Glassman's experiments. This, claim his harshest critics, leaves him free to do whatever he wants as long as he keeps calling it "Zen," a freedom they consider perilous for a community leader.

"If I had to choose between being something called 'spiritual director' and being 'business manager,' I'd choose the business," Glassman says. "That's how I want to teach. It looks radical because we're shifting from a Japanese form. If we use a Cistercian model, it's not radical. If we use a Chinese model, it's not radical. Sitting together is definitely the most intimate way of being together. No doubt. But work-practice affords me more possibilities of working individually with students. It gives me an opportunity to work with who they are, or who they think they are. I know what people think are their own limits. I see potentials that they don't. I see the buttons. They stand out in all of us. It's easier for all of us to see them in each other than in ourselves. But we don't always give others the opportunity to help us see ourselves. If people come and sit zazen and get up and leave—there is no way to work with them. Sitting is the most direct way to let go of body and mind. But without a laboratory it's very, very difficult. There's no feedback. I agree with Yasutani Roshi, who said that zazen can be a trap. He used to say, 'The dolls in the window are doing perfect zazen but they are not opening their eyes.' And I've seen that in groups where zazen is emphasized in an extreme way. You can be a zazen freak without putting emphasis on really opening up, and that brings a bigger problem because you get attached to the form. And the form becomes a substitute for life. As a teacher, zazen doesn't give me enough interaction. Work-practice is not necessarily the best way, but the way I'm going to be doing it."

Glassman assumes, perhaps idealistically, that everyone comes to a Zen center to learn zazen. Using a definition derived from Hui Nêng, the Sixth Patriarch of China, he presents zazen as the elimination of the separation between subject and object. According to Buddhist doctrine, this separation is essentially not real but the fictive projection of the self. The elimination therefore refers more specifically to the notions of self that generate this illusion. For Hui Nêng zazen is a state of mind that can be cultivated anywhere; in his day there were no such special places as zendos. "People see the work-practice as a means by which they can then do 'real' practice," says Glassman. "But the work-practice in and of itself has to become zazen. We are not doing anything 'in order to'—what we are doing *is* the practice. In Japan you had only the monastic practice. Lay people came to the temples, but there was really no concept of a strong practice outside the monastery. There are always going to be people who want to go to a zendo and sit and leave and not talk to anybody, including the teacher. They don't want any interaction. They want a church or a synagogue or a temple—a place to go and get some peace and quiet and leave. Zen can offer that. You can sit and derive from zazen a sense of well-being, but that is not the marrow of Zen training.

The issue here is: is there a Zen practice that doesn't really get into your life-style? Can I practice Zen in some way without its affecting me, affecting the way I live? I don't think you can have true practice without that interaction. And the issue for me is what form that takes. It's very explorative, and for me it's taking the form of business right now. Then we'll explore social action."

A famous Chinese quotation captures the Zen ideal of enlightened presence in the midst of ordinary activity: "I draw water. I chop wood. How miraculous!" But for Americans, Zen was anything but ordinary. ZCNY initially attracted many students between the ages of forty and sixty who had been among the first generation of American Zen practitioners. For those inclined to spiritual practice in New York's greater metropolitan area, not much was more special than the silence of Zen, the luxury of sitting in elegant zendos listening to words of esoteric wisdom, waking before dawn to Japanese gongs.

One of Glassman's toughest tasks has been to disabuse his students of a persuasive attachment to the specialness—and preciousness—of Zen training. It was D. T. Suzuki, who, with typical foresight in 1936, while addressing a conference on world religions in London, asked the questions for contemporary Zen everywhere: "How can I construct my humble hut right here in the midst of Oxford Circus? How can I do that in the confusion of cars, buses, and all kinds of conveyances? How can I listen to the singing of birds, and also to the leaping of fish? How can one turn all the showings of the shopwindow displays into the freshness of the green leaves swayed by the morning breeze? How am I to find the naturalness, artlessness, utter self-abandonment of nature in the utmost artificiality of human works? This is the great problem set before us these days."

Work-practice has been one way that Glassman has addressed this problem. Though it has met with strong resistance within his community, Glassman has done little to appease the mounting dissent. Allowing the demands of the business to take top priority, he has regularly missed scheduled sitting periods and has often been unavailable for seminars on Buddhist texts and for koan study. For several years the subject of his talks was commonly work-practice and the Greyston Bakery. The ZCNY calendar, from 1980 on, records a steady variety of programs that include retreats, liturgical study, classes, workshops, and ecumenical events; but starting in 1982 Glassman himself gave the impression that very little interested him as much as the bakery. If one wanted to study with him, the bakery was where to find him. He called it "Zen," but many others did not.

Glassman had initiated several livelihoods at Zen Center Los Angeles, but work-practice was never accepted as a prime mode of Zen training and after his move to New York, ZCLA's livelihoods dissolved. "In the early days in Los Angeles most Zen students considered work-practice as a means to support themselves," he explains. "They used the term, but they didn't really consider it a part of training. And you saw all the seniors as they were being trained leaving the work-practice to go on to 'serious' training. The feeling was that once you got to a certain level you could do 'real' Zen training. And you hear that attitude a lot here. At the last council meeting a senior monk was still saying, 'I'm worried about the tail wagging the dog,' and I keep saying, 'the tail *is* the dog.' It is for me. That's where I'm training. It doesn't mean that I'm not training in other ways, but this is essential."

During an evening discussion in the zendo at Greyston, a nonresident psychologist in her fifties who comes regularly from her townhouse off Park Avenue questioned Glassman on the objective virtues of work-practice. Presenting a case for the therapeutic value of free time, she asked why "working" was better than "messing around." Quoting Dogen Zenji, Glassman answered, " 'To study the enlightened way is to know the self. To know the self is to forget the self. To forget the self is to be enlightened by all phenomena.' There are lots of different ways of doing that. There is no particular value to my style. A fish swims and a bird flies. Does one have more value than the other? I like to keep us on the edge, but for some that edge might be five hours of zazen or work or whatever. For someone else, it might be one hundred. Everybody should go up to his limit—and then a bit more. Overdoing it is too much. If you underdo it, you don't learn anything about yourself. Where is that edge? You can't compare two people. I've never understood the concept of not liking work. For so many people, what they do not like in life they call work."

Underlying the resistance to work-practice and hard work has been an independent antagonism to the bakery as a business, as a competitive enterprise that pulls ZCNY into the corporate structure of capitalist America. Here Glassman is in many ways at odds with students of his own age. Unlike most of them, he maintained his distance from the cultural revolution of the

1960s. He was twenty-nine years old in 1968 when he began Zen studies. That was the year that saw Robert Kennedy and Martin Luther King, Jr., assassinated, the biggest build-up of American troops in Vietnam, race riots in American cities, Lyndon Johnson at the White House besieged by antiwar demonstrators, the Russian invasion of Czechoslovakia, and the Democratic Convention in Chicago turned into a battlefield. The vision of a world run amok that catalyzed a collective quest for radical sanity did not tempt Glassman into the wholesale rejection of accepted values as it did for so many of the new religionists. While the disenfranchised white middle class freely combined drugs and alternative lifestyles with Eastern religions, Bernie Glassman put on his suit and tie every morning, said goodbye to his wife and kids, and drove to McDonnell-Douglas to work on space industry products under contract to the American military.

For Glassman there has never been a contradiction between Zen and business, Zen and corporate structures, between spiritual and material. These are the standard oppositions formulated by Zen students who accused their own Judeo-Christian institutions of having been so co-opted by bureaucratic and material interests that they were rendered spiritually ineffectual at a time when they were most needed. Advocates of the new religions had come from mostly middle- to upper-class families, well off, well educated, and steeped in business. Glassman's circumstances were modest by comparison. His parents were Jewish immigrants from Eastern Europe: his father was a printer by trade who raised his five children in a middle- to lower-class section of Brooklyn. Neither material accumulation nor middle-class status were his to reject.

The first fifteen-member board of ZCNY, chosen by Glassman, consisted largely of middle- to upper-class college graduates and professionals; two were respected writers and five held doctorates in the humanities. For most of these board members the pursuit of spiritual ideals complemented an elitist social vision in which any consideration of money—that necessary evil—was a vulgar intrusion. With the exception of a former Jesuit seminarian turned Wall Street broker, Glassman was the odd man out.

"When Zen was introduced in Japan," he says, "its inherent cultural context was art—aesthetics. You had the Confucian ideal and a feudal system. In our culture it seems correct to me that business is the world we most associate with." And for Glassman, business—working together—provides a sense of community that wasn't available to lay groups in Japan. Yet as the first board members of ZCNY exemplified, the context for Zen when it was introduced into the United States was, if not specifically art, the larger realm of humanitarian interests. But unlike the support art received in medieval Japan, art in the United States has been pushed to the cultural edge by science and business. To steer his ship away from this elite edge and head into the American bull's-eye, Glassman had to antagonize the professional, humanitarian, well-established, middle-aged, and middle-class sector of his community. And while they had no intention of moving into Greyston or devoting their lives—monklike—to Zen practice, they still comprised the major donors of ZCNY.

"The true assimilation of Zen will be getting it into a milieu that exists in this country," says Glassman. "What's going to make it Zen? If we can use the word 'Zen' it only makes sense if it's something not based on an ego-structure. In terms of Zen and business, it will be as we say in Zen: first mountains are mountains, and then mountains are not mountains, and then they are mountains. In the third phase, the separation is gone. There isn't an 'I' and 'the mountain.' On the outside the bakery may not look different from other bakeries, but actually I think that even on the outside it would look different, feel different. Because at the same time that all this work is going on there is also a release of the ego-structure, a letting go of the self. That has to be part and parcel of the whole process. The actual expedient means are not so easy to know. But the bakery is being run with that intention. So new forms develop. We have to get it all together, but getting it all together *is* the teaching. That's a hard one for people to grasp."

Getting ready to leave his office, Glassman unlocks his legs and says grinning, "I believe in management by meandering. I did the same thing at McDonnell-Douglas with my division. I wandered around a lot, sticking my big nose in everything." His nose is big and bulbous and his cheeks full fleshed. Bushy black eyebrows frame large brown eyes that are sometimes brooding, even mournful. Everything about his physical presence is rounded, except his hands and feet, which are oddly long and bony.

In an outer office he stops at the desk of his attendant monk, a forty-three-year-old former microbiologist who gave up her cancer research at the Sloan Kettering Institute to be on Glassman's staff. Slumped in front of a television monitor, she disconsolately watches a Pronto computer program flash

ZCNY's precarious financial balance direct from Chemical Bank. "That's her soap opera," observes her Zen master on his way downstairs to meander through the production floor.

Another episodic drama that has engaged the membership at large concerns the role of the Greyston mansion itself. The sale of Greyston has been considered four times in its short history as a Zen seminary. Three times these proposals were brought to the governing body by Glassman and voted down. While Greyston's enormous maintenance costs have always entered into the discussions, money has not been the sole issue. Glassman has always been ambivalent about the role that the mansion itself has played in the formation of the community, and ever since the bakery began he has wanted to consolidate living and working areas. In the spring of 1985 a council of senior students approved putting Greyston up for sale with the intention of buying residential property close to the bakery. As usual Glassman wasted no time. The next day he was driving around Yonkers looking at houses and talking about the virtues of consolidation. "Who knows? Maybe we'll end up at Greyston. And that would be fine, too." Paraphrasing Zen master Ikkyu, he adds, "If you don't know where you are going, you can't get lost."

The following year, with no prospective buyers in sight, he began transferring community activities from Greyston to Yonkers. Of all his unexpected moves, abandoning the mansion surprised many of the original members most, even more than his starting a bakery had. Zen claims that ultimately there are no beginnings and no endings, no birth, no death; but leaving Greyston would certainly close a chapter in ZCNY's history.

That chapter began before Bernie Glassman returned to his hometown as Tetsugen Sensei. At least five members of the original board of directors were New York residents who had come into contact with Maezumi Roshi and were ready to roll out the carpet for his first dharma heir. In keeping with Japanese customs regarding lineage, Maezumi Roshi was the first abbot of the Zenshin Temple and therefore the original occupant of ZCNY's high seat.

Born in 1931, Maezumi Roshi is only nine years older than Tetsugen, but having developed one of the most extensive and public Zen communities in the United States, he is often identified with the older generation of Japanese teachers who first introduced Zen to the United States. A slight, dignified man, he has the refined facial features associated with Japanese nobility. He speaks English slowly, which doesn't make him easy to understand, and he always seems ready to listen. By the end of the 1970s he was listening to the complaints of East Coast students disillusioned with their Zen teachers. By 1978, as Tetsugen was making plans to leave Los Angeles for New York, Maezumi Roshi suggested to these people that they not only study with Tetsugen but help organize his new center. As one person recalled, "Roshi has a way of asking you to do something that makes it more like a privilege than a favor."

For idealists a request to build a community from scratch, whether issued by Maezumi or not, was a privilege in itself. For East Coast students older than Glassman, an American Zen teacher was still something of a contradiction in terms; to support this ambitious young utopian was to put one's own shoulder to the Americanization of Zen. According to Glassman, "Maezumi Roshi deliberately stayed away so that we would not be influenced by Japanese flavors." Maezumi himself had high hopes for his favored son and for how his lineage would be represented by this American heir. His own father was a respected member of the Soto establishment, and both his brothers are priests in Japan. He, too, had a lot riding on Tetsugen.

People in New York were captivated by Tetsugen's conviction that anything was possible, and there was no shortage of money or people to get ZCNY going. The community's first purchase was a three-story brick building on Mosholu Avenue in a middle-class section of Riverdale. The ground floor was converted into a zendo and an office; the apartments above were shared by resident members. The Glassman family rented a modest house nearby. Two months later Columbia University put the twenty-six-room Greyston property on the market for $600,000. Designed as a summer home for the Dodge family in 1868 by James Renwick, Jr., the principal architect for St. Patrick's Cathedral, the estate had been donated to Teacher's College of Columbia University by its founder, Grace Hoadly Dodge. At a cost of $175,000, the Mosholu building, which sufficed as a basic facility, had already absorbed the first donations, but Greyston offered a new set of possibilities.

As an invitation to Zen practice, Greyston would make a sensational drawing card. Cloistered from the urban ghettos of the South Bronx as well as from the rough southern tip of Yonkers, it offered a rare corner of peace and privacy in New York City. Opponents of the purchase feared that "the middle way"—the Buddhist tightrope between absolute and relative realities—would be subverted by the "upper-middle way." They argued for more humble environs that would limit the size of the community and honor the traditional simplicity of Zen, or at least for something less reminiscent of the palace that Shakyamuni had left behind. But even those most skeptical of buying the mansion agreed that the prominence of Greyston, with a respectable social standing all its own, would attract an established membership. However Greyston was approached, it was clear that it would need a large constituency if it was to support itself.

During these discussions Glassman remained oddly quiet. Greyston was special; it would impose its own identity on an embryonic community. That identity was guaranteed to help establish ZCNY, but it was no blank page. In the midst of these discussions, Maezumi Roshi arrived for a visit. In Greyston he saw a showcase for Zen in America, one that would validate Zen Buddhism for Americans in their own materialistic terms and also indicate to Soto headquarters in Japan that the mission to transmit his lineage to the United States had been accomplished. A board member who had to vote on the Greyston purchase recalls: "You simply don't go into this kind of purchase without thinking that the head guy can pull it all together. All the ingredients were there to encourage people to come and sit, and then Maezumi Roshi comes along and says, 'Go for it, this guy Glassman can handle it.' There was strong opposition to buying Greyston, but it was Roshi's confidence in Sensei's capacity to represent the highest attainment in Zen that was so convincing."

The down payment on Greyston was made with large donations from very few people; Columbia University held the mortgage, and Maezumi Roshi's description of the showcase continued to be both vilified and extolled. Certainly Greyston did its job. It was imposing though not threatening, and no one was asked to check his middle-class lifestyle at the door. Indeed, few of ZCNY's members had been privy to such grandeur. To some Greyston itself was more attractive than anything called "Zen practice"—a splendid refuge dubbed "The Zen Hilton" where the 4:45 wake-up bell could be ignored in favor of French toast at 7:30.

A schedule of daily meditation, monthly retreats, classes, and workshops started immediately. Twenty-three retreats were offered in the first twelve months. The schedule itself simulated a rigorous monastic regime, but with new students Glassman was the perfect, obliging host. Waiting to see what would emerge, he was as patient as he was skillful. Zen enthusiasts may have captivated their audiences at Greyston's communal meals with stories of exemplary devotion, such as that of Bodhidharma, who faced the wall for nine years, or of Eka, who proved his zeal with an offering of his self-amputated arm, or of Japanese aspirants, who would sit knee-deep in snow for a week before gaining admittance to the temple to pursue "the great matter of life and death." But in 1980 the slightest of entry trials would have all but emptied Greyston's halls.

Glassman's style in the beginning was so accommodating that he was perceived by long-standing Zen students as too relaxed, too permissive; he didn't present "real Zen"—an accusation he seems to provoke no matter what he does. During the first winter ten residents were employed outside the community, leaving after the morning practice period for jobs that included teaching school, editing Russian journals, working on the Long Island Railroad, and nursing at Roosevelt Hospital. Another ten students were supported by ZCNY and helped run the center out of the Mosholu office. The schedule was followed faithfully by the monastics, who created an atmosphere of hard-core practice that was cohesive enough to absorb personal irregularities. Still, several men—men being more prone than women to identify Zen with samurai rigor—thought it sacrilegious that students who slept in weren't roused from their beds or that the "encouragement stick" was not used to hit people nodding off on their cushions.

For the first two years the residency remained small, while workshops and talks were often attended by more than fifty people. Glassman commanded attention from an elevated platform in the service hall of Greyston, placed in front of a row of arched windows that looked out over the dramatic cliffs of the Palisades. For Sunday dharma talks the assembly was asked to "please stand" for the abbot's entry. To the accompaniment of brass gongs, he situated himself as two attendants arranged his robes. On winter afternoons, with the hall flushed with streaks of red from the western sky, the high seat seemed just a little higher; yet even his adversaries admit that when Tetsugen talks dharma, he needs no seat at all. In addition, he was the only American Zen teacher in the metropolitan area, and even if the qualities of enlightenment remained ineffable, he talked smart and thought fast in a way that New York intellectuals appreciated. They came to his talks, nodded with sagacious approval, and left. The more adventurous moved in for an occasional retreat, but very few ever considered giving up their worldly lives for full-time Zen training.

Greyston's civilized style came as close to the mannered aristocratic aesthetics of Japanese Zen as America allowed. It did function effectively as a showcase, but Bernie Glassman never quite pulled off being lord of the manor. He has little affinity with the WASP courtesies of the immediate neighborhood and minimal interest in talking about such abstract things as art or politics. A reserved man, he is impatient and somewhat uneasy with small talk; he takes little pleasure in social events within the community and even less for those that he's occasionally obliged to attend on the outside.

While the showcase continued to attract new students, financial resources dwindled. The large donations that accompanied the first wave of enthusiasm were not repeated and cash-flow crises were frequent. Speaking with the authority gained from his corporate past, Glassman informed a board with little collective business sense that "if an organization doesn't have a cash-flow problem, it is not growing." Nor was it his job to placate the anxieties of a middle-class student body with its inevitable leanings toward financial security. More than once he indicated that keeping the community on the financial edge helped create the very unpredictability most suitable for Zen training.

In June of 1981 ZCNY was offered a one-year contract to run the kitchen concession for the exclusive Riverdale Yacht Club, which caters to Riverdale's most wealthy residents. ZCNY needed money, but the proposal antagonized members who did not endorse serving the rich as an appropriate expression of Zen practice. Zen practice, retorted Glassman, was about cultivating an attitude of service without discrimination. For a teacher who had defined one aspect of his job as making students "uncomfortable," of tugging away at their preconceptions, the Yacht Club offered a perfect opportunity: it fit virtually no one's idea of service. It was also an opportunity to cultivate Greyston's neighbors and to assuage their suspicions about "the Zens," as they called them. For one year ZCNY staff cooked and served dinners to club members, but when special events taxed their limits community volunteers were recruited. Club members applauded the quality of service but wages averaged only $2.50 an hour. Students confronted their own fixed attitudes toward the very rich and toward where and with whom the practice of Zen applied. At the same time more neighbors started attending events at

Greyston with a newfound sympathy generated by their personal association with the Greyston residency. But by the middle of that winter, with the
mathematically minded Zen teacher compiling the Yacht Club statistics, a
new direction was clearly in the wind.

That same winter ZCNY began preparing for Glassman's abbot installation ceremony, which took place on June 6, 1982. "Abbot installation" is
the prosaic translation of what the Japanese call *Shinsanshiki*—"ascending
the mountain." Although the incoming abbot said that Zen practice is "always a matter of ascending and descending at the same time," the ceremony
called for Maezumi Roshi to descend the mountain on the eve of June 5th,
vacating the high seat for his dharma heir.

Maezumi Roshi may have stayed away so as not to impose Japanese flavors, but for the Shinsanshiki and its 250 guests, among them a contingent
of Soto priests who had flown in for the ceremony, the aromas of old Japan
were in full force. Neither customary etiquette nor the Japanese accent on
detail went unobserved by the incoming abbot. Special incense holders and
flower arrangements were set out on newly constructed altars covered with
silk brocade. Guests received gifts of books and sumi drawings wrapped in
handmade silk-screened scarves and placed in white bags on which their
names were written in calligraphic script.

This adherence to custom reflected Maezumi Roshi's persistent concern
for an orthodox and meticulous transmission of his lineage. "In the Soto sect
there is a traditional study for dharma transmission," explains Glassman.
"In the times of Dogen Zenji these studies were very extensive. In Japan, as
Zen spread and temples popped up all over the place, they needed more and
more priests and the studies got shorter and shorter. But Maezumi Roshi
went back to the way it was in Dogen's time, and the amount of studying we
did was more than an average priest would do in Japan today. The one thing
Roshi really wanted to do with me, I think, was to make sure that at least one
teacher in his line could not be faulted in terms of formal study. The Japanese
are very particular. He had me study aspects of Soto liturgy that many Soto
priests are completely unfamiliar with. Even things like the Shinsanshiki. In
Japan there's a way of getting around everything. Traditionally, part of the
Soto training was to be the head monk for three months. But there were so
many temple posts to fill that the monasteries changed the rules and said,
'okay, you only have to be head monk for a week.' They have been skimping

on everything. Very few people do a formal Shinsanshiki. It's never been done in this country the way we did it and that's because of Roshi. He wanted to set an example with me, and he wanted to pass on as much of the old ways as he could before they disappear. There are all kinds of things that most people in this country will never know about. Some things will get written up by scholars, but we won't know them directly, by example."

While guests were suitably impressed with Greyston, the ceremony, the gifts, and the sit-down luncheon that followed, most were unaware of the significance of the kinds of details Glassman had arranged. The timing and sequence of brass gongs, bells, wooden mallets, and drums were particular to a Shinsanshiki. A neighbor's home served as the symbolic resting place for the new abbot, who prior to the ceremony traditionally refreshes himself at a layperson's house after traveling on foot to his new temple. The presentation of poems at the temple gates and the order of the procession that followed were all prescribed: ZCNY's board of directors led off, followed by Soto Zen clergy and Japanese and Americans affiliated with the Soto lineage; then came representatives of Buddhist, Christian, and Jewish communities, including Brother David Steindl-Rast; Cambodian monk Maha Gossananda; Korean master Soen Sa Nim; Baker Roshi, then abbot of San Francisco Zen Center; Kwong Roshi, abbot of Sonoma Mountain Zen Center; and Dean Morton, of the Cathedral of St. John the Divine. Tetsugen was flanked by his attendant monk, Peter Muryo Matthiessen, and Maezumi Roshi, whose outer robe was majestic purple. With the hand-held banners and colorful garments, the ornate regalia recalled the Heian Buddhism of medieval Japan rather than the monochromatic aesthetic associated with Japanese Zen. The color, however, was somewhat lost on the new abbot himself, who is color-blind and sees bright colors in more muted tones.

Taking the high seat, Tetsugen listened as the certificate of appointment from Soto headquarters was read in Japanese. "Standing on the lion's throne," he answered, repeating a Japanese script edited for this American event, "this humble monk Tetsugen offers this incense, burning in the golden burner. I offer its merits to the successive presidents of the United States, to the justice and freedom of our nation, to the peace of the world and mankind, to the harmony of all beings." For those Zen students unfamiliar with the standard liturgy of Jewish or Christian services—and there were many—the fleeting image of Richard Nixon or Ronald Reagan in the midst of this ceremony co-opted for a moment all the glorious expectations of Zen in America. For how long and under what circumstances Japanese customs would be replicated was fast becoming a thorny issue for American students. For the Shinsanshiki, however, the old alliance between Japanese Zen and political leadership was mostly shrugged off as a polite gesture of hospitality to the Japanese guests.

Tetsugen's opening remarks emphasized that although the Shinsanshiki might appear to be filled with things symbolic, there are no symbols. The heart of the Shinsanshiki is *jodo*, or "dharma combat," in which "dragons and elephants in this assembly" are urged to "contemplate the prime principle of reality" and invited to test the realization of the high priest. During the jodo a young monk rushed forward, banged his head three times against the altar, and asked, "How can I not bang into things like this?" Tetsugen replied, "Open your eyes." The monk banged his head three more times, with eyes wide open, and repeated the question. "Open your eyes," Tetsugen replied. "Sensei, if there is nothing at all," asked another man, who was wearing a gray robe over a pin-striped suit, "how did you find your abbot's job?" "I got it through the *New York Times*."

W. S. Merwin then offered a poem on behalf of Aitken Roshi and the Diamond Sangha in Hawaii. The ceremony ended with the reading of a telegram from an old priest in Japan who apologized for his absence "due to circumstances beyond control"; by the time the telegram was read the old priest had peacefully passed away.

The Shinsanshiki was grand. The Riverdale residents and the ecumenical clergy were duly impressed. The professionals, the poets, and the middle-class membership that Glassman had courted were all there to witness his ascent to the mountain. With his legitimacy so publicly confirmed, the view from the top must have indicated clear sailing ahead. But as Glassman's favorite koan asks: where do you go from the top of a hundred-foot pole?

Glassman went to a defunct bakery just north of the Bronx-Yonkers line and leased it for two years. A $175,000 loan from a founding member catapulted twenty-five resident trainees into the nitty-gritty of commercial baking. Four monks were dispatched to San Francisco to train at the Tassajara Bakery, while others concentrated on equipment and sales. Glassman trained a dozen people to use the first of four Apple computers, which was then fed a list of every gourmet shop and restaurant in Manhattan. Not one

D. T. Suzuki. Photo courtesy of Ruth McCandless.

D. T. Suzuki and Nyogen Senzaki, circa 1947. Photo courtesy of Ruth McCandless.

Haku'un Yasutani, circa 1967. Photo © Tim Buckley.

Haku'un Yasutani, circa 1973. Photo courtesy of the San Francisco Zen Center.

Shunryu Suzuki at Tassajara, circa 1969.
Photo © Robert S. Boni.

Shunryu Suzuki at Tassajara, circa 1969. Photo courtesy
of the San Francisco Zen Center.

Nakagawa Soen, circa 1970. Photo courtesy of Maurine Stuart.

Robert Aitken and members of the construction crew at the Palolo site, 1987.
Photo © Francis Haar.

Robert Aitken, circa 1982. Photo courtesy Robert Aitken.

Robert Aitken and others at sesshin held between the two samu training periods that focused on the Palolo construction, 1987. Photo © Francis Haar.

*Robert Aitken and Koun Yamada at Koko An Zendo, 1981.
Photo © Francis Haar.*

Jakusho Kwong in the kitchen of Sangha House at Genjoji, 1984.
Photo courtesy of the author.

Jakusho Kwong and his wife, Laura, standing in front of Shunryu Suzuki's memorial rock, 1983. Photo courtesy of the author.

Jakusho Kwong, circa 1968. Photo courtesy of the
San Francisco Zen Center.

Taizan Maezumi, Bernard Glassman, and Lou Nordstrom inside Greyston
zendo preparing for Glassman's abbot installation ceremony, 1982.
Photo © Peter Cunningham.

Bernard Glassman and Taizan Maezumi in front of Greyston Seminary, 1981.
Photo © Peter Cunningham.

Bernard Glassman officiating a Buddhist service at the Zen
Community of New York, 1982. Photo © Peter Cunningham.

Bernard Glassman, 1982. Photo © Peter Cunningham.

Bernard Glassman and Taizan Maezumi sharing a meal at Greyston.
Photo © Julie Thayer.

Maurine Stuart and Nakagawa Soen at Zen Studio Society, New York. Photo courtesy of Maurine Stuart.

Maurine Stuart offering incense at the altar of Cambridge Buddhist Association, 1989. Photo © Julie Thayer.

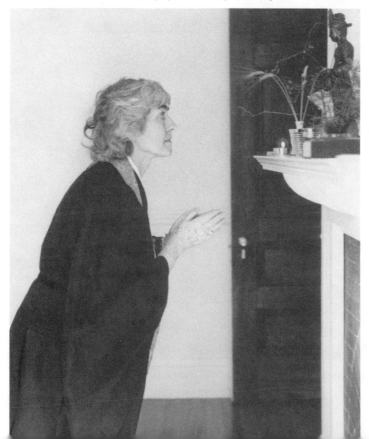

Maurine Stuart in the zendo of Cambridge Buddhist Association, 1989. Photo © Julie Thayer.

Richard Baker, circa 1965.
Photo © Robert S. Boni.

Richard Baker in Germany, circa 1985.
Photo courtesy of Jürgen Tapprich.

Richard Baker in Japan, circa 1968. Photo courtesy of the San Francisco Zen Center.

Richard Baker in Thailand.
Photo courtesy of Richard Baker.

Richard Baker and Philip Whalen in Santa Fe, New Mexico, 1987.
Photo © Ulricke Schmidt-Aberjan.

person on ZCNY's staff was familiar with professional baking, a problematic fact for everyone except Glassman, who insisted that "if you put your mind to it you can do anything." The new abbot put on coveralls and led work crews who removed massive quantities of debris to prepare for the installation of rotating ovens, mixers, racks, and dishwashers. Trade magazines cluttered the Mosholu office. When the Tassajara apprentices returned, they led all-night baking crews at the Greyston kitchen. The experimental samples were delivered daily to soup kitchens and church organizations. Sweet-smelling cakes permeated dawn zazen.

By 1983 new residents could no longer live at Greyston and work outside the community; they entered a "seminarian program." They were assigned jobs, roommates, cleaning tasks, and dishwashing schedules and, in addition to a full day of work in the managerial or production spheres of the bakery, were expected to sit zazen regularly as well as participate in evening classes and weekend programs. In addition to room and board, residents received monthly stipends of $100. Although alimony payments, therapy bills, clothing allowances, and vacation spending monies were provided by the community, Greyston was no longer anyone's Zen Hilton.

With the bakery consuming the time and energies of the teacher and the residents, nonresident members felt increasingly isolated from the community. Some felt "seduced and abandoned" by a community that initially promised to accommodate and support their spiritual practice wherever and however they chose to pursue it. A sportswriter who had studied with Japanese teachers before coming to ZCNY recalled: "In the first two years, Glassman took great pains to create the idea that this was the opposite of an autocratic situation. The myth was that the student could have it almost any way that suited his or her inclination. If you wanted strong Rinzai Zen, great. If you wanted to come and sit and have no relationship with the teacher, great. If you wanted to be a monk and live with your wife, fine. If you wanted to live at Greyston and watch soap operas all afternoon, that was fine too. If you wanted Judaism or Catholicism, we'd provide that, too. Not only did he permit all that, but he constantly adjusted the definition of Zen so that it was consistent with any or all of these preferences."

But by 1983 it seemed to nonresidents that the bakery was the only place that the teacher was teaching. "He betrayed my vision of Zen," said the disillusioned writer. "You can call anything you want Zen, but I felt like I signed up for basketball camp and the counselor decided to teach tennis." Yet when the student acquiesced and decided to study tennis, he found that Glassman still wouldn't play by the rules. He told Glassman that he kept taking the net away. "Well, yes," Glassman replied, "that's my job, to take the net away." At first the answer seemed impressive, but six months later the writer left to practice at a nonresidential center where life revolves around dawn and evening zazen, convinced that to study at ZCNY was to study Glassmanism, not Zen.

A defender of Glassman's claims that there is method in this madness: "Life is inconsistent, always changing, never what you expect or want. So he concentrates on internal stability in the midst of change. And he's the boss. So he keeps changing it all around. It always comes down to faith in the teacher. Either you trust that his moves are the functioning of his realization for the benefit of others or you think that he is a capricious, irresponsible egomaniac. That choice is personal, not subject to objective judgment, and no one is one hundred percent free of doubt. Only dead people are perfect, and it's easy to have faith if your buttons are never pushed."

While the debate over Glassman's teaching style continued to preoccupy his students, ZCNY was increasingly faulted by the membership for measuring its success solely in terms of bakery sales. For the first quarter of the bakery's first year, Glassman's optimistic projections were characteristically twice as high as the actual income. Later projections were similarly unrealistic, and even as the bakery became more successful, its profits continued to be eclipsed by the total overhead. In addition to buying the bakery building, new equipment, vans, and so on, ZCNY was still meeting the interest payments on Greyston as well as the $175,000 loan to start the bakery. In 1986 ZCNY closed their financial records in the black for the first time. Total expenses of $650,000 were met by $500,000 income from the bakery, with the difference covered by dues, program fees, and donations.

Even when bakery sales were down, though, lavish praise from the outside helped sustain the new enterprise. Wholesale buyers as well as culinary pros from schools and restaurants were impressed with both the quality of the goods and Glassman's managerial talents. The in-house ratings were somewhat less flattering and more difficult to assess since they came from students who had little or no business experience and were trying to define Zen practice through bakery work. "The difference between Greyston and other bakeries is that money is not the bottom line," said a twenty-six-year-old former monk and bakery manager who left the community to pursue a career in baking. "Without constant consideration to money, inefficiency is rampant. After all, a straight business can't turn around and receive donations on behalf of its spiritual contribution to society or get loans as a not-for-profit religious organization. I can't say whether or not the Greyston Bakery is 'Zen training.' I only know that for a manager it was totally frustrating. In an ordinary bakery cost considerations are the constant reference, and that can be a teaching too." This same baker was fired from his first straight job when six dozen cheesecakes were ruined by incorrect scaling. When he had been a baker-monk, similar mistakes had been written off as opportunities for learning and had never carried the vaguest threat of unemployment. Soon, fortified by this lesson, he got a job with one of Greyston's most formidable competitors, and within three months of leaving ZCNY, this same monk who had lived on stipends for virtually all his adult life was making $40,000 a year.

While the conflict between profit motive and learning experience is a common problem for the bakery staff, Glassman has continued using the bakery as his laboratory, placing people in new jobs at the expense of conventional organizational wisdom. "Just when you get comfortable with a job, when you think you know how to do it right," explained a student who had been working at the bakery for three years, "he gives you something to do that makes you feel dumb all over again. Then after a while you begin to feel that you can do anything. At first you have these ideas about what you can and can't do. I can drive the van but I'll never learn the computer. I can make the Danish but I can't do sales; I can be a Zen student but I can't be a baker. You begin to see yourself differently, to think about yourself differently, to give up your attachments to fixed ideas about yourself. And there has been a loss of 'efficiency' in running the bakery this way. Sensei has always said that this was a training, not a profit-making enterprise, but the community has been under extreme financial pressures. We are trying to support the place and we are the livelihood, so it can be confusing to switch gears between profit and practice."

One Saturday morning, wearing a brown beret and a blue down jacket, Glassman drove a delivery van down the Major Deegan Parkway to deliver breads to D'Agostino's and Sloan supermarkets throughout Manhattan. "In a Japanese monastery the tenzo is the cook," he explained. "We say that the most experienced person, or the most attained monk, should be the cook. And that when people eat the food they will taste that attainment. And how does that happen? What is the training of the tenzo? Certainly that training is not happening here yet. It's not so simple to get it all together to get to a place where that can happen. Jishu [his attendant] is preparing to lead a one-month training period and she is studying *The Diamond Sutra*. She has always been curious about how it starts off—Shakyamuni got up, he cleaned himself, he got dressed, he got his bowl, he went into town, and *then* he started to teach. And it finally struck her that it was all preparation. You have to get it all together, and then you can teach. We can look at that in many ways—like we have to get our community together before we can even teach ourselves—but getting it together *is* the teaching. That's a big problem for a lot of people. They miss the fact that getting it together is it. We have a wonderful koan about that: how can the water buffalo jump through the window when his tail can't fit through? That koan is considered one of the most difficult. This bakery has brought us into contact with business leaders like Peter Grace. A religious leader accepting Zen doesn't have the same effect. This country has a built-in acceptance of business. In order for Zen to really get its bearings in this country, it has to adapt to what's happening in the society. So many people still want the magic of an Oriental teacher. They say to me, 'I'm not at ease with a Japanese teacher, or Tibetan, or Korean.' But when they see an American Zen teacher doing business, it's not magical enough."

Glassman grew up on the border of Brighton Beach and Coney Island, half a block from the Atlantic Ocean. His father had come from Russia, his mother from Poland. He is the first and only son, born when his four sisters were nine to sixteen years older. Standing in the kitchen of the same apartment in which she was raised, Edith, his eldest sister, explains, "We weren't that religious. Still we were Jewish, and after four girls you might say that when Bernie was born it was like Jesus Christ arrived."

When Glassman was seven his mother died of cancer. The family was "more socialist than Jewish," and for one year following his mother's death, the boy went alone to the synagogue to say the mourner's prayer. Zen lore is filled with outstanding figures who lost one or both parents in childhood, learning life's crucial lessons of impermanence and suffering at an early age.

The lives of Dogen Zenji, Bodhidharma, Hui Nêng, Nyogen Senzaki, and others offer parallels to Glassman's, but he is not inclined to credit any event with dramatic significance and further disclaims that suffering turned him toward Buddhism. "For a lot of people, suffering is the standard entry to Buddhist studies. I never felt that it was for me. In fact, no religious, personal, or social experiences that I know of add up to a linear evolution toward Zen."

Glassman's family contends that for the only boy the maternal gap was more than filled by his four older sisters. Glassman observes that this theory may not hold up under therapeutic scrutiny, but then he gives a Talmudic shrug that suggests some skepticism about therapy itself. He has displayed no more interest in the psychological motives of his adult life than of childhood, but a psychotherapist who has studied with him for five years once described Glassman as "a guy who always gets what he wants, but sees himself as always wanting what he gets."

Unlike many of his students, he has never engaged in any kind of therapy. He has recommended short-term therapy for several students but in general displays little interest in the origins of behavioral patterns or in psychological descriptions: "If you want to find out why you behave in a particular way, go to a therapist. If you want to find out how to let go, practice. Because we have personality traits, because we are human, we say in Zen that we're always defiling the precepts. We are always dirtying up the empty glass. Just by using it. By allowing it to fulfill its function. So our job is to keep cleaning it and that's the way it is. As long as we realize that our practice is to keep it clean and that it will get dirty, then we're observing the precepts. And then in our practice we have to go to the place where there is no glass. And in that very state, although we are constantly cleaning the glass, there is no cleaning and there is no glass. Both exist at the same time. Zero and one exist at the same time. I'm not so interested in the question why. I'm more interested in how. There is a tendency in this country to make the Zen teacher into a therapist. And there will be Zen teachers who will be trained in psychology, and how they use psychology will be their valid expression of Zen. But that's not who I am, not how I was trained."

A studious interest in how things work formed early. By age ten he was taking apart radios and television sets, devising experiments with electricity, and repairing household appliances. As assistant to a television repairman in high school, he learned that ninety percent of the times that a television was reported broken the set was unplugged. As he says of one's original nature, "Unless you turn the switch on you don't know it exists."

In 1960 Glassman received his B.S. in aeronautical engineering from the Polytechnic Institute of Brooklyn. For a philosophy course he had been assigned Houston Smith's *The Religions of Man* (1958), and it provided him with his first introduction to Zen. In the section on Buddhism, Smith records both the "loving legend" that has encased the life of the cosmic Buddha and the human story of Siddhartha Gautama, "the man who woke up." He portrays Siddhartha as a hard-working, pragmatic teacher, disciplined, revolutionary, comparable to Socrates. "Every problem that came his way was automatically subjected to the cold, analytical glare of his intellect. . . . The remarkable fact, however, was the way this objective, critical component of his character was balanced by a Franciscan tenderness so strong as to have caused his message to be subtitled 'a religion of infinite compassion.' "

Polytechnic's humanities program was a required concession to American educational pluralism and did very little to contradict the ideological separation between the humanities and sciences that has dominated Western thinking since Descartes. Yet Smith's portrait embraces both sides of the spiritual-science dichotomy, applying supreme analytical powers to the diagnosis of human suffering and to its remedy—a systematic map to liberation called the Eightfold Path. For the class of 1960 no account of Shakyamuni could have been more convincing, since Buddhist hagiography more often than not invokes a divine reverence for Shakyamuni that inhibits mortal description.

Smith ends the section on Buddhism with a brief description of Zen that, influenced by D. T. Suzuki, emphasizes the use of koans as a method for awakening the mind from the deadening effects of habit. Glassman recognized that here was something he wanted. Before graduating, he made three promises to himself: to visit a Zen monastery in Japan; to visit a kibbutz in Israel; and, influenced by Eugene O'Neill's play *The Iceman Cometh*, to spend some part of his life living on the streets.

Having accepted an offer from McDonnell-Douglas in his senior year, he sailed for Israel the following summer and met his future wife, Helen Silverberg, on board ship. The twenty-year-old college student from Minneapolis wrote home from Tel Aviv that she was dating a young man who had recommended Somerset Maugham's *The Razor's Edge*. In her letter she told her conservative Jewish parents that the novel's idealistic hero, Laurence Darrell, who leaves behind the vacuous preoccupations of English society to follow the Vedanta path in India, was a lot like Bernie himself. Mrs. Silverberg flew to Israel in alarm.

Two years later the bride-to-be absently said to her mother, "What if I'm marrying someone who ends up becoming a Zen monk?" They married in 1963 and settled in Santa Monica, California. According to Helen, their friends were an eclectic group of itinerant boat-dwellers, accomplished eccentrics, including a mathematician obsessed with elegant proofs, and a suicidal pianist turned optometrist. "It was very much a men's group," she says. "Buddies. Bright young men. They sat around our living room drinking beer, eating pizza, smoking cigars, reading Alan Watts, and talking about enlightenment." By 1966 Glassman and his friends were making periodic visits to the Japanese Temple in downtown Los Angeles where the elderly Bishop Togen Sumi had been sent by Soto headquarters to preside over the Japanese-American congregation. One Saturday afternoon Glassman asked Sumi Roshi about the walking meditation that is done between periods of sitting. Sumi Roshi spoke little English and referred the question to his attendant monk, who answered, "When we walk, we walk." The young monk was not yet Maezumi Roshi and Bernie Glassman didn't see him again for almost two years.

When *The Three Pillars of Zen* appeared in 1965, it had a major impact on Glassman as it had on many readers of Zen. Compiled by the American Zen teacher Philip Kapleau Roshi, it combined basic Zen texts with the first how-to instructions for Westerners. No longer could an American read about Zen and not know where to begin.

After reading *The Three Pillars of Zen* Glassman started doing zazen at home. One evening, as he sat before an unlit fireplace in the dark, he began to experience himself disappearing. "I began to have a sense that I was losing myself—like whoooosh. And I panicked. I didn't want to lose myself. I thought I was going crazy. And there was a real sense of fear. I went into the bedroom and turned the lights on and woke Helen up. I couldn't stay in the dark. I was terrified. It took the whole night for me to calm down. And I stopped sitting. And I remember at that time wishing there had been someone to tell me that it was okay to go on. I was afraid to do it alone."

The Three Pillars of Zen begins with a translation of the introductory talks of Kapleau Roshi's teacher, Haku'un Yasutani Roshi. Two years after the book was published, the Theosophical Society of Los Angeles sponsored a talk by Master Yasutani; the translator was Taizan Maezumi. Yasutani talked about letting go—the importance of *being* the infinity of no mind. Glassman recalls that a woman in the audience stood up and said, "But if that were true, then you'd be completely gone."

Glassman recounts, "And Yasutani Roshi said, 'Yeah, that's right.' But the woman spoke as if being 'completely gone' were an absurd, crazy statement. And he just said, 'Yeah.' And that response was very powerful for me: 'Yeah.' Like no big deal. That's just the way it is. I had been slowly getting the idea that 'letting go' was what it was all about. But it wasn't until Yasutani Roshi's talk that the weight of it struck home and the whole thing made sense to me—what was *really* required. And then seeing that the woman couldn't grasp the words, that they were so removed from her idea of common sense that they didn't mean anything—that had a big impact, too."

The Three Pillars of Zen also provided Americans with an introduction to Dogen Zenji through the essay "Being-Time," excerpted from the *Shobogenzo*, "The Treasury of the True Dharma Eye." Written in ninety-five fascicles over a period of twenty-five years, it was completed shortly before Dogen's death in 1253. Kapleau Roshi wrote that although "Being-Time" is "perhaps the most abstruse section" of the *Shobogenzo*, it is "peculiarly relevant for students of Zen living in the science-oriented twentieth century, revealing as it does in a unique way the meaning of time and the universe." Noting the similarities between Dogen's insights and contemporary physics, Kapleau Roshi then addressed the critical difference: "Dogen's realization, being a Self-discovery, liberated him from the basic anxieties of human existence, bringing him inner freedom and peace and deep moral certainty. But, as far as can be seen at this time, no such inner evolution has followed in the wake of these scientific discoveries."

Glassman had participated in the American dream of dominating space by developing instruments that could analyze it, measure it, traverse it, even dent its supreme anonymity. His studies of quantum theory offered scientific validation for what the Buddhists call the truth of "non-knowing" and proof of the basic oneness: the universe could no longer be fragmented into separate, isolated particles. While interplanetary research was taking him as far into outer space as he could get, three pages of Dogen indicated that if mind and the objects of mind are the same, then the whole universe in its totality and particularity, in all of its past, present, and future expressions, was his to "be"—but he had to travel inside to know it. Glassman says, "Here was a guy writing in the thirteenth century who had *experienced* what modern physics was just beginning to discover!" Indeed, he had surpassed what modern physics was about to discover, for as he wrote in another section of the *Shobogenzo*: "A practitioner of zazen passes beyond the entire universe at full speed and is greatly honored in the abode of the Buddhas and patriarchs."

Following the talk at the Theosophical Society, Glassman signed up for a retreat led by Yasutani Roshi, but his best intentions could not overcome crippling leg pain exacerbated by a college judo injury. After one day of sitting like a frog with his knees closer to his ears than to the floor, he left with the true if somewhat feeble excuse that one of his sisters had just flown in from the East Coast. He rushed home in time for cocktails with Edith on the patio with an unannounced resolve to conquer the form of zazen. From then on car pools to the office and Saturday afternoon football games on television were occasions to stretch his muscles into the lotus posture.

Taizan Maezumi was then attracting American students to the meditation meetings he led at his small house on Serrano Street. With the uncompromising zeal of a new convert, Glassman wanted to drop out of graduate school to devote more time to Zen studies. But since he had taken a leave of absence from McDonnell-Douglas to complete his doctorate, a $300-a-month stipend from UCLA was the Glassmans' total income. Helen, pregnant with their second child, argued for a more pragmatic approach. As it was, her husband's fervid new interest was already threatening her sense of well-ordered domesticity, and Maezumi's plans for a residential center didn't help.

In the summer of 1970, following Tetsugen Glassman's ordination, Helen traveled to Japan with her husband, eager to sightsee and determined not to practice. For Glassman Japan was a very familiar culture. "Nothing ever felt foreign. There was never anything strange about Japan or about Zen, as there seemed to be for others." Helen, being one of those others, continued to experience things Japanese as cloying and restrictive. Zen had become their bone of contention; they separated on returning to Los Angeles and he moved into the new center. "He's willful, stubborn," says Helen. "When he wants something, he's a sledgehammer." More than anything, he wanted Zen teachings, he wanted enlightenment. "I was a fanatic," he says. "I had nothing else on my agenda."

Six months later they reunited on the condition that Helen and the children live at the Zen center, but a common commitment to Zen practice was slow in coming. Tetsugen's talents for accomplishing the Buddha Way may have been a source of rejoicing for his teacher, but his wife had a different response. "*Bride* magazine," she says wryly, "does not tell you how to deal with your husband's kensho experience." Soon she began dealing with it by giving zazen another try. After five years of steady zazen Helen became ordained, formally entering the lineage of her husband and his teacher. Maezumi Roshi gave her the name Yuho, which means "Subtle Dharma." An effusive and articulate talker, she laughingly explains that "Maezumi Roshi usually gives a name that he wants you to grow into."

The succession to which Glassman is lineage holder descends through Maezumi Roshi and his father, Baian Kuroda. In addition to being certified by his father, Maezumi Roshi also received dharma transmission from Yasutani Roshi and Osaka Koryu Roshi. After studying with Koryu Roshi, a lay Rinzai teacher, for four years, Maezumi went to Sojiji, one of the two main Soto training centers, before coming to Los Angeles in 1956. On trips back to Japan he continued his koan practice with Koryu Roshi, and in 1972, after twenty-five years of study, Maezumi Roshi received Koryu Roshi's seal of approval. Maezumi met Yasutani Roshi for the first time in Los Angeles in 1962 and immediately asked to be his student. For the next ten years Maezumi Roshi studied with both teachers.

During an "Introduction to Zen" workshop, Glassman attributed the type of preliminary talk he was giving to the Harada Roshi-Yasutani Roshi influence. Dai'un Harada Roshi did sitting practice for many years as a young monk before straying from the Soto fold in his search for an enlightened master. After studying at a Rinzai monastery for seven years, he left to go to the Soto university, and then, determined to pursue koan study, continued to wander until he went to Nanzenji, a Rinzai training compound in the eastern hills of Kyoto. Here he completed koan practice with Master Toyoda Dokutan (1841–1919) and received this master's seal of approval. At age fifty he became the Soto abbot of Hosshin Temple, demanding vigorous koan practice from his Soto students. He is considered responsible for reforming the Soto sect, for shaking his monks loose from the intoxication of complacent sitting.

"Very different styles flow into the ocean," said Glassman in the workshop. "Each one of us has all these different aspects, but when you get to know yourself, you see that certain aspects are emphasized and you will be attracted to those that are dominant in you. There are many different ways of studying. The fact that everything is different is what we mean by the oneness of life. The heart practices differently from the eyes, the ears. Koryu Roshi emphasized wisdom in everyday life. His forte was in powerful sitting, deep, centered concentration, and the emphasis of his school is called *prajna*, or the 'wisdom' of awakening. In studying with him the spirit was always aimed at the wisdom aspect of what's happening. He penetrated into the heart of the matter. Yasutani Roshi has the reputation of having always driven toward kensho or awakening—understanding what life is about—but there was a big difference in the flavor of these two teachers. Yasutani Roshi demanded a meticulous understanding and study of what's happening, and Koryu Roshi didn't care for that at all. Koryu Roshi just wanted you to grasp the spirit. He didn't allow for discursive thoughts; he didn't want to clarify your understanding through discussion. There are virtues with each style, but some people always complain. Some people said that Yasutani Roshi took too long in the dokusan room, that he was too thorough. Some people thought Koryu Roshi was too fierce. Seated in dokusan he seemed towering and his voice was very loud and the demands he made created a tension that could be frightening. He was the fiercest teacher I ever met in dokusan, but outside the dokusan room he was the most gentle man. Both Koryu Roshi and Yasutani Roshi were very gentle people."

Above a yellow tiled fireplace in Glassman's spacious and well-lit private interview room at Greyston are five framed photographs: Harada, Koryu, Maezumi, Yasutani, and Kuroda. Sitting cross-legged on a blue sofa, surrounded by religious books and fresh flowers, Glassman looks frequently at these portraits as he recalls his early experiences with Zen practice. In 1969 Yasutani Roshi assigned him the koan *mu*—"the barrier set up by the ancient masters to help break through the gateless gate"—which Glassman describes as "working on becoming *mu* itself and then, without leaving that state, seeing what it is." Before the year was out, Glassman was left in charge of the new community while Maezumi Roshi returned to Japan for one and a half years to complete his own studies with Yasutani Roshi. In May 1970 Maezumi Roshi returned briefly to welcome Koryu Roshi to Los Angeles. "At that time," recalls Glassman, "since Maezumi Roshi was so close to finishing his own koan studies with Yasutani Roshi, I was resolved to resume my koan practice with Maezumi Roshi—until I heard Koryu Roshi's first talk in the zendo. I was blown away by it. Not that I could understand it. It was in Japanese. But that didn't matter. Maezumi Roshi translated—sort of. But it wasn't in the words. It was his style of presentation. I was intrigued. I wanted to work with him in that dokusan room. That talk was so powerful and so immediate that I decided to start right in."

Before the sesshin ended Glassman had passed through the barrier. "I passed *mu* in my first sesshin with Koryu Roshi in Los Angeles and apparently it was a very clear passing. Very deep. By the fourth night of sesshin I was ready. Maezumi Roshi was running the zendo and he knew and he just pushed me over the precipice. So I went into dokusan and I passed it and Koryu Roshi and I were crying and hugging, and I think for me that was the deepest feeling of love I've ever known."

Under Maezumi Roshi, Glassman completed koan study in 1976. "The way I've worked with the koan *mu* has certainly been tremendously influenced by the way Koryu Roshi worked with me. There are many different ways of working on koans and particularly on this first one. I don't know that I can honestly say that one way is better than another or that I know which way is best, but I was very influenced by his demand for total concentration, single-mindedly pushing toward one point, not giving any room at all for discursive thought. I worked with him almost twenty years ago, and there have been periods when I didn't work that way with students, when I thought that style was too pushy and could be too harsh, but I seem to come back to it, though not necessarily with everyone, and I keep seeing how effective it is."

Maezumi Roshi inherited from Yasutani Roshi the belief that teaching is the best way of learning and therefore insisted that Tetsugen start teaching almost immediately; he requested that he run the zendo, give talks, and officiate at services. "I wanted as many people as possible to encounter The Way," says Glassman, "but I didn't want to be a teacher. That was my biggest dichotomy. My teacher requested that I teach. I began teaching in 1970. I was too young, but that's how he trained me."

In Los Angeles Glassman is remembered for his tough, aggressive style of teaching, a style influenced by both Koryu and Yasutani. "I followed a standard textbook way of passing *mu* which doesn't happen all that often. And in a way I got trapped by that. It took me a few years to realize that it doesn't happen that way all the time. I was naive and thought that 'I' worked really hard. So I thought all you had to do in the zendo was push a person really hard and that 'it' would happen. And, also, I felt that it was extremely important for some kind of opening to occur. In this I was influenced by Yasutani Roshi. I felt that openings were critical and that you really had to push. And I saw a lot of effect from doing that. I saw that by pushing people in certain ways you really could get them to let go and they really did have some kind of experience. So there was reenforcement for this style. Then, over the years, I began to see the shallowness and decided that it was not the best way of doing things. It's very dramatic and you gain a lot of power and everyone's having these far-out experiences, but over the long run my own sense was that it wasn't where Zen practice was at."

Although Glassman refers to the Harada-Yasutani line as the one that most influenced Maezumi Roshi's teaching methods and therefore his own, it is Maezumi's relationship to his "source teacher," his biological father, Kuroda Roshi, that moves Glassman the most. This is the relationship that most expresses the actualization of nonseparation—the foundation of Zen—and this intimacy is what Glassman sees as the heart of dharma transmission. In response to a question about teacher-student relationships, Glassman once told a woman who had come to a formal interview with an infant strapped to her breast: "The relationship that I have with Maezumi Roshi is more intimate than the one between you and your baby."

Glassman's own memory of Kuroda Roshi is one of seeing compassion in action, "watching him accept people who came to him without discrimination, without judgment. To see his availability, his openness to others, his patience, his capacity to give and to comfort—and you got to see that in his daily life, in his house, with his family, with all the different people who would visit. Yasutani Roshi was probably the sharpest teacher in terms of prajna wisdom, the clearest. His understanding of dharma was truly brilliant. And as for Koryu Roshi, I never met anyone with that kind of *samadhi*, that kind of sitting power. But Maezumi Roshi always said that he learned the most from his father. He lived with him. He learned day-to-day functioning. How do you respond to somebody coming unexpectedly? How do you respond to somebody burning down the temple? To somebody stepping on your prized chrysanthemum? Now when Maezumi Roshi talks, I can hear Yasutani Roshi or Koryu Roshi, but when he acts, I see his father."

Although Glassman's lineage incorporates lay and monastic paths of Zen training, Maezumi Roshi adheres to the orthodox belief in the supremacy of the monk's vows. This belief has never been stated more unequivocally than by Dogen Zenji, who claimed that "even if a monk violates the monastic precepts, he is superior to a layman who does not break his precepts." And it has retained a strong hold even among those teachers who have been the most outspoken critics of the corrupting forces of monasticism. Following Koryu Roshi's death in 1985, Maezumi Roshi explained that receiving this lay teacher's seal of approval was a recognition of understanding, but that his own lineage was through his father and that he, like Yasutani Roshi and Harada Roshi, still considered the monastic context in which he was raised the most serious expression of Zen practice. According to Maezumi Roshi, Harada Roshi used to say that "if you really get involved, you cannot help but become a monk." And Maezumi Roshi explained: "for me, being raised in a temple and within a very strong Soto monastic tradition, the idea of monasticism is very common and natural. In this country we are involved in the question of lay and monastic, but in Japan there was one very important difference. In Japan monastic practice also became a way by which a monk acquired his status. It's a route to going home and taking over the local temples. In this country it's different. The purpose of practicing together in a community or a center is different. But now we are in a kind of transitional period. And in a way it is always a transitional period. A few years ago, just having men and women practicing together was a big thing. And monks and laymen. That's another big thing. These are radical changes taking place. We cannot generalize so easily."

Glassman Sensei has also expressed faith in the supremacy of monastic vows. But the superimposition of this ideal onto communities that are essentially secular has provoked conflicts in both the Los Angeles and New York centers, where monks have been relieved from the traditional bans on marriage, sex, and intoxicants. However widespread sex and alcohol were for Japanese monks, the abuses of the ideal were, at the very least, carried out with a sense of discretion, whereas in the United States these departures have been openly sanctioned. In theory, regardless of lifestyle, ordination implies that the vow to help all sentient beings will be the guiding principle of one's life.

In the actual day-to-day functioning of the New York and Los Angeles centers what has distinguished the monastics, besides shaved heads and distinct robes, has been a superior status in the organizational structures. In both communities the perception of monastics comprising an "in-group" has attracted those interested in organizational power and its association—however tenuous—with both spiritual authority and spiritual virtue. But monastics have proven themselves no more committed to Zen practice than laypeople. At ZCNY three of the present monastics were ordained by other teachers, and only two of the seven monks ordained by Glassman have remained at the center.

Combining monastic vows with secular lifestyles has nonetheless served two functions. It has introduced the monastic dimension of the Japanese Zen tradition to the United States, where it may someday figure prominently. It has also been a skillful means for establishing the authority of Zen teachings both within and without the communities. At ZCLA as well as ZCNY, newcomers to the Zen workshops have been much more willing to trust the authority of the instructor if he or she has been ordained. In 1985, in recognition of how misused the term "monk" had become, Maezumi Roshi tried to replace it with the term "priest," which is appropriate for the Japanese—as well as Protestant and Jewish—custom of married clergy. "Monk" has been officially deleted from public records but has stayed very much in colloquial use in both communities. In 1986 Glassman returned to New York from a meeting in Los Angeles and announced that Maezumi Roshi wanted celibacy to be part of the monastic path. There had been three students at ZCNY who had planned to enter the novice program. After that announcement there were none.

While the question of spiritual status remains confusing to communities of monastics and secular practitioners, Glassman has created parallel paths designed to give lay practitioners a sense of progression that is built into novice training. "We say that there's no place to go and nothing to learn, but most people benefit from some sense of progression," he explains. "When I came to New York I felt that we needed to create some rites of passage for people to be comfortable in their practice. You can't forget about the form. That doesn't work. At ZCNY there is no one uniform practice. Different paths can be addressed, but the form can be misleading. There are traditions where the form is secular, but surrender to the teachings through the teacher, the guide, or the guru is total, complete. And in a way, that's true monasticism. And in the same way, you can have monks who wear robes but with no sense of surrender at all. The same thing is true with celibacy. You can interpret it strictly to mean no sex. But another way of understanding celibacy is in terms of availability, of being wholeheartedly available to the teachings, to the teacher. And again, you can have celibate monastics who are not available. It gets tricky. You have to have the form. But just having it isn't enough either."

In all Glassman's teaching modes, paths, and organizational structures—which he restructures continually and unabashedly—there is an underlying concern with dharma succession. "Anyone can teach Zen," he says, "but the unique vow of a lineage holder is to maintain the lineage." Specifically, this means acknowledging individual dharma heirs. The commitment to maintain the lineage is Glassman's priority. In his current view, not all heirs will be Zen teachers. Poets, plumbers, philosophers—and bakers—can be Zen teachers insofar as their work inherently expresses their attainment. "I want to open it up," says Glassman, who foresees many successors but has none to date. These would-be teachers will receive *shiho*, a Soto term for transmission, but the Rinzai *inka* will be reserved for only the deepest level of spiritual realization. In Japan the terms shiho and inka have been roughly equivalent; both indicate a final, formal recognition by one's master. But inka is now being used by Glassman as the highest step on the Soto ladder. This change was introduced by Harada Roshi and used by Maezumi Roshi. "These descriptions may change tomorrow," says Glassman, "but I want to create ways for people to question themselves. All these structures are expedient means. If you decide not to use a structure, that's an expedient means, too. I see the problem with structures, but I see more problems without them."

Community affords Glassman the familial conditions for the intimacy that occurred in the transmission between Maezumi Roshi and his father. In 1983 the Glassmans left their own house and moved into Greyston, occupying a suite of rooms on the second floor. Like all the rooms at Greyston, theirs are never locked and students are free to wander in and out of their apartment. Although the model of Chinese masters laboring alongside their students was incorporated into Japanese Zen, it is unlikely that any Japanese abbot has come close to embracing a lifestyle that has as much parity with his students as Glassman has. In Japan intimacy is not necessarily associated with informality; Glassman's style of familial informality is particularly American.

"I want you to know who I am," Glassman told an assembly of students in the Greyston zendo. "I want you to see me at my best and at my worst. It's very standard that anyone who is really serious about practice will discover that their teacher is human and you either deal with it or you don't. It depends on how close you are to the teacher. I was extremely close to my teacher. The only times I was discouraged in my Zen studies had to do with the human character of my teacher. The closer you are to the teacher, the harder it is to deal with his humanity. Half the time the student breaks away. Very, very rarely is realization matched by actualization, and it can get discouraging."

Asked by a monk how he had resolved those difficulties for himself, Glassman answered: "Part of it was tied in with what Dogen Zenji said: you find a teacher and you don't look at what you consider negative aspects—not necessarily negative but what you *consider* negative; don't pay attention to those and study as hard as you can. I was very rigid in those days, so I just dove in. I took everything I could get from Maezumi Roshi. I was there to chew him up. There was no way for him not to transmit the dharma. And I just said to myself, okay, I'll study as hard as I can and then I'll get enlightened. But not so simple, huh? In order to accept somebody else's humanity, their so-called weaknesses, you have to accept your own. Not so easy. Roshi knew, for example, that I didn't approve of the way he used to drink and I never drank with him—well—not never. But in any relationship, as we uncover each other's weaknesses—I don't like that word 'weaknesses'—but, as we uncover the places in the other person that we don't want that person to have, because we don't want to face the fact that we have them in ourselves, we either work with them or we walk away. Like a marriage. In dharma it's the same. Those aspects are always there. That's what the practice is all about—giving into the humanness in all of us, the 'isness' of who we are. Everybody has the ability to work with these things, no matter who they are, and you either stay or you don't. I don't believe there's ever been a teacher-student relationship that didn't have doubting moments."

Assessing a teacher's realization seems to be the favorite game of Buddhist students, although one seasoned player compared it to playing tag in a hall of mirrors. Another student left ZCNY after telling Glassman, "Enlightened people can't be fat!" While ZCNY has not experienced the turbulence that has marked other centers, including Maezumi Roshi's, it has not remained indifferent to the investigations concerning what it means to be a Zen master and what it means to be a Zen student. In 1984 the Zen centers of Los Angeles and San Francisco initiated reforms that would allow greater student control over the operations of the community. Glassman Sensei's response to this was swift and direct: "I'm going to become more autocratic," he announced softly—and repeatedly.

"In Buddhism," Glassman explains, "we study the world of differences, that's the world of form; we study the world of emptiness, the realm of oneness; and we study the relationship, the mapping, the isomorphism between those two, which is called 'harmony.' These are the Three Treasures: the Buddha is oneness, emptiness; the dharma is form; and the sangha is the relationship between the Buddha and the dharma, which says that they are really the same thing. Form is emptiness and emptiness is form. Nowadays we use *sangha* to refer to community. So all the members of a community make up the sangha and this is theoretically one of the three treasures. But the term 'sangha' originally meant 'the community of *enlightened* disciples' that formed around the Buddha. The enlightened sangha does not include people who wander in on Sunday mornings to hear a talk or who come to the zendo a couple of evenings a week. They may call themselves Buddhists or Zen students or whatever, but a community based on the Buddhist treasures must rely for its principal guidance on the realization of the teacher. Otherwise you have a secular community. That might be a very nice thing, but it's not what I'm interested in and it doesn't allow me to fulfill my commitments as a lineage holder. You can't get the best part of a teacher and deny who he is at the same time. Here I was being asked not to express Zen teachings in terms of the bakery or work-practice. So it felt like the best thing to do was to be much *more* expressive of who I am, if I can. It's up front.

"The notion of a sangha taking over—becoming the driving force—won't work unless it's an enlightened sangha—that is, unless it's a fully integrated Buddha-Dharma-Sangha. That's not impossible, but it is so hard for that to happen that, as I see it, it's safer if it's weighted the other way, on the side of the teacher. If there is a strong, enlightened teacher things will continue because there will always be a couple of students around a real teacher. If a student doesn't have confidence in the realization of the teacher, then it can't work. But that confidence has got to ride out the judgments of personal behavior. If it doesn't, the student should leave. At a certain point each student really has to ask himself or herself what he or she is doing in a Zen center. At ZCLA and San Francisco all these nice people came together, many were married couples, many had small children, and they evolved a way of life. And this way of life itself became very attractive to others. For many people it became more attractive than Zen practice. And at a certain point, like any other community, the consensus is for stability, security, protection. That's human nature. As the masses grow their needs will be defined by their interests. It happens in every tradition. The questions being raised about the behavior of the teacher are not unimportant, but my own feeling is that if a student is really determined to accomplish the way, is wholeheartedly set on knowing what this life is about, those questions will fall into place."

The autocracy of the Zen master has its counterpart in surrender as an ideal form of spiritual practice. In Japan surrender to the master is taken for granted not just for the attainment of Zen teachings but for the attainment of harmony with the entire universe. It has existed between Zen master and disciple with no more urgency or virtue than between warlord and samurai, feudal landlord and serf, mistress and maid, or boss and employee. Americans, however, show little instinct for the kind of submission and obedience that has been indigenous to Japan as well as to any area that has come under the influence of Confucianism.

At ZCNY the monastic ideal of 'doing what the teacher says' has rarely been achieved with any consistency by the monks and far less by the laity, for whom this Japanese prototype has set an unworkable standard. Yet without any real recourse to monastic orthodoxy, Glassman continues examining seven hundred years of Japanese Zen convention while reinventing practice forms for contemporary America. "In the monastery," he says, "the illusion is that the monks have a desire for nakedness. In a monastery they all share the same illusion. In this country we don't know what the rules are. Zen monks here won't know what they are for a couple of hundred years. I'm very critical, too. I have very tough standards. I don't think any of us are monks. I have this sense that as Americans we're very attracted in some kind of intellectual way to a notion of a committed monk but that in our guts we're householders. There's nobody that I know of as a monk who puts the Buddhadharma above his own householder life. There's no comparison with the Trappist monks. Those people are appealing to us, but there's nobody I know who really wants to live like that."

Glassman still strongly believes in community as the way for Zen practice in this country, but community based on work-practice. "Most people who get involved with Zen in this country are like parishioners. So you get some kind of parish Zen. And there's nothing wrong with it. In Japan you have parish Zen, too. Temple Zen. Those people are not really Zen practitioners. And it took a while for us, as American teachers, to realize that very few people coming into a Zen center were really committed to working with us. Over and over I've talked with teachers in this country who realized they didn't have a monastery. They had people coming and going. So what's the model? The monastery was not just a way of operating a strict practice mode. Living with the teacher meant that practice was all through the day. How do you really form a spiritual life without that kind of intimacy? The needs of the parish are important. But you don't get the same concentration of energy with the parish as you could with monastics, and even in a community like this, making extensive accommodations for parishioners can really drain the energy. So there's that tension between the parish and the monastery, the laity and the ordained. It's in many traditions and every major religion has lots of accommodating paths. How do you work it out? Well that's what we're trying to figure out, and it's a very transitional time. I used to have ideas about American Zen. Now I don't. I see the experiments going on. I don't know where they're going. I don't know the feeling of this whole community yet and what the community means to everybody and what their involvement is. It hasn't taken shape yet. What does membership in a Zen community mean? It certainly will be different five years from now."

Yes, but is it Zen? That is a question that promises to continue to haunt ZCNY. Although its membership has generally been more receptive to social action than to the bakery business, in the most recent discussions about the Greyston Family Inn the question was asked again: Yes, but is it Zen? A woman who joined the Greyston residency in the summer of 1986 objected five months later to the center's direction of social action, claiming that baking alone was true Zen practice. And the question will no doubt be asked of another of Glassman's projects, which is to fulfill his vow to live on the streets. He has already suggested the possibility of a homeless sesshin. Those brave enough to sign up would live on the streets with no money, food, or identification papers while asking the old question, "Who am I?"

While the Greyston Family Inn is eligible for funding from city, county, and federal agencies, some financial advisors have tried to convince Glassman that his program is timely and attractive enough to secure funding from the private sector. This option would keep the project free from the machinations of local politics and bureaucratic restrictions, which by religious convention are considered the very dregs of worldly existence. But this argument has held no sway for Glassman, who says, "All the things that people say are not Zen are the things that I want to get involved with."

The Master took the high seat in the Hall. He said: "On your lump of red flesh is a true man without rank who is always going in and out of the face of every one of you. Those who have not yet experienced him—look! look!" Then a monk came forward and asked, "What about the true man without rank?" The Master got down from his seat, seized the monk, and cried: "Speak! speak!" The monk faltered. Shoving him away, the Master said: "The true man without rank—what kind of shit-wiping stick is he!" Then he returned to his quarters.

Rinzai Gigen

"Your lump of red flesh" is your own body. This is "a true man without rank." All right? Everybody has a rank of some sort; but the rank Rinzai is speaking of is rankless rank. It is all right to have a rank, but this is rankless rank. This true man without rank "is always going in and out of the face of every one of you"—this is probably very difficult for you to understand.

This true man goes in and out of each pore of your skin, in and out of your whole body—not only in and out of your face. And don't make the mistake of thinking there are two things here: the true man and yourself. They are not two! It is only that the expression is misleading. Recognize this true man! "Those who have not yet experienced him—look! look!" Have *you* looked? Well?

"Then a monk came forward and asked"—he asked for all of us. This translation says that Rinzai "cried," but in the original it reads simply "said." No need for a loud voice; a mild, soft voice is all right. What Rinzai said is wonderful, if we look at the original Chinese. The Chinese character meaning "speak" also means "Tao." "Speak! speak!" also means "Tao! Tao!" This translation says the monk "faltered"; but the original says he "bowed his head." And, finally, the Master said: "The true man without rank—what kind of shit-wiping stick is he!"

Nakagawa Soen

MAURINE STUART

When Maurine Stuart talks about "practice," it may refer to either Zen studies or playing the piano. A former concert pianist, she spent hours of every childhood day doing "practice, practice, and more practice." After that, Zen studies offered nothing new in the way of discipline, concentration, spontaneity, or will. "I always felt that I was an instrument just as much as the piano," she says. "To know formal Zen practice simply deepened that. Just as you must have your technical equipment to be an artist or a musician, so the technical equipment of Zen is zazen. It provides a fundamental feeling that you are based in your own true nature, and from this comes the faith, the confidence, the courage to let whatever you are doing work through you. You're not doing it, it's doing you. From this foundation, you can feel that doing-Zen in mothering, cooking, playing the piano."

President of the Cambridge Buddhist Association in Cambridge, Massachusetts, Stuart Roshi still teaches the piano as well as Zen. In 1982 Nakagawa Soen conferred on her the title "roshi" in a private ceremony between Stuart and himself. An informal transmission, the ceremony was lacking in standardized procedures and remains unrecorded in Japan. Yet Soen Roshi's stature loomed so large among the first generation of American adherents that his recognition of Stuart, however informal, was enough suddenly to capture the attention of the Zen Buddhist community at large. Furthermore, an American roshi is such a rare phenomenon that every instance substantiates the transmission of Zen to the United States, locates it on the map, and offers a particular vantage on the transmission process as well as the teachings themselves. That Stuart is a woman in a tradition dominated by men did nothing to diminish curiosity.

She had been quietly teaching Zen in the Boston area for ten years before her last encounter with the late master in the summer of 1982. His instructions were: "Please tell everyone that Soen has made you a roshi." As news of her title spread, the questions proliferated. Did this qualify as a "real" transmission? Or was this Soen Roshi, the ultimate Zen trickster, offering one last outrageous paradox, happily assured that American students would grind their teeth over this koan for years to come? Or was this Soen's heretical warning to Japanese and American students alike about the fallibilities of formal transmission? And if so, did that diminish his recognition of Maurine Stuart?

Soen Roshi formally transmitted the dharma to five people, all of them Japanese men. His unconventional procedure with Stuart has led some members of Zen clergy in both Japan and the United States to disqualify the authenticity of her transmission. That women have historically been excluded from the official wings of the Zen School has made it all the more easy for them to do so. But to disaffiliate Stuart still begs the question of Soen's authority. Soen Roshi was not just a seminal influence in America; on both sides of the Pacific he is considered one of the truly great Zen masters of this century. And he earned a reputation for peculiar methods long before he honored Stuart. His creative relationship to Zen form could be as profound as it was playful; but whether or not his intentions were understood never jeopardized their integrity.

Stuart's transmission contradicted established ethics, but not the variegated dimensions of Soen's Zen, making its status all the more difficult to categorize. She has accepted the title as an indication of genuine transmission but has never called herself Soen Roshi's dharma heir nor a holder of his lineage. Rather, her dharma transmission specifies for her a horizontal understanding between teacher and student independent of the vertical concerns of Zen genealogies. By Stuart's assessment, Soen intended this title to sanction her authority to teach Zen, which had not been legitimized by her training as a Zen student or her ordination in 1977 as a Rinzai Zen priest. Yet for using the title roshi, she has been faulted by those Buddhists who identify orthodoxy as the best means to safeguarding authenticity. Zen training cannot circumvent the transformations exacted by cultural adaptation; but conservatives consider the protective guardianship of orthodoxy essential to Zen's early attempts to define itself in the New World.

"Zen trying to define itself is not Zen," says Stuart. "Zen must be flexible, must respond to time, place, and circumstance. In Japan dharma transmission became too concerned with status, with real estate, and with temple properties. True transmission is about recognizing the spirit, not the totem."

In the past few years an increasing number of formally licensed teachers have tacitly acknowledged their respect for Stuart Roshi by inviting her to teach in their meditation halls and allowing their students to study with her in Cambridge. These approvals have come from men whose own spiritual authority, according to Stuart, has been invested with too narrow a version of dharma succession. "These signals of slow-coming acceptance don't affect me personally one way or the other," she says. "But I do think they indicate a healthy change of direction. Zen has a wonderful tradition. But if we are tyrannized by it, it is not Zen."

In her sutra book, Soen Roshi made a single calligraphic ink stroke that translates as "heart-mind." From Soen Roshi to Stuart Roshi: heart-mind. For Stuart, this is the essence of transmission. It has nothing to do with gender or Zen bureaucracy.

"When I first saw Soen Roshi I knew that this man was right for me," she says. "That had nothing to do with the fact that he was a roshi—the esteemed abbot of Ryutakuji. It was seeing him bow to the sun, seeing his respect for a teacup, for the tea, for the server, for the bamboo ladle. Those were his credentials. Finding a teacher is a very personal matter. An American asked the Dalai Lama how one could identify true teachers, and the Dalai Lama said, 'Watch them. See how they behave.'"

With the acquisition of her title, the new roshi cautioned students not to change their behavior toward her. "No fuss," she said. "I'm just an ordinary woman." A Zen teacher may well be an ordinary woman, but historically there is nothing ordinary about a woman Zen roshi, a detail of Zen history that Stuart does everything to downplay. When a feminist from the Diamond Sangha in Hawaii visited the Cambridge Buddhist Association, she asked to give a talk on "Women and Buddhism." Stuart says, "I thought that she would talk about all the wonderful women in Buddhist history. Instead she talked about how there weren't any." Too often women expect Stuart to agree with their vision of an oppressive pantheon of Zen men: patriarchs, masters and monks, poets, priests, and warriors. It is not, however, the job of a Zen teacher to affirm obstacles. Nor, in her experience, has being female been problematic for Zen practice or a professional career in music. "There was never anything I thought I couldn't do," she offers as a simple statement of fact.

In 1984 the Providence Zen Center held a conference entitled "Women in Buddhism." Organized by students of the Korean master Soen Sa Nim, it evolved from general agreement that American women practicing in male-dominated traditions could benefit from discussions, from sitting silently together, and from exposure to authoritative female leadership. Having already shown little patience for women who harp on the masculine aspects of Zen, Stuart reiterated the importance of female participation in Buddhism, and she told a mostly female audience stories of Chinese Zen nuns and of American women who helped introduce Zen to the West.

Born on March 3, 1922, Stuart was twenty to thirty years older than most of the women at the conference. She had raised three children while making her way through two male-dominated careers without the benefit of the feminist ideologies that have bolstered a younger generation of women. The conference drew few participants who had pursued even one career with the same determination with which Stuart had pursued two, but to varying degrees it attracted women committed to investigating their personal, social, and spiritual lives in terms of feminist thinking. Discussions often centered on the ways in which practices that have historically been shaped and transmitted by men could become more accessible to women. Common subjects were childraising as Buddhist practice, the gender politics of Buddhist organizations, and the imposition of the monastic male model onto secular students. Of general concern was how to introduce female strengths to the samurai ideal, and whether or not the participation of women would substantially influence the unfolding of Buddhism in America.

The answers to some of these concerns were readily apparent: of the six teachers leading this conference, four had trained in Japanese Zen traditions, and by conservative Japanese standards, three (including Stuart) had not received legitimate accreditation to be independent Zen teachers—a fact that was neither questioned nor even discussed by the two to three hundred women in attendance. Having been consigned to the cultural peripheries for so long, these women were clearly not concerned with the rigid codifications of systems that had served men only. Zen lineages have been so exclusively male that by definition female inclusion cannot be "traditional." For many women practitioners this fact alone invalidates the assumed alliance between tradition and legitimacy. In addition there are men as well as women for whom this doctrinal alliance has been contaminated, if not altogether destroyed, by personal experience, and the conference drew its fair share of women disillusioned with legitimately sanctioned male teachers. Only with the introduction of Zen to the West are practitioners divided equally between the sexes. Whereas men have wrestled with the ethical polemics posed by orthodox transmission and its alternatives, these women suggested that the subject held little to no interest.

In formal black robes Stuart had cut a dramatic figure on the podium. A solid, compact woman, she holds her shoulders, neck, and head very erect. Out of clerical vestments, she wears colorful dresses, makeup, and jewelry. "Makeup!" exclaimed an unadorned Zen monk in her thirties after meeting Stuart at the conference. "I was so delighted to see her wearing makeup. And earrings! She's not an aging hippie. She's a professional woman from a different generation."

With the trappings of Japanese Zen culture under examination, makeup and earrings were not the only surprise. "Why robes?" she was asked. "Why Japanese chanting? Why bowing in something called a 'zendo'?" An American female roshi, apparently, was expected to advocate radical stylistic departures from Japanese Zen, but Stuart maintains that true freedom is in the form, that the tradition empowers the practice, and she has no difficulty identifying herself with her stern Rinzai heritage. On a break between scheduled talks she looked around a noisy common room filled with women and children. "You can't throw away the form," she said. "It doesn't work. Not in Zen. Not in music. Not with raising children."

At the end of the conference, she changed into loose pants and let her shoulder-length hair down for the return drive to Sparks Street, the colloquial name for the Cambridge Buddhist Association. She was not altogether pleased: "Too much talk talk talk. Not enough time to sit together." Asked to return to a similar conference next year, she accepted on the condition that she colead three days of silent sitting and leave before the talking began.

Slipping into the driver's seat of a Datsun Maxima, she laughed at all the different images that people have of women and of Zen masters. Makeup, diapers, pots, and pans may mark the ordinary territory of a woman, but, she said, "There has never been anything very conventional about my life." In fact, with her hair flying sensuously in the wind and with an obvious delight in taking the wheel, she had just transformed into an American road queen. Watching the speedometer glide past the legal limit, she admitted to driving fast—"to feel that edge."

The Cambridge Buddhist Association (CBA), founded in 1958, has incorporated the shift in the United States from an armchair interest in the philosophy of Zen to the activity of Zen training. Initially the association was established for the nonsectarian instruction of Buddhist meditation. This remains its ideological foundation, but under the direction of Stuart Roshi it has been characterized as "a Zen center." Clarifying this popular misconception, she explains: "I am a Zen teacher. The CBA is not a Zen center."

Half hidden by spruce and hemlock trees, 75 Sparks Street is a stately three-story Victorian house. Except for the live-in caretaker, the membership here is nonresidential, with many members, including Stuart, living in the immediate neighborhood of Old Cambridge, an area rich in political history. Around the corner is the Henry Wadsworth Longfellow House, which before a cannonball announced the beginning of the British bombardment of Boston, had been part of "Tory Row," a string of luxurious houses whose residents had little foreknowledge of the battles to come. And no one suspected that the same neighborhood would claim another kind of historic turning, that some of Cambridge's most prominent heirs of the American Revolution would enter 75 Sparks Street two hundred years later to seek the ultimate source of liberation in the teachings of Shakyamuni Buddha.

The Victorian structure of this zendo hardly softens the aesthetic austerity associated with Japanese Zen. In empty white rooms, on bare hardwood floors, are two parallel rows of black meditation cushions. The upper two floors house students during monthly retreats. In between retreats and daily zazen, the house is empty, quiet, and, as the Japanese say, "clean as a Zen temple."

Off the back entrance a family-style kitchen faces a vegetable and flower garden. In a Marimeko dress and plum stockings, Stuart peruses a kitchen cupboard filled with teas. Holding her glasses up like a monocle, she examines the labels on packets of herbal, berry, and twig teas, Japanese green and Chinese black teas. A gourmet whose private library includes several hundred cookbooks, she has a passion for everything there is to know about food, from new recipes to the botanical history of vegetables, marine farming, and the culinary habits and cuisines of cultures around the world. She selects red currant tea.

With the slow regal grace of a diva, she carries the tea tray up a wide oak staircase and into a comfortable meeting room. Setting down the tray, she sits forward in an armchair and crosses her legs. Her rounded hands have acquired the heavy padding that comes from strenuous piano playing, and she cups them primly over her knee. Stuart has been described as "half lion, half kitten," a contrast that appears even in her physical presence, for demure and even dainty gestures are offset by bold black eyebrows and a square-jawed chin that can assume the stubborn determination of an Irish cop.

Born in the Canadian prairies, she grew up in Keeler, Saskatchewan, a tiny village set in the midst of summer wheat fields and impassable winter snows. North of Moose Jaw, it inhabits the same flat, uneventful landscape that passengers on the Canada via Rail arrange to sleep through in favor of the more dramatic Rockies. But even as a young girl, summoned by receding horizons, she would pack up cold pancakes and wander into the fields to sit quietly for hours at a time. "There was always that need in me," she recalls, "to feel that the dimension of my mind extended to this whole universe— even when confined in a little five-by-five-foot cubicle as I so often was at the piano. That feeling began in the prairies."

Stuart's father owned the last private bank in Canada. Having held out against the government conglomerates, his bank was of much greater service to the local farmers than the restrictive, impersonal government banks, and it proved particularly beneficial during the droughts of the "dirty thirties." Maurine's early years were divided between the town and a 640-acre farm owned by her mother's father, a renegade socialist to whom she refers as her first teacher. Born in the United States, Sam Haight pioneered his way to Canada, leaving behind the sulfurous indoctrinations of his father, a rabid hellfire-and-brimstone preacher. North of the border, Haight proclaimed himself an atheist, skillfully deflecting the efforts of the local minister who visited regularly to warn against the damnation of nonbelievers. All too familiar with the subject, Haight switched it from God to gardening and sent him off with baskets of fresh vegetables. "He looked after his farm meticulously," recalls Stuart, "and with such love and care that every single blade of grass and every piece of manure was treated with respect and used to replenish the land in a wonderful Buddhist way. Even the devastating droughts didn't disrupt his methodical and loving care for the animals and plants and people in his presence. Very impressive."

The house Stuart was born in had no plumbing and no electricity. But it was filled with paints and brushes, books and musical instruments—urban luxuries to the striving prairie communities. After settling in Keeler, Maurine's mother had limited her own musical endeavors to the cultural education of her three children. Before she was three, Maurine, the eldest, insisted that her mother teach her to play the piano. "It was my demand for it. I always got very impatient for things to get on. You should gobble up the whole world in one bite, so to speak. You should learn everything, do everything, never take a nap. I had lots of energy and always wanted everything to go faster than it did."

If things aren't moving fast enough now, it's not because she has slowed down any. A 1986 February snowstorm left the streets of Cambridge treacherous, but it didn't prevent her from attending the 6:00 A.M. Friday sitting. After doing zazen with the few students who were able to get to the zendo, she went to the kitchen to make a pot of French roast coffee. Outside, spruce boughs, anchored by snow, were barely visible through the frosted windows, but she didn't cancel her plans to drive to Exeter Academy in New Hampshire. Since 1983 she has been teaching zazen at this exclusive boarding school, which has a reputation for academic excellence and conservative patronage—the Harvard University of secondary education. Exeter is not a school where one might expect to find zazen, yet Stuart's classes attracted so many more students than had been expected that the religion department had to reconsider its curriculum. Despite the driving conditions, she foresaw no problems with returning to Cambridge in time for a board meeting of the Ahimsa Foundation, an organization that funds animal protection. Next on the agenda was an appointment at Sparks Street at 6:00 P.M. with a student from Rhode Island, followed by the 7:30 sitting she would lead. Her students protested. Exeter would not expect her. The roads were too icy. The day was too long. A handsome forty-seven-year-old woman who translates Scandinavian literature into English scolded her sixty-four-year-old teacher: "You simply cannot go on with this kind of schedule and not in this kind of weather." Stuart took her cup and saucer to the sink, washed them, and placed them on the drainboard. She put on a long black coat with shoulder flaps like bats' wings and left four dejected Zen students standing at the kitchen doorway. Turning at the back entry she winked and quoted Robert Browning: "Grow old along with me, the best is yet to come."

Stuart's teaching style is to listen for the individual beat. In the middle of a recent retreat, in her deepest full-bodied baritone, she implored students not to adhere to the rigidity of Zen practice at the expense of spontaneity. Quoting her former piano teacher, the late Nadia Boulanger, she said, "Don't play as if you've swallowed the metronome!" A staunch advocate of laypeople's Zen, she makes a point of seeing students at their homes and workplaces, even trudging through knee-deep snow to visit the former CBA caretaker in his yurt in the New Hampshire woods. "Her visits leave the house feeling a little different," said a young mother. "It isn't quite the same as it was." Stuart represents the CBA and specifically the zendo, the physical and archetypal location identified with Zen practice, and these visits help dissolve the hard-edged dichotomy between one's home and the zendo, between daily life and formal Zen. The young mother continued, "It's a dissolution of privacy and that can be threatening, but when you face her in dokusan it makes for more intimacy. My hidden places do not reside in my home, but having her in my home makes me more willing to entrust her with the hidden places of my mind."

Stuart's teaching takes various forms. A young man who now works in a restaurant received cooking lessons from Stuart. "I learned more from her over a pot of soup than I did in the zendo," he said. "It suddenly seemed so simple that this whole practice is about how we cook our lives." Before adopting two Korean children, one student received weekly piano lessons from Stuart at her home. Formerly a public relations liaison between the Massachusetts Institute of Technology and the Boston business community, she said that Stuart's message in Zen and piano training was the same: " 'Let go. Don't let up.' She pushes harder in Zen practice, but there's the same suspension of judgment, the same acceptance, the same confirmation. In sesshin we contend with my demons; in my lessons, it's my fingers. But I learned about the way she gives from the way she plays the piano; whether it's zazen or music, there's an expansiveness in the form and the more *you* give, the more *it* gives."

"There's not so much difference between teaching Zen and teaching the piano," Stuart says. "It's a question of being with each person, of helping them find the way themselves, of helping them to become their own teachers. I was so fortunate in having wonderful teachers, great musicians, and to pass this on is very important to me. I enjoy the contact with students and making music together and seeing the light go on. Someone starts off feeling so dumb; they don't understand what's going on, why they're being asked to do certain exercises, and then you see this change and they come alive and begin to get it. I can't *give* anything to anybody. Teaching is about being present. Just being there."

Another woman revived her Zen practice through studying the piano with Stuart. She had once attended a talk by a Zen monk in San Francisco who, holding up one finger, had said: "Consider doing this for the rest of your life." The woman didn't do zazen again for ten years. Recently, she interrupted a piano lesson to say: "Playing the piano is just like zazen." Replied Stuart, "*Everything* is just like zazen."

This wasn't always so for Stuart. When she started Zen studies, her children were four, seven, and nine years old, and she battled with a conflict that has more often than not plagued young mothers engaged in Zen training. "It was part of my struggle to feel that there was my family and then there was my practice, and for a while I didn't put the two together very well. When I went off to sesshin I sometimes felt disloyal to my family, and when I was with them I felt I should be practicing. I was going to every sesshin I could, but periodically I would think, if only I could go away to a monastery. But finally that wasn't my way of practicing, and my teachers made me aware that my life involved other people and that it was the quality, not the quantity, of my practice that was important. There were times, at the end of a sesshin, when I wouldn't want it to end, when I didn't want to leave, and then I could understand renouncing the world. And that was a very big pull for me. To walk away—from everything. But I realized that was too easy. To come back and deal with everything—that's the big practice. One week of sesshin, as difficult as it was in the beginning, was so easy compared to my everyday life. Dealing with small children—that was difficult."

Her husband, Ossie Freedgood, a toy manufacturer and artist, was never involved with Zen nor in his wildest dreams had he ever imagined himself married to a Zen Buddhist priest. Yet to all appearances, the Freedgoods seemed to have overcome the problems that surface all too easily when only one partner is involved with Zen studies. To what extent these later precipitated their separation in 1986 remains a matter of private concern. "My life is no one else's life," says Stuart. "I must do what I have to do. Some students were surprised when Ossie and I separated and a few were disappointed. But any model is an unworkable model. It means you are looking outside, not inside. Your life is your practice, your life is your koan. Once I went to New York to see Soen Roshi. 'How did you get here?' he asked. 'I drove my car,' I said. 'And how are you driving your life?' he asked. *That's* the question."

The following year she resumed her maiden name. Her marital commitments had precluded the possibility of residing at Sparks Street or running a residential center. She does not now consider either of these options, however, convinced that residential centers generate dependencies that inhibit the self-reliance required for Zen training and perpetuate an infantile relationship to society. Wary of the false homogeneity that can regulate behavior at residential centers, she encourages students to express their Zen practice unobtrusively in the community at large and warns against "the elitism that comes with being exclusive Buddhists."

"In Japan," explains Stuart, "the monastery was another aspect of a community-oriented social system, and one didn't join up in order to fulfill a need to belong or to identify with a group. There is nothing wrong with those feelings or with those needs, but I question the use of a Zen center as a place to work them out. My experience with residential centers in the United States is that they attract very immature people. They have been set up along the lines of Japanese male hierarchies, and the Americans who have a need to be in the protective shadows of these systems are not particularly mature. Unless you have a strong sense of self, you cannot understand letting go. Keeping an open mind does not mean standing in the middle of the street and getting run over by a car anymore than it means getting run over by another human being. American Zen students are a little confused about the ego. They think they're supposed to check it at the door like a hat. Of course you have your ego, otherwise you wouldn't be here. You have to have that ego in order to want to clarify your life and understand it. But from what I've seen in the residential centers, this confusion has served to maintain an unhealthy dependency on the teacher."

According to Stuart, the exclusivity promoted by the residential centers also generates a tendency toward "professional Buddhism," in which the richness of life is too often subverted to fixed authoritarian definitions at the expense of personal exploration. "The residential communities that I know," she continues, "have bred a kind of solipsism with regard to Buddhism. The vast scope becomes narrowed down to a very limited interpretation of things. But then that limited view becomes the whole scope for the residents. This does not encourage the open-hearted way of Buddhism as I understand it."

Her faith in lay practice in no way tempers the severity of traditional sesshin. For those students who can arrange it, routine life is suspended each month for retreats that are conducted with strict adherence to the monastic rigor of her Rinzai heritage. The month-by-month consistency of this intense practice period epitomizes the training path she has mapped out, and its role is crucial to her presentation of laypeople's Zen.

"Formal practice is absolutely necessary: zazen, dokusan, sesshin," says Stuart, "but my separation from my husband has left me more time to be with students in casual circumstances—to cook and eat together at my home, to go to the movies together, to garden together. This, too, is very much part of Zen training. In the days of Rinzai, every place was a place for confrontation. Koans were used to enliven zazen when it got too soporific. But long before formal koan systems evolved, the spontaneity of teaching dialogues were a crucial dimension to the vitality of Zen training. How much love and compassion do you feel for the teacher when the teacher says, 'This floor that you have just washed is so dirty it must be washed again.' Then what? Big ego. Where did it come from? Where will it go? What happens to the cook if I bow and smile and ask, 'Do you have the soup ready?' What happens to the cook if I don't smile and don't bow and ask, 'Do you have the soup ready?' Who responds? Who changes? These are wonderful opportunities. But we do not have to live together exclusively to have them. I believe in the intense intimate working-living situation between teacher and student, but we need breaks. Students need to take their practice out into the world, to families and jobs. And I need a place with a piano, a place to make music. And I need some space to myself, some privacy. I have lived with others all my life."

Because of her exceptional talent, a wealthy couple sponsored Maurine's education when she was eleven years old by sending her to the Riverbend

School in Winnepeg, Manitoba. At this strict English-style boarding school she entered into the first of several significant apprenticeships. "I had one teacher who could have told me to put my toes into the icy waters of the Red River each morning, and, yes, I would have. The real teachers in my life inspired me to find out things for myself, to go more deeply. If I trusted them, I was ready to do whatever they asked. I was so sure they knew what they were doing. I would practice from five in the morning until late at night because they made me feel this is a wonderful thing to do." Her religion instructor was the one teacher whom Stuart did not trust. She excelled in academic subjects, particularly math and science, but consistently flunked courses in Biblical scripture. "I failed because I asked questions," says Stuart. "When it came to Biblical scripture I did not unequivocally accept. That attitude was considered delinquent, and flunking me was my punishment."

At Riverbend, acquiring the social manners of English society was the underlying agenda of the educational program. Emotional displays were considered vulgar and home offered no relief. Myrth Stuart's repeated instructions to her daughter were: a lady never complains and never explains. "Music saved me," says Stuart. "It's where I expressed my emotions passionately. I always felt that if I got angry all of my education would be taken away from me. If I had ever said to anyone, 'You know, I don't like working fifteen hours a day. It makes me tired and it makes me angry,' then they would have said, 'If you don't behave you can go home to Saskatchewan and hole up in the fields.'"

Much as she loved the prairies, Saskatchewan did not offer the life Stuart had in mind. On graduating from Riverbend, she joined its music faculty and continued studying at the music school of the University of Manitoba. At the same time, she started performing on the concert circuit, traveling alone throughout the western parts of the United States and Canada. Of the many awards she received, the most prestigious came in 1949 from the French government: to study at the American Conservatory in Fontainebleau with Robert and Gaby Casadesus and with Nadia Boulanger. Sitting in her living room on Mount Auburn Street opposite her own piano, a Mason Hamlin, Stuart says, "What a lady Nadia Boulanger was! She was a passionate teacher, an inspired teacher. The more gifted you were, the harder she made you work. Of course, she was teaching us all kinds of technical things and inspiring us to look into the literature of music and quoting from every composer you can imagine all the time, but it was her own enthusiasm, her own amazement and wonder and humility, that was so thrilling."

Regarded as the greatest music teacher of this century, Boulanger died in 1979 at the age of ninety-two. Although her teaching crystallized her reputation, it was her conducting prior to the Second World War that first brought her international acclaim: she was the first woman to conduct the philharmonic orchestras of Paris, London, and New York, the Boston Symphony, and the Philadelphia Orchestra. According to Stuart, her genius rested in her sensitive use of herself as an instrument, a vehicle for the music, never the other way around. These are the same terms that Stuart uses for Zen practice and they suggest just how contiguous music and Zen training have been for her.

What Stuart also shares with Boulanger is a passion for the art of teaching; indeed, she started teaching during the summer when she was twelve, partly to earn some money and partly from a sense of responsibility to pass on what she had learned. "People gave me so much. All my education was free. And my teachers always said, 'Pass this on to someone else. Don't think about repaying us.'"

In Paris Stuart also took lessons from Alfred Cortot, who was acclaimed for his renditions of Beethoven and Chopin but whose career had been sullied by his agreement to play for Nazi officers during the German occupation of France. His lessons were separate from the government scholarship, and before leaving Paris Stuart spoke to him about payments. She was told, "I have only chosen to teach people I wanted to teach. You must never think about paying me for a lesson."

In Paris she lived in cheap pensions, first around La Cité Universitaire, later in the workingmen's quarters of Mont Rouge; she also stayed at Maison Canadien, a government residence for Canadian students that housed a curious mix of young artists, musicians, and university students, among them Pierre Eliot Trudeau, later Canada's prime minister, whom Stuart remembers as "quiet, not at all political, monkish in fact." She managed to squeeze leisurely afternoons into a 'metronomic routine,' spending them in museums, cafés, and bookstores. One afternoon she came across *The Story of Oriental Philosophy* by L. Adams Beck, pen name for Elizabeth Barrington. Published in 1928, the slim green volume contains a final chapter on "The Teachings of Zen." Barrington's references to art made her version of Zen easily accessible to the young music student:

The Chinese realized when Buddhism came with its doctrine of the Indwelling Spirit that here was the whole secret of the philosophy of art. This Buddhism taught that "to the eye of the flesh, plants and trees appear to be gross matter. But to the eye of the Buddha they are composed of minute spiritual particles," and that "grass, trees, countries and the earth itself, all these wholly enter into Enlightenment."

Thus all was spirit, and the office of art was to make that spirit, that wonderful efflux of life and vibration visible to all. Art could never be an imitative thing: it must be like religion itself, the essence of man's heart, the work of his hand: the two were in the deepest sense one.

Summing up what she calls the philosophy of Bodhidharma, Barrington continues:

There is no such person as a Buddha. The Absolute is immanent in every man's heart and this Treasure of the heart is the only Buddha that exists. Those who seek the Buddha do not find him. This may be qualified into the statement that those who seek the Truth will find the Buddha and finding, comprehend not the Buddha, but the cause which underlies the phenomena of his life and teaching.

Maurine underlined various passages in this one short chapter but only once added an emphatic "Yes!" and that was in response to Barrington's conclusion: "Meditate and do and you shall know." Another fifteen years passed before she began formal meditation, but she never traveled without this book. Having defined her art as a spiritual practice, her initial interest in Zen was to make herself, like Boulanger, a perfect vehicle.

After a year in Paris she followed the Casadesuses back to the United States where she continued studying with them in Princeton, New Jersey, while living in New York City. "I practiced all morning and in the afternoons I would set out to eat everything up—museums, art galleries, and concerts. I listened to music all the time." Nor were her tastes limited to classical music. She frequented Birdland to listen to Charlie Parker and to this day can belt out a lusty imitation of Bessie Smith.

During this period Stuart met her husband, and for the next fifteen years they lived in a large apartment on the Upper West Side of Manhattan with their children, Barbara, Elaine, and Marc. One afternoon in 1964 Stuart was vacuuming the living room with the television set on when she suddenly noticed that an old Japanese man with eyebrows like lions' whiskers was lecturing on Zen Buddhism. "It was D. T. Suzuki, and I just went right into that television and sat down beside him," she recalls.

Less than a year later, while walking toward her apartment, she impulsively detoured from her regular route. Heading down an unfamiliar block off West End Avenue, she passed a small sign on a brownstone that read "Zen Studies Society." This was 1965 when, prior to its move to East 67th Street, the Zen Studies Society was located on West 81st Street in a ground-floor apartment. Organized in 1956 by Cornelius Crane, its original function was to propagate the work of D. T. Suzuki. Crane had subsidized Suzuki's seminars at Columbia University on the condition that they remain open to auditors. Those New York intellectuals who had already been reading—and re-reading—Suzuki could now, thanks to Crane, attend his lectures.

On entering the apartment she found herself facing Eido Roshi, then the industrious young monk Tai Shimano. Tai-san, as he was called, had been attendant monk to Nakagawa Soen Roshi at Ryutakuji and first came to the United States with the help of Anne and Robert Aitken to assist the Diamond Sangha in Hawaii and subsequently toured the United States as Yasutani Roshi's attendant monk. In the fall of 1964 Tai-san spent four months in Japan considering his options before concluding that his future lay in serving the transmission of Zen to America. On New Year's Eve 1964, he arrived at Kennedy Airport with no money, few acquaintances, and no previous experience in worldly employment. But with warrior willfulness and engaging manners he soon attracted a sitting group that met regularly. Subsequently he was informed that, this being America, he needed a legal cachet to receive the benefits accorded tax-exempt religious organizations. It was discovered that with the death of Cornelius Crane in 1962 and the return of D. T. Suzuki to Japan, the society had become virtually defunct while maintaining its tax-exempt status. Tai-san had become a board member of a society that had no assets, no obligations, and by 1964 no purpose—a perfect slate for a new Zen center.

"I asked the young monk what was going on and could I come and sit and what was the schedule," Stuart recalls of her first encounter with Tai-san. "He handed me a sheet of paper and I went away. I came back for an introductory lecture three days later and I've been there—on the cushion—ever since. It was so natural to just sit."

After coming to zazen three times, she signed up for an intensive week-long retreat in which the required ten to fourteen hours of zazen each day can aggravate the knees even of the professed. "You are mad," she was told. "You don't know what you're getting into." She signed up anyway. The sesshin was held at Pumpkin Hollow, a retreat center of the Theosophical Society in Clarenville, New York, and led by Yasutani Roshi, who was then eighty years old and still wearing American sneakers and the shabbiest of robes. "That little grasshopper of a man," as Stuart calls him, had held sesshins across the United States from 1962 to 1969, and they were a far cry from the anticipated silence of Zen. This skinny Zen master, with his long head and ears like teacups, filled the zendo with his exuberance. Sesshin was for him time-out from daily life, a short-lived opportunity for *kensho*, "seeing into one's own nature." Students were exhorted with frequent and unsolicited whacks on their shoulders from the "encouragement stick." The zendo monitor burst out with "go for it," "get it," "strike while the iron is hot," and stories were told of death-defying determination such as the one about the monk who sat with a stick of incense in one hand and a knife in the other and vowed to kill himself if he didn't get enlightened by the time the incense burned out. As always—at least in the stories that are passed down—he got it just in time, pushed to the breaking point by the pain of the burning stub.

Stuart's enthusiasm was quelled in one day. This *is* madness, she thought. What am I doing here? I don't know why they're bowing. I don't know what they're chanting. I don't know what's going on. In addition, her hip injury from an old skiing accident made cross-legged sitting an exercise in nothing but pain. She telephoned her husband in Manhattan and asked him to come and get her. But having watched her finally go off to a Zen retreat after fifteen years of yearning, he suggested that she wait one more day. She told Yasutani that since she found it impossible to maintain the lotus posture, perhaps this practice was not for her. "I don't care how you sit as long as you sit," he said. "Sit on your piano stool if you like, but sit!" (Now she sits zazen in the *seiza* position, kneeling bolt upright on two round pillows and looking like a formidable masthead.)

"The second day," she recalls, "it began to take, without anyone explaining anything, and by the fifth day I was hooked." From then on she attended sesshins regularly with Yasutani Roshi, Nakagawa Soen Roshi, and Tai-san. Today she is one of several American teachers who acknowledge their debt to Yasutani while steering clear of his zendo tactics. "I thought I would just be sitting quietly, you know," she says of her first sesshin. "I had read an article by Gary Snyder on going to sesshin in Japan, and that sounded all very jolly. You sat and sat and then went to smoke with the monks and had a little cup of tea and then you came back and sat some more. I had no idea it was anything this tough. There was lots of yelling and screaming and the *keisaku*, the 'cautionary' or 'encouragement stick,' was quite frightening. This was Yasutani's style and Tai-san's too. He wanted people to get there very fast. 'You got it? Have you got it?' 'No,' I said to him one day. I thought this was a place where you were supposed to get rid of your ego and all of this just seemed to encourage it. So Yasutani Roshi and I had a long talk about that. And he said, 'Well, okay, do it your own way.' And I said, 'All right, I will.' I felt that it recreated an atmosphere of competition, confusion, and hysterics. I didn't like that. I still don't."

But even those who most resented feeling bullied toward enlightenment responded to Yasutani's sincerity. Says Stuart, "All method and style aside, the most resistant student finally knew that he was there for them, present with wholehearted effort to wake them up, that the boundless vow to 'save all beings' was compressed into this small, frail body." Despite the jarring interruptions, "There was this feeling of my mind expanding from the cushion to an infinite, clear space. And then to take that feeling into activity was such a nourishing experience. To know that you could use that as a base—like the piano—and that it was available just from sitting on a cushion, counting breaths, or whatever, and that it could provide this condition of mind—that was worth anything! You can't really be more explicit than that because then people anticipate something for themselves and you don't want them to. I say to people now, 'Have your own experience. Sit down. See what happens.'"

Stuart now conducts zazen in an atmosphere of condensed silence. "The enlightenment experience," she explains, "is after all the very heart of Buddhist practice, any Buddhist practice. Buddhism is the path of awakening. That's what it means. To emphasize this is very important and to encourage people is very important, but Yasutani Roshi's sesshins were frightening to me."

At Sparks Street there are open sesshins during which the front door is left unlocked for students to join anytime. Each year there are three or four closed sesshins when attendance must be full-time or not at all. For this nonresident sangha, these arduous Japanese-style sesshins offer a concentrated dose of zazen and working with the teacher. As sesshin leader, zendo monitor, and lead chanter, Stuart's double cushion is surrounded by the gongs, bells, and wooden clappers used to communicate all movements of a sesshin day. Like Yasutani Roshi, she does not insist that participants engage in all aspects of the routine. "If you feel some kind of resistance to bowing or chanting, don't do it. Listen. Watch. And at some point, if your zazen opens you up to trying, unselfconsciously and without resistance, then allow yourself to try. Then when you bow, don't think, 'I'm going to put my knees down and I'm going to place my head on the floor, etc.'—just do it! Just become it. Just let it happen, so to speak. The same with chanting. Just become one with it and don't think that you are doing some strange mumbo-jumbo sound. Just let it happen and then it feels natural. Not like something imposed from the outside, but something that you are doing, again 'doing' in the sense of 'being done.'"

"No looking around" is a common zendo rule. For new students, furtive observations are acceptable maneuvers. "The tradition in Japan," she explains, "is not to tell you anything and in a sense it's a good way to begin because it just sort of seeps into your core and, yes, you may get embarrassed and, yes, you may not know the correct way to bow, but by just observing and sensing and going with what is happening, you will learn. There are no rules posted here but you don't need to be told to walk quietly. You'll feel that walking is quiet. I don't need to tell you when to put your palms together. You'll see everyone putting their palms together. And then let the explanations come later. First do it. When a child learns to talk, the mother doesn't explain grammar. This is the ideal way to teach people music, too. Especially when they're little, as young as four. You just sit down and play. And then read the notes. No explanation. Just do it and see how it feels and then we'll explain it to you later."

The keisaku is used only on request and only by Stuart. Walking down the rows of sitters, she looks to see who has their palms together, indicating the request to be hit on the shoulders with the flat narrow stick. Sometimes she stops to massage someone's tense brows or shoulders. With the exception of an occasional call to 'Sit still!' the zendo remains relentlessly quiet.

During sesshin all meals are vegetarian, self-served, and eaten on plates with Western utensils. There are no second helpings, a means to cultivate an intuitive sense of need and proportion, and Stuart keeps a close watch on the affairs of the kitchen. After one sesshin meal of artichoke quiche, the cook returned to the kitchen to find a note from the roshi that read: "This is not the Ritz!" Later Stuart discovered an apology was in order. A friendly greengrocer had sent the cook home with a free bag of fading vegetables. In the spirit of accepting what is freely given and of not being wasteful, the cook had done his job well. That afternoon Stuart told the story of three wandering Zen monks, Seppo, Ganto, and Kinzan, who lost their way while making a pilgrimage through the mountains. A green vegetable leaf floating down a stream revealed that someone was living farther up the mountain. But they decided that anyone careless enough to lose one vegetable leaf was not worth meeting. Just then they saw a man with a long-handled hook racing along the stream.

Stuart applies the value of paying attention to a single vegetable leaf in and out of the kitchen. Yet, as if deliberately contradicting the monotonous adherence to Zen ideals that this and her annoyance over an artichoke quiche might suggest, she can dramatically overturn the silence and simplicity of Zen. At the end of a particularly intense rohatsu, a strenuous eight-day sesshin that commemorates the enlightenment of Shakyamuni Buddha, the roaring silence was broken by Bach's *St. Matthew's Passion*. Suddenly the Zen meditation hall was bursting with music intended for the affirmation of all of Christendom; and it was no less startling than when Soen Roshi first introduced Western religious music to American sesshins twenty years earlier.

Stuart first encountered Soen Roshi in the summer of 1968. Having been away on a concert tour, she returned to the Zen Studies Society for a regular evening sitting unaware that there was an honorary guest. "I was sitting in the zendo and all of a sudden my back straightened up and I thought, who's here? And when we stood up for *kinhin*, I looked and saw this little man and it was love at first sight. Soen Roshi was four foot ten, maybe five foot at the most, but he was a mountain of a man. I could feel this marvelous presence, and it never left me. He gave a talk in the zendo that night. It was so hot and the perspiration was pouring down his face, and I don't remember a word he said. Just who he was, sitting there, hit me full force. There was always a feeling between us that was like an open channel."

That same year Soen Roshi performed a collective jukai ceremony for a dozen students, including Stuart. In modern Japan, Shinto priests commonly perform marriage rites while the Buddhist clergy perform those of death and dying. Jukai ceremonies in Japan often number five hundred postulants at once. And since one aspect of receiving the precepts is atonement for any actions that have violated the prohibitions against, for example, killing, lying, or stealing, most are elderly postulants making their final amends before entering the buddhafields. In its short history in the United States, jukai has moved closer to the Christian ceremony of confirmation, sealing a commitment to being Buddhist and to using the Buddhist precepts for daily guidance. The personal deliberations entailed in becoming a Buddhist in a Judeo-Christian society have prompted several teachers in the United States to perform individual ceremonies. During jukai the postulant receives a Buddhist name and a rakusu, a square cloth sewn in the same complex pattern as the monk's *kesa*, or outer robe, and worn, biblike, below the chest. The putting on of either the rakusu or the kesa is accompanied by the recitation of The Verse of the Kesa:

> Vast is the robe of Liberation
> A formless field of benefaction
> I wear the Tathagatha Teaching
> Saving all Sentient Beings

Soen Roshi had given Maurine both a rakusu and the Buddhist name *Myoon*—"Subtle Sound"—prior to the formal ceremony because, as he told her, "of your devotion to Zen." For some students the collective jukai was too impersonal to make an impact, but not for Myoon. "Some people didn't feel that Soen Roshi was anything special," says Stuart. "For me, he always was. For seven years I didn't see him. But that's not so important. It's the quality of time together. He never gave the feeling that you had 'to get it.' He always said quite the reverse: 'From the beginning you are enlightened.' And that created a very accepting spirit."

During one retreat Soen Roshi spoke of watching Hari Krishna disciples dancing in the streets of New York City in flowing orange robes, singing mantras, and playing drums. Unlike many New Yorkers, Soen had been charmed by these religious street dancers, and wondering how to introduce something similar into the sobriety of a Zen retreat, he announced: "This afternoon we do *Namu Dai Bosa* dance." *Namu Dai Bosa* is a chant intended to activate the Bodhisattva spirit and raise the mind of compassion. That afternoon, during walking meditation, Soen Roshi began the chant, increasing the volume as the staid, uniform line slowly broke into swaying movements. Stuart recalls, "I was having a really great time dancing around in the zendo. At one point I thought, wouldn't it be lovely to turn this into an allemande left, as in folk dancing, when you take people's hands and weave around, and Soen Roshi stopped me and said, 'No. Don't touch. Just by yourself. Just like on the cushion.' Just dancing. He was a great artist in whatever he did."

In rural settings, Soen sometimes led the walking meditation line out of the zendo and into the woods, saying, "Look at the stars! Look at the moon!" Or he would decide the time was just right for a tea ceremony. "You know tea ceremony, with its formal style," explains Stuart, "its proper bowls, whisks, pots, proper everything! And so quiet and lovely and simple. At tea ceremony you are not supposed to wear any jewelry. But Soen Roshi would sometimes borrow women's earrings and put rings on all his fingers and instead of having tea would whisk up instant coffee. On other occasions, it was very serious, formal, absolutely *comme il faut*."

One summer day in New York, Stuart accompanied Soen to one of his favorite movies, *Fiddler on the Roof*, which he had already seen eight times. Suddenly in the middle of the movie, it was time for a tea ceremony. Reaching into a monk's pouch hanging from his neck, he pulled out a packet of miniature crackers and a little case, which had been a World War I gunpowder holder and now contained powdered green tea. He put a little on her tongue and a little on his own. Tea ceremony performed, they returned their attention to the fiddler.

In 1970 Ossie Freedgood's toy business relocated to the Boston area and the family left New York for Newton. From Stuart's earliest days in New York, the city not only supplied her demands for an exalted life but seemed to affirm her right to one. By the time she left, her spiritual home had become specifically identified with the Zen Studies Society. Leaving the city and her piano students behind was painful enough, but leaving the zendo and its community of practitioners was as wrenching as going off to boarding school all over again.

Treating Newton more as a suburb of greater New York than of Boston, she returned to the Zen Studies Society for sesshin every month. Soen Roshi was unacquainted with Zen practitioners in Boston, but he offered a simple solution: "Find Elsie Mitchell and you'll be all right." It was a prophetic suggestion, for it was Elsie Mitchell who founded the Cambridge Buddhist Association, but it was a year before the two women met. In the meantime Stuart sat alone on her living room floor, hiding her cushion under the couch and her altar in the bookshelf so as not to offend the visiting neighborhood ladies. She felt sorry for herself, having to practice without the guidance of a teacher or the support of a group. "One day in New York I said to Soen Roshi: 'I have grave doubts about what I'm doing. I sit down on this cushion every day. What am I doing?' He said: 'Your very best teacher is your own practice.' The fact that I was sitting there doubting made me go more deeply into it, made me ask, 'What is this?' And finally this was much stronger than sitting in a comfortable place where everybody was handing me the spoon, saying, 'Here, eat this.' Now I often encourage people to sit alone."

Late in the summer of 1971 she kept a journal of a sesshin that was led by Soen Roshi at the Montfort House of Renewal in Litchfield, Connecticut. Surrounded by forty-seven people, Soen Roshi made an oblique reference to the story of *The 47 Ronin* and concluded that this was indeed an auspicious number. What also struck this singular Japanese abbot was that although participation was equally divided between men and women, all the official positions such as zendo monitor, lead chanter, tea server, incense carrier, or bell ringer were assigned to men by the male attendants who had organized the retreat. Soen then requested that Maurine be "the women's representative" at the daily morning meetings of the officers and position holders. Recalls Stuart, "He asked me to attend and to speak up on behalf of the women about what was going on. And that was the beginning of something," she concludes wryly.

Following Soen Roshi's first dharma talk, Stuart wrote in her journal: "He talked about communication. Used the word 'intercourse' with Buddha and with Bodhisattvas and being mindful with no-mind. Transparent, clear. And everything will go smoothly. Wonderful *teisho*. Where is the truth? Not in the books, not in the mountain. Have the courage to throw it all away every day, every action, every work, no-mind mindfullness.

"Second day. Some trouble today. Some sleepiness. Some tiredness. But got through it and somehow got much stronger from the struggle. Always get much stronger from the struggle."

Soen Roshi usually served brewed coffee at the officers' meetings, but Stuart recorded several mornings when coffee beans were passed around instead. She recorded no discussions regarding women, although Soen did consult her on which pieces of music should end the seven days of silence. He had previously asked her if she knew Beethoven's *Missa Solemnis*, so she had brought a recording to Litchfield. "I remember him very thoughtfully saying, 'When I was in school, to hear Beethoven records was very rare. And now Beethoven is everywhere. Isn't that wonderful?' Soen Roshi loved Beethoven. He often said, 'Beethoven was a real Zen man. Transcended all his pain, all his sadness.'"

"How I love this man," she wrote on day three. "What has become tarnished is shiny when he is around. His talk this morning was about *Avalokitesvara*. A thousand arms. A thousand eyes. All the different behaviors again of everyday life. Absolutely pure *namu*. Transparent. No thought. No sleepiness. Difficult, yes. But it's continuous and it will go on."

Stuart sets the worn journal down in her lap to pick up one of her Persian cats, and her commanding presence fades out with the afternoon light. "At one meeting," she recalls slowly, distantly, "we were speaking about the *Missa Solemnis*, and I told Soen Roshi that I felt that Beethoven had transcended the form of the Catholic mass, that he had taken a form and gone beyond it, which is what we're doing all the time. And in order to be so free with the form, he had had to work with it in every detail just as we do in our practice of continuously sitting, of continuously working. He immersed himself completely in old church music and then threw it all away. Let it all go in order to let it speak through him in a completely free form." Picking up the journal, she reads: "This then became a religious experience for all searching people not just for Catholics. The Kyrie was supplicating, the Sanctus, joyful thanks."

Soen Roshi also led these forty-seven practitioners in the collective chanting of the sound *mu*, which became louder and louder with each protracted exhalation. In a large group the magnification can overpower the ordinary boundaries of self, and losing track of one's personal voice can trigger both exhilaration and panic. For Stuart this practice induced sensations of alienation and aggravated previous associations with theatrical zendo tactics that urged—as she saw it—a materialistic greed for 'getting it.'

"But one afternoon, when Soen Roshi was doing it with us," she says, "I felt him giving himself to mu so completely that suddenly I just couldn't be a listener anymore. It just took me up and threw me around. This was a very important experience, because we are outside so much of what we do. Maybe not when we make music and maybe not when we make love, but in so much of mundane experience we're too much outside of it. And suddenly that feeling of being absolutely in it came through to me, through this mu-ing, which I had resisted like mad."

"Sept 2nd. In the morning *teisho*, Soen Roshi said all thought and conjecture are the enemies of zazen. But out of zazen grows all thought. Then in dokusan, he said to me, 'Just go ahead quietly in your zazen. Step by step without thought of good or bad, success or failure. Carry this into the present and saturate your everyday life with it."

That same morning Soen had talked about the Gospel of Saint Thomas, in which heaven is described as a kingdom liberated from dualities:

They said to Him: Shall we then, being children, enter the Kingdom? Jesus said to them: When you make the two one, and when you make the inner as the outer and the outer as the inner and the above as the below, and when you make the male and the female into a single one then you shall enter the Kingdom.

"He liked Saint Thomas better than all the rest of the New Testament," Stuart explains. She recorded in her journal: "He related one part of it to Rinzai: 'Of course, the kingdom of heaven is within you, not in heaven, not in the ocean, and Rinzai said the same. Inside and outside. All one breath. Mind like crouching lion or diamond-cutting sword. Hardest is softest. *Sunyata*: hardest and softest.' I have never felt for anyone in my life what I feel for him. He makes me happier than anyone in the whole world. Much clearing in my loneliness."

"Sept 3rd. Dokusan. What is mu? When Mount Fuji smiles, I will tell you. When my mind can become pure enough to really unite with that mountain, we will all smile together. That mountain of a man. Mount Fuji. Me. You. Christ on the Cross. The pure-mind Christ on the Cross saved himself and all others. Pure mind way. Came that we might have life and more abundantly. Bodhisattva mind."

Old photographs that Stuart had tucked into the journal fall loose around the couch. There are post-sesshin group photos that show a younger, slimmer, dark-haired Maurine, but the only pictures she is interested in are of Soen Roshi. "I remember going into dokusan and Soen Roshi said, 'Smile Kannon. How old is Kannon Bodhisattva? Bodhisattva of compassion. You. Smile.' He was a monk and a poet. It didn't make any sense to him to forsake a moonlight walk in order to maintain rules and regulations. What does the day ask? What does the moment require? Who needs what from me? This was his teaching. This is what I learned from him. People have asked me what is my method of teaching. I have no method. It's just completely according to the circumstances, where an individual is coming from; what is his or her background, temperament, capacity."

Within a year, Stuart's solitary zazen in Newton began to attract others. The first neighbor to drop in casually noticed a meditation pillow and asked for an explanation. Stuart placed another pillow on the floor, and this same woman is still doing zazen. She began bringing friends to Stuart's house, and soon zazen was held regularly two mornings a week. When the group outgrew the living room, it moved downstairs to the children's playroom, which accommodated about fifteen people.

The Chestnut Hill Zendo, as it came to be called, was like many groups that had started spontaneously all over the country to support individual meditation practice. Living rooms, playrooms, garages, and stables for zendos; bed pillows and bath mats for meditation cushions; Pyrex bowls for temple gongs; oven timers to mark sitting periods—these were all part of the makeshift accommodations to homespun Zen. But the inventive conversions did not always work for all members of the family. Sitting in the kitchen one day, Ossie Freedgood was approached by a disheveled young man looking for the bathroom. "Are you new here?" he was asked. "No," answered Ossie, "I live here."

In 1971 Maurine finally found Elsie Mitchell, who by then had already spent fifteen years quietly disseminating Buddhist teachings. Born in 1926, Elsie Mitchell was raised in a Boston family that traced its history through the Transcendentalists and cultivated a steady indifference to any organized religion. At Miss Porter's, a preparatory school in Connecticut renowned for its blue-blooded students, Elsie was subjected to, as she put it, "a thorough indoctrination in a sort of all-purpose Protestantism." Echoing Stuart's response to scripture classes at Riverbend, Mitchell has recalled that, "Bible readings, hymns, and lengthy sermons (twice on Sundays) were major features of the school curriculum. I found them drab, alien, and unpersuasive." But in the school library, Elsie came across *The Story of Oriental Philosophy*, the same book that would introduce Stuart to Zen some ten years later in Paris.

For Mitchell, Buddhism was also a gateway to Christianity, and the dialogue between these two traditions has continued to preoccupy her interests. As an English language tutor at Harvard University's Yenching Institute in the 1950s, she befriended many Asians—Buddhist and Christian—who persuaded her that an Asian journey was in order. In 1957, on the first of several trips to Japan, Elsie and her husband, John Mitchell, recorded the ritual chanting of Zen monks at Eiheiji, the Soto training complex in Fukai Prefecture founded by Dogen Zenji in 1244. Folkway Records later released these recordings in an album called *Zen Buddhist Ceremony*. Four years later they returned to Japan and Elsie had *tokudo*, a ceremony in which she became an ordained Soto priest.

In Cambridge the Mitchells started attending lectures on Zen by Dr. Shinichi Hisamatsu, the first Asian Buddhist scholar to conduct seminars at the Harvard Divinity School. Before leaving Japan, Dr. Hisamatsu had founded a meditation group for lay practitioners in Kyoto, and he remained a firm believer in nonsectarian, laypeople's Zen. "It is not real Zen if it cannot be practiced without the support of others," Dr. Hisamatsu had told his class, "or if it can only be done in a certain special place. Only you can find the answer to your koan, only you can make your life a true expression of Zen Mind. Or No Mind."

Not content with explanations only, the Mitchells asked Dr. Hisamatsu for guidance in Zen practice. A small group began to meet weekly in the Mitchells' house; in addition to a few American academics, most participants were Asian students from the Yenching Institute. They were joined periodically by visiting scholars, among them D. T. Suzuki, who had come to Cambridge for an extended visit after leaving Columbia University in 1957. Two years later this group became the Cambridge Buddhist Association; its ideals had been established by Dr. Hisamatsu, and D. T. Suzuki became its first president.

After meeting Elsie Mitchell, Stuart began to attend the CBA meditation meetings while continuing to lead sittings at the Chestnut Hill Zendo. She also returned regularly to New York to study with Tai-san, who in 1972 received dharma transmission from Soen Roshi and was thereafter called Eido Roshi. But Soen Roshi's directive—"Find Elsie Mitchell and you'll be all right"—turned out to be a little more complicated than it sounded. The two women remained circumspect, relating with the same gracious formality that characterized the Mitchells' house, in which they met. Then one night Maurine became ill and fainted in the zendo. Mrs. Mitchell took her into the kitchen and asked if there was anything she could do for her. "I asked if she would be my friend and if I could call her Elsie." The next day Stuart received a book by messenger. It was the poetry of the Christian Buddhist Maraquita Platov, and it was inscribed "from Elsie."

"From then on she really asked very much from me in an extraordinary way," recalls Stuart. "She asked me to conduct the meetings in her zendo, she asked me to take over the library, and she asked me to take over the correspondence with all the people who wrote to the Cambridge Buddhist Association with questions, which made me have to study. She kept giving me more and more responsibility, more opportunities. In this way she has been my most important teacher since I've lived in Massachusetts."

Stuart's frequent references to Mitchell as her teacher have created more ambiguity with regard to questions of transmission and lineage. Her students have little or no personal contact with Mitchell and do not locate her within the Rinzai tradition that they have identified for their teacher. In 1984 Stuart gave a public talk that opened by paying homage to her teacher, Elsie Mitchell. A transcription was sent directly to a Buddhist magazine. Much to Stuart's annoyance, the magazine published the piece without the homage. No one disputes her claim that she "learned" from Mitchell; it is her deliberate designation of Mitchell as "teacher" that challenges notions of Zen training. "You cannot teach someone," says Stuart. "You can only help them ripen their own spirituality. In this way Elsie has been my teacher. It is not about the Rinzai lineage. By focusing too narrowly on lineage, it is possible to miss the spirit of dharma transmission. I am not a lineage holder. I am in the Rinzai tradition. And this is what I transmit."

At the same time, Elsie Mitchell, a Boston Brahmin who conducts her life with an impeccable sense of urbane anonymity, insists that Stuart is *her* teacher.

Stuart's impatience with the kind of stringent adherence to form that questions her debt to Mitchell extends to the state of modern Zen in general.

With Zen spreading rapidly in the United States, there developed well-founded efforts on the part of Zen organizations to guard against the American tendency toward sprawling informality as well as the insidious confusion between informality and simplicity. When taken too far, however, the preoccupation with form endangers genuine practice, and the liberation born of discipline all too easily suffocates in the name of tradition. "Where is the school of Ikkyu?" Stuart asks wistfully.

Zen master Ikkyu (1396–1481), the illegitimate son of the emperor, took advantage of his immutable royal status to shun the Kyoto establishment. His own teacher, Keno, having refused to accept a certificate that recognized his spiritual attainment, removed himself from the competition for patronage and disciples and lived like a hermit on Lake Biwa, at the physical and cultural edge of Kyoto. At age fourteen Ikkyu came to this hermitage to study Zen with Keno. Of his own generation of monks, Ikkyu wrote, "With much satisfaction they glory in their monastic robes, and though they wear the habits of a monk they are only laymen in disguise. Let them put on cloaks and robes, and the robe becomes a rope which binds the body, while the cloak becomes an iron rod to torment it."* Debunking both Zen decorum and the refined aesthetic that marked the degenerate termination of the Japanese middle ages, Ikkyu socialized with persons of every rank, displaying irate impatience with the destitution of the poor and the pride of the rich. Disarming the political and religious aristocracy by associating with the masses, he popularized Zen with irreverent and witty public theatrics. He also left behind a collection of poems that attest to his heartfelt integrity and severe personal morality. Despising hypocrisy and small-minded righteousness, Ikkyu drank sake, ate meat, loved women, and fathered several children before becoming the abbot of Daitokuji, the Rinzai compound still located in the northern end of Kyoto.

For Stuart, "Where is the school of Ikkyu?" is a rallying cry to be true to oneself, to remember that practicing Zen does not mean to forsake the inside for the outside. And to be true to herself includes being true to Mitchell. "Elsie saw possibilities for me that I didn't see for myself," explains Stuart. "She attuned me to my own possibilities. That's where the teaching comes in." When a member of the Cambridge Buddhist Association asked Stuart to

*Heinrich Dumoulin, S.J., *A History of Zen Buddhism*, translated by Paul Peachey (Boston: Beacon Press, 1969), 185.

perform her wedding, Stuart replied that she was not ordained. Mitchell suggested that as the growing Buddhist community could use a priest for such occasions, perhaps Stuart should speak with Eido Roshi about filling that role. "Yes," replied Eido Roshi, "I think it's your karma."

Her ordination took place in 1977 on Bodhi Day, December 8th, the day that commemorates the enlightenment of Shakyamuni Buddha. Eido Roshi officiated at the ceremony, which was held at Dai Bosatsu, the Zen Studies Society monastery in the Catskill Mountains, and gave Stuart the name Chico, "Wisdom Light." After this, at Eido's suggestion, she was called sensei. In Japan priestly ordination in neither the Rinzai nor the Soto sect qualifies one to teach, and in Japan, moreover, the Rinzai sect never even used the term sensei. Presumably this divergence from historical usage was Eido Roshi's way of helping authenticate Buddhism through American systems of accreditation. It was neither the first nor the last time that the elasticity of nomenclature facilitated the adaptation of Zen.

In 1976 the presiding president of the Cambridge Buddhist Association died. Dr. Chimyo Horioka, a Shingon priest and curator of the Boston Museum of Fine Arts, had been president of the CBA for the ten years following D. T. Suzuki's term. Stuart was asked to take over. With her acceptance, the trustees decided that it was time for the CBA to have its own residence, separate from the Mitchells' home, so that it could function as a training center. The Sparks Street house was purchased with private contributions, and costs are covered by contributions and monthly membership dues of twenty-five dollars.

Elsie Mitchell is the latest patron, and probably the last, in a long line of very generous sponsors in Maurine Stuart's life. And she presents to Stuart the koan she has struggled with all her life. How do I accept this generosity? How do I express my gratitude?

Both Stuart and Mitchell represent the Cambridge Buddhist Association and envision it as a singular American offering to Buddhism in the West. Although the CBA is still, in theory, a nonsectarian Buddhist organization, from D. T. Suzuki to Dr. Horioka to Stuart Roshi it has focused on the dissemination of Japanese Zen Buddhism. Yet unlike either the lay organizations in Japan or those Japanese lineages debilitated by temple conglomeration, the CBA has never contended with the monastic model. It was not organized to counter the corruption of the priesthood or the degeneration of monastic vitality. In Japanese Zen the uphill struggle to maintain lay organizations through time is partly explained by the inability to gather momentum outside the long shadow cast by the monastic ideal. When the Cambridge Buddhist Association was founded, there was virtually no Buddhist monasticism in North America. It was never intended to address the needs of the counterculture or to serve as an alternative to anything, which allowed its integrity as a lay organization to flourish. Not only did its secular presidents disavow the exclusivity of monastic practice, but teachers like Soen, who helped spawn the Zen monastic tradition in the United States, fully supported the intention of the CBA to activate Buddhist practice within the mainstream of society. Soen and Yasutani, both of whom were affiliated with the CBA through the Mitchells, had so questioned the benefits of monasticism in Japan that a rigid belief in orthodox monastic practice was not theirs to impose.

Five years after Stuart's informal transmission ceremony with Soen Roshi, she said, "The more I think about it, the more I realize how much this title of roshi was Soen Roshi's way of acknowledging the Cambridge Buddhist Association. He asked me many questions about how we were practicing. He spoke over and over of his respect for Elsie Mitchell and for Dr. Horioka. He spoke about how important our contribution was. Not to impose Buddhism, or to impose a way of life, but to take this practice into your very life, whoever you are, wherever you are." Elsie Mitchell, with a quiet modesty of her own, insists that "Soen Roshi made Maurine a roshi purely because of her own attainment. It had nothing to do with the CBA."

In May 1979 the CBA signed a purchase and sale agreement to pay $225,000 for 75 Sparks Street. Immediately following this agreement, the CBA ran into unexpected resistance from local residents who rallied to prohibit the purchase, claiming that it would further the "deterioration of the fabric of neighborly life, which in Cambridge is already delicate."

Because fifty-two percent of Cambridge property was already tax-exempt, there was reasonable concern about the effects on the economic health of the community with the addition of yet another tax-exempt institution. In fact, the city was in the process of trying to remedy its depressed tax base, but at the time of the purchase agreement no legal recourse had been ratified. A more pressing concern to local residents was the disturbing vision of hordes of spiritual seekers causing congested traffic on an otherwise exclusive one-way street, defiling the sanitized humdrum with exalted rev-elry—"like those tattered troupes who play tambourines and dance in the streets," explained one resident, apparently referring to Hari Krishna devo-tees.

The civic-minded Mitchells were most sensitive to the financial situation and had always intended to pay "in lieu taxes" for the CBA's share of com-munity services.* As for the crowds, noise, traffic, and chanting, the history of the CBA indicated that these prophecies were unfounded. The CBA had functioned out of the Mitchells' home virtually unnoticed by neighbors for twenty-two years; while it did intend to intensify its schedule and increase membership, the patterns of behavior were not likely to change. And with some exceptions, none of which had ever occurred in the Mitchells' home, the more a zendo is occupied, the quieter it gets. The neighbors still brought their complaints to the city council, however, and an injunction was placed against the sale.

Elsie Mitchell charged that the opposition stemmed more from fear of the CBA's religious views than from its institutional nature. She accused the council and her neighbors of discriminating against an Eastern religion and of refusing to educate themselves on the distinguishing characteristics be-tween a religion and a cult. The neighbors, many of them professors at local universities, prided themselves on being liberal humanitarians and were in-dignant at being accused of bigotry. A professor at the Massachusetts Insti-tute of Technology explained that, influenced by the CBA, his children might become vegetarians; another professor acknowledged agitated visions of ro-mance between his teenage daughter and "one of them." Yet another asked, "What happens if my children see someone in robes?" And although the cur-rent membership of the CBA was safely identified as being mostly "married and middle-aged," it was conjectured that a change in group leadership could generate "undesirables" in the future.

The dispute was finally argued in a civil court and monitored by the local press, arousing interest with headlines such as "Cambridge Homeowners Try to Block Buddhists" and "Buddhists Told Don't Meditate Here." The neighbors contended that they wanted to preserve an "old-time, small-town atmosphere where people chat over fences and have impromptu barbecues." According to Elsie Mitchell, "the barbecue set was not traditional for Cam-

* In lieu tax is an optional, reduced payment for tax-exempt properties.

bridge," and she suggested that the difficulty lay more accurately with the transformation in the neighborhood from old Bostonians to a younger, bourgeois, professional class whose social ambitions were threatened by anything that neither confirmed nor enhanced an ascending status. "People in their thirties to fifties," explained Mitchell, "were not interested. They were determined and closed. The old Bostonians stayed in Cambridge precisely because of its open intellectual milieu; the young people are too nervous and insecure about their academic careers to be open. People over seventy were either for us or willing to listen. Old Cambridge drew people who wanted an idiosyncratic life." Supporting Mrs. Mitchell's claim, a member of this diminishing population of Cambridge elders sent an unsolicited contribution to the CBA to "help defray the legal expenses in connection with the recent unpleasantness."

Other letters were sent directly to the city council from ecumenically oriented clergy in support of the CBA and in praise of "the wisdom and compassion cultivated by Buddhist teachings." The pastor of the First Congregational Church wrote that "in no time during my six-year association with the CBA did anyone seek to undermine my Christian faith or impose their Buddhist beliefs."

On November 20, 1979, a court ruling ordered the building department to issue the CBA an occupancy permit forthwith. The *Boston Globe* reported that "the Cambridge Buddhist Association, a group of middle-aged believers, can legally meditate at its Sparks Street home."

Having felt the sting of Boston's mercurial liberalism, John Mitchell, treasurer of the CBA, called the court ruling "a victory for religious freedom." Although the most indelicate references to the "cultists" had been judiciously kept out of the press, the public transcripts of the trial corroborate that religious discrimination played a part in this zoning dispute. Taking the witness stand, John Mitchell was asked to formulate, "in fifty words or less," the principal beliefs of Zen Buddhism. He was asked about services, ceremonies, and the "accoutrements of the religion." He was also asked if Zen had a "principal treatise or book that might correspond to the *Holy Bible* in the Christian religion." Dissatisfied with Mitchell's response of "innumerable tomes," the lawyer asked, "Where can we find the tenets of Zen Buddhism if we were to look?" Mitchell then explained that one aspect of the religion was that the tenets were not put into words. "You do experience them.

You don't express them." This prompted the defense to admit that they were trying to establish whether or not the activities of the CBA were "religious." John Mitchell informed the court that the Commonwealth of Massachusetts had in fact already recognized Buddhism as a religion; still the request continued for exactly what books led to an understanding of Zen. Continuing a line of inquiry that annoyed sympathetic members of the ecumenical and academic community by its use of Christianity as a moral standard, the government lawyer asked if any fealty was paid to a supernatural being and, "in order to get a reference point," asked Mitchell in which branch of the Christian religion he was raised.

"If you were going to attempt to demonstrate personal commitment to Zen Buddhism," John Mitchell was asked, "is there any particular way that you would have to modify your behavior from that of a law-abiding citizen of Cambridge who practiced the Christian religion?" The CBA had aided Japanese scholars and Tibetan refugees, as well as other Zen Buddhist centers in the United States, without any trouble, but the problem here was supposedly the size and noise of the zazen meetings. In any case, John Mitchell, an English Catholic born in Austria, reassured the court that the ethical values of Zen Buddhism complemented the highest ideals of Christian probity.

What remains an occasion of private irony, attributable perhaps to discreet New England manners, is that deleted from the trial was any mention of *Sun Buddhas Moon Buddhas*, Elsie Mitchell's personal account of "A Zen Quest." Published in 1973, it records her immersion in the Christian-Buddhist dialogue and has a foreword by Dom Aelred Graham, the Benedictine Prior whose own book *Zen Catholicism* had been published ten years earlier.

Undeterred by the opposition and confident of legal confirmation, the Cambridge Buddhist Association had moved into Sparks Street in May before the trial ever began. The installment of the two-thousand-book library, the caretaker, and the caretaker's dog had been cited by the press like an admonishing litany throughout the summer news coverage. The formal inauguration was scheduled for June 12th. Members of the CBA and of the Chestnut Hill Zendo and friends from the Harvard Divinity School had been invited to an opening ceremony.

The expected guest of honor was Eido Roshi, but he did not appear and no formal opening ever took place. The relationship between Stuart and

Eido had been disintegrating for five years. In 1975 and 1979, as well as later in 1982, the Zen Studies Society had been rocked by rumors of Eido Roshi's alleged sexual liaisons with female students. In the midst of enthusiastic preparations for the gala opening of Dai Bosatsu, the first Zen monastery in America to replicate traditional Japanese architecture, these allegations resulted in an exodus of students, including six monks. Stuart had traveled from Newton to New York frequently during that winter of 1975 to 1976 to help in the preparations. "The monastery was in process and everybody wanted to contribute and be a part of it," she says, "and suddenly something exploded. I couldn't believe it, and I just thought, surely, he'll change."

Soen Roshi was due in the United States for the opening of the monastery, which had been named after the mountain where he had lived his "impermanent life in an impermanent hut," and Stuart, along with other members of the sangha, planned to clarify her confusion directly with him; in the meantime, she was determined to give Eido Roshi the benefit of the doubt. In the ten years she had known him, he had demonstrated extraordinary dharma gifts, and his dedication to seeding Zen in America had secured from Stuart an incommutable gratitude: "Here is this tireless young monk, I thought, who has given up his life in Japan, who has suffered loneliness and isolation in America, who is doing everything he can to help us on this path."

The opening ceremonies took place on July 4, 1976, at the end of a one-week sesshin and amid the national celebrations of the American Bicentennial. Dozens of priests flew in from Japan, Baker Roshi came from San Francisco, Philip Kapleau Roshi from Rochester, and Aitken Roshi from Hawaii; Joshu Sasaki Roshi came from Los Angeles, as did Maezumi Roshi, with his senior student, Tetsugen Glassman. Soen Sa Nim, the Korean Zen master, was there and so was Chogyam Trungpa Rinpoche, the late Kargyu Tibetan master. But Nakagawa Soen Roshi did not appear. For Zen romantics his absence indicated yet another act of enlightened spontaneity that further revealed his realization. Others have claimed that Soen Roshi, alerted in Japan to the exodus of monks, deliberately boycotted the ceremonies. Amid all the fanfare, however, relatively few tried to second-guess the enigmatic Soen Roshi, and the festivities continued late into the night, aided by a healthy supply of sake, "the water of wisdom."

According to Stuart, during the course of that sesshin Eido Roshi made a public confession of his bad behavior. "In a teisho, he said something about how Bob Aitken knew what kind of person he had been," apparently alluding to his time in Hawaii in 1964 as a young unmarried monk, when his dalliances with women had caused a rift with Aitken Roshi. "He didn't say it outright," explains Stuart, "but everyone assumed he was referring to sexual misconduct, and he said how deeply sorry he was, and tears streamed down his cheeks, and I was crying, too, and I thought, oh this is wonderful, everything is going to be all right."

She returned to Newton confident that Eido, who was forty-three at the time, would mend his ways and mature into the trustworthy teacher that Soen Roshi had foreseen in him. Without hesitation, she went to New York frequently to maintain her studies with him. Although Soen Roshi had always been her "heart teacher," her ties with Eido were strengthened by years of practicing together and by his being Soen Roshi's dharma successor. But in 1979 there was another eruption of allegations that Eido Roshi had abused his responsibility and authority by sexually exploiting female students. This was accompanied by another exodus, which included a young couple who sought refuge at Sparks Street before it was legally open. Throughout that winter Stuart had maintained some communication with Eido, strained though it was. On a trip to New York in February 1980, she was informed of the latest plans for Dai Bosatsu: women could attend sesshin there but not *okessei*, the intensive three-month training periods. "I got absolutely livid," she recalls. "How could he say that to me, a woman who had been ordained by him at Dai Bosatsu, who had worked hard with all the other women to make that place happen, including the woman who gave two million dollars to build the monastery, which was supposed to be a monastery for men and women, laypeople and monks, not just male monks. For me, that did it."

What continues to be particularly difficult to untangle is the responsibility of silent participation, that twilight zone of knowing and not knowing and not wanting to know. Stuart was not alone in wrestling with these ambiguities; they pervaded the sangha, and questions of personal responsibility were generally no less enigmatic for the students who left than for those who stayed. Nor were the allegations limited to sexual misconduct. They spread to financial mismanagement and incorrect behavior toward Soen Roshi. Eido's opponents claimed that Soen Roshi was deliberately misinformed about what was going on. In the fall of 1982 another round of accusations, allegations, denials, and subsequent departures was documented in a series of letters sent by individual students to the membership of the Zen Studies Society and in letters that were exchanged between Eido Roshi and some of his senior students. Included was a letter from Eido Roshi to sangha members denouncing the cruel actions that had been directed toward him and his wife, Aiho. Enclosed with this letter was another that he had written to the director of the society, a recent defector after seventeen years. Eido Roshi denied the accusations, categorically listing them under the headings: "1. On Soen Roshi, 2. On the bookkeeping and accounting of finances, 3. Dokusan and seduction." In a further attempt at clarification, Eido posted this exchange on the bulletin board of the New York Zendo. The controversy, a matter of public concern, is still unresolved.

The troubling question of sex and spiritual leadership within Zen sanghas entered the public domain in the spring of 1983, when an article on San Francisco Zen Center appeared in *Co-Evolution Quarterly*. At that time Richard Baker Roshi, the presiding abbot, was on a leave of absence. While an infraction of the teacher-student relationship was, at most, the tip of an iceberg, it was the precipitating cause for his leave. The same article noted that Eido Roshi's sangha had been repeatedly split by accusations and subsequent denials of his sexual relations with female students. About the same time, the Zen Center of Los Angeles—which, like its counterpart in San Francisco, had represented one of the largest, liveliest, and most stable Zen communities—began its agitated descent. Again, the precipitating cause was the male teacher's affair with a female student. In this case the teacher himself, Maezumi Roshi, made the disclosure at a regular staff meeting with no apparent anticipation of disapproval. Maezumi Roshi never claimed spiritual merit for himself for abstention from women or alcohol, but his personal life became the catalyst for a collective crisis of faith from which his center has been slowly recovering. Another article in the same issue of *Co-Evolution Quarterly* depicted the illicit sexual exploits of Baba Muktananda, the esteemed Indian Swami who advocated yogic asceticism and claimed that the kundalini energy that generated enlightenment was released through celibacy. A few months later a similar story unnerved the students of a prestigious Theravadin teacher.

To the concern of some practitioners and the complete indifference of others, rumors continue to implicate Zen teachers. There are now self-appointed arbitrators of true and false teachers as well as fortune tellers of the New Age who swear that the real turmoil within religious communities has not yet begun. What this means is hard to assess, but without doubt the concurrence of similar eruptions from so many Eastern traditions confirmed the need for serious examination. Within the Zen communities this provoked such general acceptance that it was time to drop the idealized myths of Zen and look at the actual situations, to put the practice into practice—which always requires pulling up the anchor.

Beneath the polite, restrained etiquette derived from the Zen of Japan, some ponderous deliberations regarding moral authority have been steadily brewing. These questions have not been restricted to sanghas with public problems or to resident students. The concerns are generic and the stakes are high, for the inquiry seeks nothing less than the direction of American Zen. Echoing the reflections of many Zen students, Stuart asks, "Who teaches you? How am I taught? What does it mean to be a teacher? What does 'transmission' mean?"

When Japanese teachers came to the United States in the 1960s, it was impossible to separate the personality of the teacher from his cultural context and from the teachings; it was a package deal. In order to make what she now deems a necessary distinction, Stuart pits the absolute reliability of practice against the relative vagaries of human behavior: "We sit zazen because we have absolute faith in it. We do sesshin because we know that for centuries and centuries this has had a profound effect on the efforts to realize our essential selves—what we call buddhanature. We chant the *Diamond Sutra* because we know that when you chant with your whole being it has the capacity to center you deeply and to help you realize the Way. And if you see that someone is not reflecting the dharma, then question. This is a human being. This human being has all kinds of flaws. The practice is what you throw yourself into. Unconditionally. Without any question. No doubt. The practice is the teacher. *Your* practice is *your* teacher."

Stuart insists that sex was not the issue at the Zen Studies Society, but rather the misuse of people. "I felt that everyone in the sangha had been betrayed. I wasn't judgmental about sex, or about a teacher having sex with a student, but in this situation it was an unloving act. It was the misuse of sex and of women and the manipulations that were so devastating." A woman now in her mid-thirties who left the Zen Studies Society in 1980 said: "Of course the issue was not sex. Do you think that so many men monks would have walked out on their teacher on *our* behalf? On behalf of the women? Do you think those guys were that enlightened? No. They got burned out by their delusions just like we did."

In communities that have lived through disruptive teacher-student relationships, members tend to agree that while sex itself has not been the key issue, it throws into relief the question of moral authority. At the same time, because Zen must pick its way through the stickiest recesses of Judeo-Christian morality if it is to take root, it will continue to be reexamined through the issues of money, sex, and power. "Our American democratic traditions will have a very important effect on the role of the teacher," says Stuart. "One of the most important changes that will come out of our American heritage is that students will stand up to their teachers and say no. Wherever teachers are misusing students for the sake of sex—using sex in the name of practice—wherever this is perpetrated, women have to stand up and say no. This is a very serious matter, not just among teachers but in those communities where men feel they have permission to act in the same way."

No born rebel, Stuart's own route to independence was through dutiful obedience. "Would I dip my feet in the icy waters of the Red River now? That attitude of submission had to be rebelled against. My husband used to tell me that when he first met me half my person was my teacher, that I automatically said, 'Whatever they say, that's it.' As I learned from my Zen teachers, this was a more Oriental way of doing things. For me, the process of questioning was a matter of maturation, and my experiences at Zen Studies helped me."

Since 1983 Stuart has been sought out by women students uncomfortable with the relationship between sexual attitudes and spiritual authority within their own Zen centers. There are Zen students of both sexes who have identified sex between male teachers and female students as an essentially feminist issue that mirrors the perpetuation of patriarchal authority and female dependency in the society at large. Stuart insists that for her the problem is one of neither feminism nor male chauvinism: "I am concerned about this issue because these women are concerned. Their concerns concern me. Their lives concern me. The basis of a good teacher-student relationship is a very strong, intimate bond, but it is the teacher as the embodiment of the teachings who must know that you cannot abuse that relationship. This energy can be used sexually in very careful, subtle, and compassionate ways. But when it is misused the intimacy is ruptured, and this lack of quality in the teachings and in the teacher is what I object to. The teacher has an enormous responsibility. If power gets out of hand, it causes deep trouble."

So far the issue of sex has been limited to male teachers and female students, but Stuart warns that it could easily be the other way around and has refused to support the rampant moral righteousness that often accompanies complaints about male teachers. "For me sex is not an available teaching method. This is not a way for me to interact with students. There are young men who get crushes on me and I must be careful. But this is a personal decision not based on sexual politics or some objective morality. Sex can be a teaching method, no doubt. The question of sex between students and teachers has nothing to do with a moral standard. Without setting up any rules or moral injunctions, what comes out of good, deep, strong practice is a feeling of deep compassion for other human beings."

According to Stuart, underlying the moral expectations of Zen teachers is a confusion between realization and psychological understanding: "There are different levels of reality. It is definitely possible to have deep realization and no understanding of yourself on a psychological level. You must make the distinction between an enlightenment experience and an enlightened person. Having kensho cannot be used as a way to judge or choose a teacher. And if you keep things on a psychological level, you cannot understand what makes life magical. I hope Zen doesn't get psychologized right out the window."

One psychological perspective offered by Buddhism is conveyed in the words of the Rolling Stones: "You can't always get what you want, but in the end you get what you need." "You get what you need precisely because what you get *is* what you need," says Stuart. "This is the *absolute* law of the dharma—for the teacher, for the student, for all sentient beings without restriction. What happened between me and Eido Roshi is the best thing in the world that could ever have happened. I emerged from it with a much stronger feeling that the practice itself is the most important teacher. Soen Roshi had always said, 'Don't hang on me. Don't idolize me. Look to the universe. Look to the stars, to the sun. I am just a person. Just because I have a title doesn't make me finished. Never finished. I am training, you are training. We are training together.' Whatever the situation is, you have to find out what you can learn from it. What is in this teaching? The fact that *you* can learn from it, that *you* can make it a teaching, doesn't justify or qualify or explain the behavior of the teacher. And you don't walk into the fire and burn yourself over and over again. Everything can be a teaching. That doesn't make everything or everyone a teacher. Crises are to be used. They force questions. Disillusionment is wonderful for growing."

In the summer of 1984 Stuart led a women's sesshin in California. She herself doubted the benefits of limiting participation to women only but told the San Francisco Bay Area organizers, "If you feel that there will be some special quality in our being together as women then let's do it and find out what happens." What happened had such a profound impact on Stuart that she returned there to lead sesshins for women twice a year for several years in a row until she felt that they had outgrown their usefulness. She now recalls that "many of these women had somehow been intimidated by sesshin atmosphere and also had become somewhat fearful because of things that have happened in relation to male teachers. I discovered that these women felt a new kind of strength when there were just women and a woman leader, when they felt less judgment about how they were behaving. They were not up against a kind of macho style where they were made to feel that if they could not endure there was something wrong with them. In a very good sense, they were warrior women cutting off delusive ideas about who they are, who we are. They had a great sense of their own strength and of their own warmth in supporting one another. I hate this word 'sharing,' but women really opened to each other, were there for each other, and there was a profound intimacy between all of us. The practice itself was so strong and so warm and intense and it did have a special feeling of being women together. So much of Zen practice has this quality of coldness in it. It comes from the samurai tradition, but it's not useful for us."

One participant of the all-women's sesshin had been practicing at San Francisco Zen Center for twelve years. An ordained priest, she was a supporter of Baker Roshi's, but her curiosity about a female teacher was connected in part to the turbulence at her own center. "Physically, there was much greater ease," she remembers. "If a man comes into your bedroom, you feel like you have to be dressed. If a woman comes in, well, it's okay to be half naked. In sesshin, you can come apart. And it felt more private with just women. I felt more permission to be emotionally naked."

At the sesshin a woman became consumed by a traumatic event in her childhood. While silent tears are not uncommon, this woman sobbed noisily, without restraint. A student from Maezumi Roshi's center in Los Angeles commented: "Rather than feeling that our zazen was being interrupted, that we were being inflicted upon, there was a sense of going through it with her, of supporting her, and she was not embarrassed. I can't imagine a woman feeling that she would be given that permission by men in other zendos or by male teachers."

Women are not alone in identifying Stuart as emotionally nurturing. A psychotherapist who began studying with her while he was still a student at Harvard said that the fact that Stuart was a woman definitely allowed him to open up emotionally, to cry more easily, to be less evasive than usual about events that made him sad. "In the beginning," he says, "I was very conscious of her being a woman. And I brought to that all of my projections of mothering and emotional comfort. And I used them to make the kind of connection I needed then. But as time went on, all the classic gender distinctions fell away. Now when someone asks what it is like to have a woman Zen teacher, I can barely relate to the question."

While many students have come to Stuart for a warm, maternal response, she has also been criticized for being too complying, for offering a "soft touch" rather than the "tough love" associated with Japanese Zen. Even women from other centers who seek the support she is reputed to provide have held her instincts against her; for these students, wielding the Buddhist sword of compassion that cuts off delusions has regained their favor over what they see as Stuart's maternal indulgences. For her supporters, this criticism reflects the sorry state that even women have fallen into, whereby the standards of Japanese Zen remain so qualified by its masculinity that behavior associated with feminine archetypes is disparaged.

A woman in her thirties from San Francisco Zen Center said that she had "actually heard women express discomfort with the way Maurine will massage someone's shoulders during zazen instead of using the keisaku. The tradition is for men to walk around the zendo holding the bottom of this phallic rod at the crotch and whacking each other with it. Is that *Zen*? Is it *Japanese*?" Another woman from the same center who has been a monk for seven years said, "All you have to do is sit in her zendo to know that Stuart Roshi is a Zen teacher. But she is not working with a monastic model. And she is a woman. Both aspects diverge from orthodox Japanese style. At our center we are definitely used to a tougher, harsher response to what we see as our dilemmas. And that has confirmed our ideas of orthodox Zen practice. But I think we need more loving kindness in Zen. If that's what you call 'Episcopalian,' fine. If we need to explore love through the Christian tradition, or the Tibetans, or the Vedandists, let's do it. There is a warrior spirit that is crucial for spiritual attainment in any tradition. But there has been too much 'toughness' that is not translating from Japanese to American culture."

Outside the zendo Stuart remains faithful to the tradition of Zen by her refusal to define fixed political or ethical positions, thus frustrating the inclinations of some of the same women she has attracted. Whether it is in response to her own womanhood or to questions of sex within and without Zen communities or to questions of zazen itself, she insists that "in all of life *you* have to find out if it's good for you. The Buddha said this himself. You must test it. Heart to heart. If it's no good for you, it's no good. Find out. Nothing is safe. The teacher can't make anything safe. The teacher is there to inspire the student, to say, 'Don't give up. Hold to it. Practice.' I can't do it for you. I'm here. I'll sit with you. I'll listen to you. I'll hit you with a stick. But you must practice.' Zen is not safe. Letting go is a big risk. People are scared out of their minds to let go. To really let go of everything. To let go of *everything!* That's the big one, isn't it?"

The sixth patriarch was once pursued by the monk Myo as far as Mount Daiyu. The patriarch, seeing Myo coming, laid the robe and bowl on a rock and said, "This robe represents the faith. How can it be competed for by force? I will allow you to take it away."

Myo tried to lift it up, but it was as immovable as a mountain. Terrified and trembling with awe, he said, "I came for the Dharma, not the robe. I beg you, please reveal it to me."

The patriarch said, "Think neither good nor evil. At that very moment, what is the primal face of Monk Myo?" In that instant, Myo suddenly attained deep realization, and his whole body was covered with sweat. In tears, he bowed and said, "Besides the secret words and secret meaning you have just now revealed to me, is there anything else deeper yet?"

The patriarch said, "What I have now preached to you is no secret at all. If you reflect on your own true face, the secret will be found in yourself."

Myo said, "Though I have been at Obai with the other monks, I have never realized what my true self is. Now, thanks to your instruction, I know it is like a man who drinks water and knows for himself whether it is cold or warm. Now you, lay brother, are my master." The patriarch said, "If that is the way you feel, let us both have Obai for our master. Be mindful and hold fast to what you have realized."

Yamada Koun

RICHARD

BAKER

On his hands and knees washing the floors of his pink adobe residence in Santa Fe, New Mexico, Richard Baker pauses long enough to observe that "housekeeping is so time consuming!" Backing out of the bedroom, he washes the area that connects the two small rooms of his private upstairs apartment, then turns and eyes his study. There is barely enough floor space to walk on, let alone wash. Half the room is taken up by a long, low table with papers, a computer, and two printers; on the far end are close to a dozen address books catalogued according to location: San Francisco, New York, Germany, Japan, and so on. Everywhere are piles of books—on the desk, on the edges of full bookshelves, under a chair, and in neat towers all over the floor. Wringing out the sponge into a bucket of soapy water, Baker laughs and says, "I never thought I'd see the day when I would consider hiring a housekeeper."

Not so long ago his housekeepers came free. As abbot of San Francisco Zen Center from 1971 to 1983, Baker Roshi maintained households at each of that center's three locations: Page Street in San Francisco; Zen Mountain Center, the monastery in Carmel Valley known as Tassajara; and Green Gulch Farm in Marin County. Of the two hundred and fifty to three hundred residential students, nine were his personal aides and attendants.

Baker's study proves impassable and he moves his bucket out to the balcony that leads to his rooms. Lining the ledge is a collection of hats that are used in more modest moods to cover a gleaming shaved head. According to Baker, "wearing different hats" in America is perceived in terms of "identity," whereas in Japan it is perceived in terms of "role," which is independent of identity. His headgear includes baseball, cowboy, and Borselino hats, Mexican sombreros, and Kid Coogan caps. He continues, "By emphasizing identity, Americans don't handle roles very well. In Buddhism it is roles that are emphasized, and once you're released into roles, there is freedom from identity. You know what Keith Richards once said about Mick Jagger: 'He's a lovely bunch of guys.' "

Baker Roshi now leads the Dharma Sangha, a group of twenty to thirty members who live in the Santa Fe area but not at the center. There are no full-time secretaries, no receptionists, no cooks, no personal attendants. Its four-man board of directors includes no students. As abbot of San Francisco Zen Center, between the abbot's budget and use of community-owned residences and resources, he lived in a style that he estimates could be duplicated by a private citizen with an annual salary of close to half a million dollars a year. Then again, the Buddhist teachings begin with the recognition that the true nature of life is change, that permanence is a delusion. And washing floors is okay, even fun. "You might as well enjoy doing what you have to do," he says, reflecting Zen at its most pragmatic.

Under fire from his students, Baker Roshi resigned his position in December 1983 as abbot of the largest and best-known Zen community in the United States. He was denounced for misusing the abbot's authority to go beyond the appropriate duties of his office and faulted on issues of money, sex, and power. He was also accused of misusing the center and its membership to promote personal status in the world at large. Baker has agreed to some of the facts that provoked his resignation, but his interpretations have differed widely from those of his detractors. His own understanding of himself as a man of integrity has remained intact.

Indicative of its preeminence, San Francisco Zen Center is known as just Zen Center. Founded in 1962 right in the crux of the transition from Beat Zen to Zen training, the long interlocking history of Zen Center and Richard Baker has absorbed most—if not all—the issues basic to Zen in America: the nature of spiritual authority, dharma transmission, the relationship between enlightenment and personality, the American experiment of combining monastic tradition with communalism. While these issues have concerned other American Zen centers, the internal conflicts they incite are to be found in religious congregations of every denomination. Even the rise and what he calls "the meteoric fall" of Richard Baker reiterate a theme classic to American literature, testifying to the prophetic warnings about the unreliable nature of rank. But two circumstances account for the widespread public interest prompted by Baker's resignation. One is that Zen Center was viewed from the outside as a model community, the fulfillment of all the promises of

Buddhism in the New World. Its San Francisco businesses, especially the Tassajara Bread Bakery and the restaurant Greens, were so successful that from a Protestant perspective they confirmed the virtue of clean, hard work. Between the businesses and the properties, Baker estimates the assets that he created for Zen Center over a period of fifteen years at $25 million with an annual $4 million gross income. Although California was an agent of success for every kind of Aquarian experiment, Zen Buddhism had an uphill struggle for acceptance throughout the nation; for the thousands of Americans who came into contact with it, Zen Center offered reassurance. It appeased cynics of Zen and New Age communities as well as Judeo-Christian skepticism toward the Oriental influence. It provided residence for Buddhist scholars and hosted respected intellectuals and religious leaders. Jerry Brown's association with Richard Baker and Zen Center was public knowledge during the time that he was governor of California. From Hollywood to the New York art world, people with the most tangential exposure to Zen referred to Baker as *the* roshi. The high-visibility role that Baker's center played in the diplomatic relations between American culture and Buddhism extended far beyond the boundaries of the community itself.

The second circumstance has profound implications for Zen practice in the United States: for the first time the collective judgments of a student body took precedence over the authority of the teacher. While various congregations of Western traditions choose and change their spiritual leaders, community control over leadership has remained antithetical to Japanese Zen tradition. What happened at Zen Center in 1983 was widely acclaimed as a quantum leap toward the Americanization of Zen. Yet what this means remains equivocal and unresolved. Is it Zen coopted by the bureaucratic machinations of a democratic process? Or is it Zen modernized, surgically removed from the obsolete autocracy of the Zen master?

For his part Baker Roshi has not always accepted his circumstances with the same equanimity with which he now washes the floor, and the present is still largely preoccupied with his past affiliation with Zen Center. Yet, while the abbacy defines a role attached to time and place, dharma transmission imparts responsibilities with no end, and he has continued to do what he was chosen to do by his teacher, Shunryu Suzuki Roshi. "I don't teach Zen because I am particularly good at it," he says. "I teach it because it is what I do."

He came to New Mexico in 1984 with half a dozen students, "a motley crew who went into the desert in shame and disgrace," as one of them put it. For these desert exiles, the rambling, neotraditional adobe purchased for $385,000 by the Dharma Sangha with monies raised by Baker provided rather extravagant accommodations. The house was sold by a friend of Baker's, a wealthy self-styled seeker who had built a private meditation wall off the western wall of a courtyard two hundred feet below the house. The inclusion of a built-in zendo made the property so appealing that for Dharma Sangha's abbot it would have been cheap at twice the price. "And besides, it's only money," he explains with the kind of insouciance toward the subject that infuriated his former students. The only other residents have been Miriam Bobcoff, a studious forty-year-old woman who spends her days working at the Oliver La Farge Public Library in downtown Santa Fe, and Philip Whalen, one of the original and most respected Beat poets. Until his return to San Francisco in October 1988, Whalen functioned as head priest, filling in when Baker was out of town.

In photographs Baker can affect what he calls his "raccoon mask" with his deep-set eyes made deeper by a prominent nose and black eyebrows. Yet in person he bears no resemblance to a furry little animal. New England-born and Harvard-educated, he is a large, imposing man with all the confidence of his patrician heritage and the charismatic charms of a flamboyant and commanding intellect. It has been said that when he enters a room, power follows right behind. He thinks out loud and talks fast and is at once restless and probing, as if testing the limits of a private voltage regulator. "Ninety percent of what I do can be explained as the avoidance of boredom," he says. This may well explain why despite enormous changes in the scale of his job, he continues to thrive on self-perpetuating chaos, rushing in late for appointments, making and receiving dozens of calls on his designer telephones, working on too many essays, letters, and lectures. In addition to the floors, these days there are the dishes, the laundry, the post office, the bank. "But," he insists, "I'm exactly the same now as I was then. I don't want a residential community. I don't like fund-raising, but I'd rather fund-raise than run a community-owned business. I don't want to create anything that *needs* people. But in terms of who I am, I haven't changed. I have no money, no savings, no income-producing job, and I live the way I've always lived because my resources are not just financial."

Since his move to Santa Fe, he and his wife, Virginia, have lived separately but remain close friends. She and Elizabeth, their younger daughter, have stayed in California, while an older daughter, Sally, has been living in Europe since graduating from Brown University. As in California, Baker continues to live in rooms cluttered with family heirlooms and personal acquisitions, and he has added new acquaintances in Santa Fe to an extensive network of old friends. At Zen Center he consistently reengaged those students who were dissatisfied or ready to move on. His attempt to accommodate everyone bespoke an American idealism about the possibilities of practice for everyone, as well as a strategic device to build the community. It also reflected a personal and anxious response to loss. "Dick can't get rid of anything," explains an old friend. "Look at his house!"

In the living room alone are art deco lamps, 1950s standing lamps, minimalist cube lamps, and spotlights. Over an art nouveau fireplace screen is a Japanese wooden fish surrounded by Hopi kachina dolls. There are two sitting areas, three couches, two coffee tables, two rugs, eight chairs. Every square foot of wall space is covered with art. The selection of each individual object may reflect Baker's obsession with the look of things, but in its entirety, it is a room that suffers from excess, put together by a man who says he cannot say no. Putting designer placemats on the table for lunch, Baker says, "There were students at Zen Center who would put a carton of milk on the table instead of a pitcher and not see the difference. You got the Orientalization of the New Age movement because people were looking for something new, but it prevented them from looking at the possibilities of change within their own culture. American Zen students were aesthetically interested in detail and craftsmanship when it was Oriental, but when I introduced Western aesthetics to Zen Center, students felt it was upper class. There was support for the $250,000 Japanese teahouse at Green Gulch, but when I restored the Victorian guest house on Page Street to its original style it was seen as some personal indulgence on my part."

For each of Zen Center's three locations Baker needed robes. He needed books; he needed to have the same books in each place. He needed housekeepers and assistants. He needed a good car for the four-hundred-mile trip between the three centers. And it had all made such good sense at the time. "I certainly have more robes than any Westerner in history," he says. "A former student once said that I have more robes than a rock star has shirts." In blue jeans, a cowboy hat, and a loose silk jacket, Baker looks like any number of Santa Fe's hip coastal immigrants. Getting ready for an evening out, he rolls up his sleeves and says plaintively, "I didn't dance enough when I was at Zen Center. I should have danced more."

With characteristic overdrive, the minute he left Zen Center he moved out in many directions at once. While fund-raising for the property in New Mexico, he tried to establish a San Francisco center on Mariposa Street, but it was too soon to compete for the Zen market in the Bay Area and that venture quickly fizzled out. Independent of the Dharma Sangha, he made plans to open a restaurant in Santa Fe. With his entrepreneurial talents publicly established with the restaurant Greens, he raised $1.2 million for the Santa Fe restaurant from forty investors, including members of some of America's wealthiest families, Hollywood contacts, and Werner Erhard, the messianic founder of EST.

From the outset, a minimalist vegetarian restaurant with large Noguchi lamps struck the local consortium as a high-risk endeavor. Santa Fe is a tourist town that attracts artists, restless dilettantes, and landed gentry from across the country, but its most reliable trade comes from beef-eating Texans. Yet the Desert Café opened in the spring of 1987 to rave reviews. Delays caused by perfecting the interior design, however, created financial burdens that the spring season could not sustain. Baker worked around the clock trying to keep the restaurant afloat until the summer season, but it closed at the end of May. As a Santa Fe businessman said, "That was the fastest loss of a million dollars this town has ever seen." Beset by investors and legal entanglements, Baker explains, with his singular sense of objectivity, "The restaurant was a total success in every way except financially."

At the same time that the Desert Café folded, the Lindisfarne Association turned over their mountain retreat center in Crestone, Colorado, to Baker, which he now directs as part of the Dharma Sangha. A four-hour drive from Santa Fe, the Crestone property comprises two main buildings on eighty acres of spectacular land 8,400 feet up in the Sangre de Cristo Mountains. Founded by William Irwin Thompson in New York City in 1972, Lindisfarne is dedicated to exploring pragmatic possibilities for the transformation of human culture. An honorary society, Lindisfarne has forty-five fellows to date, almost a quarter of whom have had close associations with Baker and/or Zen Center. Among them are Michael Murphy, founder of Esalen Institute and current board member of the Dharma Sangha; Benedictine monk Brother David Steindl-Rast, popular exponent of contemplative Christianity and former board member of Zen Center; astronaut Rusty Sweickart; architect Sym Van der Ryn; poets Wendell Berry and Gary Snyder; Stewart Brand, editor-publisher of the *Whole Earth Catalogue* and *Co-Evolution Quarterly*; and Paul Hawken, founder of the phenomenal Erewhon Trading Company and Smith & Hawken as well as author of *The Magic of Findhorn* and *How to Grow a Business*. The late Nancy Wilson Ross, who wrote extensively on Buddhism, and Gregory Bateson, the anthropologist who in 1980 left a hospital ill with cancer, preferring to die at Zen Center's San Francisco Guest House, were also fellows of Lindisfarne.

The Lindisfarne membership will continue to hold annual meetings which are intended to inspire the transcendence of artificial boundaries between nature and culture, the sacred and the profane. But Crestone proved to be too expensive and too remote—two factors that influenced the members' decision to release the property to Baker, who is currently vice-president of the board. Of all the representatives of Zen Buddhism, East and West, no one comes as close to the Lindisfarne ethos as Baker: "I didn't like war. I didn't like our government. I didn't like what people did to each other. And so I decided to create an ideal society. That was part of my motivation for doing Zen Center. And my aim was not only to bring Oriental culture to the West but to bring Western culture to Zen in America. I don't consider myself all that cultivated, but I'm interested in culture and art and science and life, and I think that all that has to be put together." How Crestone will be restructured is not yet clear; but having earlier secured Tassajara and Green Gulch—two of the most sensational properties in California—for Zen Center, and having now secured Crestone, Baker has emerged once again as a wizard of real estate.

In July 1987, in a private week-long ceremony at Crestone, Baker Roshi transmitted the dharma to Philip Whalen. The Sunday following their return to Santa Fe, teacher and dharma heir took up their places in the zendo, on opposite sides of the small altar, facing a group of about forty people, members and guests. "What dharma transmission really means," Baker told the assembly, "is really between Phil and myself, myself and Phil. Practically speaking, it means that Phil is now authorized to teach and he can wear the brown robe, which is the Japanese custom. But in a sense there is nothing that is not transmission. Your speaking is transmission, your activity is transmission, everything you do is transmission. So to become quite conscious of that and responsible within that is a very important dimension of our practice. All culture or history is an attempt to establish some kind of societal order and we are involved in that order. And Buddhism is an attempt to create a kind of order within that order. So what is transmitted within practice itself is also societal order."

Whalen has the fresh-faced look of a toddler—which is all the more exaggerated by a shaved head and narrow shoulders that slope down to a big belly; yet he moves with a perpetual shuffle, one feature in an extensive repertoire that he calls his "ancient and musty ways." Perusing the aisles of a local Santa Fe supermarket, he and Baker appear as the oddest version yet of Don Quixote and Sancho Panza. While Whalen has graciously played the role of loyal retainer, he makes no bones about preferring a more solitary life to the social whirlwind his Zen teacher likes to generate and is more inclined toward a conservative view of Zen than Baker. "I'm too old to start a monastery," he says. "But I'd like to run as much of a traditional number as the traffic can bear. What we Zen teachers have to offer is zazen."

Richard Baker was born on March 30, 1936, in Biddeford, Maine, on a street where every big white house was occupied by his cousins. His grandfather's brother owned six clipper ships that made regular runs east of the Bosphorus, and Richard grew up with Oriental chests and Chinese Buddhas displayed for aesthetic pleasure only. His parents were tough-minded rationalists, and his father used to say, "Ministers and priests are people who can't do anything else." Baker grew up the eldest of four children (he has a half brother ten years his senior) and traces his American roots to the *Arbella*, the first boat to arrive after the *Mayflower*. On the *Arbella* was his direct ancestor, Thomas Dudley, four times the elected governor of the colony of Massachusetts Bay, and with Benjamin Franklin, James Monroe, and Oliver Wendell Holmes included in the outer limbs of his family tree, Baker says, "A lot of people have always assumed that I was born with a silver spoon in my mouth. I wasn't. One of the qualities of my New England upbringing was that it was considered wrong to be rich. So much of the early money in America was made from the rum slave trade that there was a feeling that money was ill-gotten and that any show of it, like new furniture or new cars, was vulgar. For my family, being middle class was a moral position. That was the flavor. There was never any 'putting on the dog.' You became a doctor or a lawyer or a teacher or a businessman, but you did not try to be rich or successful."

His father, Harold Munroe Baker, had studied engineering at the Massachusetts Institute of Technology and, shortly after Richard was born, returned to Cambridge with his family to do graduate studies at Harvard in science and education. After teaching briefly at Harvard, his father took up posts in Indiana and later, when Richard was in high school, at the University of Pittsburgh. Each summer the family returned to Richard's maternal grandmother's house in Maine. "When I went back to New England, I had the feeling that I owned it, that I owned America. It was a feeling that I had when I was a kid—and that all these other people were guests."

In addition to being a scholastic genius, Richard's father had been the youngest ham radio operator in the United States and, by the age of twelve, one of the top young pianists in New England, but he was never ambitious and he never accomplished much. "He was kind of a Milquetoast in a way. For all his brains there was a kind of resignation that went with it. The whole atmosphere in my family was: never put yourself forward."

To settle a debt that George III of England owed Baker's mother's family, the crown turned over a land grant for thousands of acres in what is now New Hampshire, Vermont, and Maine. Even as late as Baker's own boyhood, the family owned more than twenty thousand acres in the White Mountains: "When I was little and the family would return to Maine, we would be driving along and my mother would say, 'When my mother was a little girl, her family owned this part of the state.' And every place I went, everybody was a relative. I am the first family member born in New England who left and was raised elsewhere. Everyone else stayed in New England and I had the feeling of starting over. I am always willing to start from scratch. My interest was experimenting with social forms. I knew that a number of my ancestors had helped write the constitution—and I felt that it had all gone awry. So I thought, I have to start over again. Buddhism offers the opportunity to start and say, what's an ideal way for people to live? So that question was rooted in a kind of traditional feeling. The shadow side of Zen Center was my desire to create a way of life and a society and an institution. It sounds so grandiose, but starting Zen Center had something to do with starting America. Not only was America started as an institution—and as an idea in recent memory—but it was very much specifically in the memory of my relatives. That made it even more forceful."

Elizabeth Dudley Baker wrote poetry and worried that her son would never marry because he was so difficult and always alone and asked too many unanswerable questions, like "Why does our moon swim across the lake?" When he was six, there was a fire in his grandmother's house, and after that he appointed himself chief guardian, getting up every night to patrol the grounds and check the stoves. When his parents found him wandering around in the middle of the night, they took him to a psychiatrist who suggested that the boy spend more playtime with other children. By the time he was twelve he was taking six books out of the library three times a week. "I read differently. I saw the world differently," he says, "so it was hard for me to have friends."

While Richard was at Harvard studying European history and architecture, classmates took to calling him "the outsider" after Colin Wilson's popular book of the same title, which had just been published. Wilson writes, "At first sight, the Outsider is a social problem. He is the hole-in-corner man." The outsider's lonely salvation lies in holding out against the cultural assumptions that make up what others call "reality." Wilson draws his composite picture from the works and lives of, among others, Nietzsche, Kierkegaard, Dostoevsky, Blake, Camus, Sartre, H. G. Wells, Ramakrishna, Gurdjieff, and Siddhartha Guatama. Through the existential nightmares of detachment to the detachment that makes available religious awakening, and through the disembodied experiences of metamorphosis, crime, and injustices of the soul, Wilson concludes that the maligned journey of the social misfit may just end in sainthood. It was the formative years of Wilson's outsider rather than the later glimmers of sainthood that earned Baker the comparison to the book's elusive hero. A few years ago, he ran into a former classmate who told him that friends at Harvard thought he was crazy: "You weren't ambitious, you didn't care about grades, you didn't seem to care about anything."

"It's true," says Baker. "People would ask me what I wanted to do and I would say, 'Well, I'd like to design my own house. And I'd like to have fresh flowers in my house everyday.' That's what I used to tell people because I couldn't think of anything else to say."

After three years he left college for a year and joined the merchant marines. On his return to Harvard he studied with Orientalists John K. Fairbank and Edwin O. Reischauer. During one lecture, Reischauer, the man credited for saving the Japanese temple-city Kyoto from American bombs, read Basho's famous haiku:

Old pond
Frog jumps in
Watersound

"I was sitting there," recalls Baker, "in this semi-satori experience of light and bliss, and then Reischauer said, 'Well. I never understood it. I still don't get it.' Shortly after that I quit Harvard forever."

In the fall of 1960, Baker arrived by bus in San Francisco with twenty-five dollars in his pocket. From the Greyhound depot, he wandered to North Beach and into Lawrence Ferlinghetti's City Lights bookstore and quickly became acquainted with the Beat poetry scene. He got a job with a book distribution company, rented a room with no kitchen, ate in cheap Chinese restaurants, and wished that he could meet "some kind of Zen master in Chinatown, maybe hang out with him, maybe observe from a distance."

The following summer he and a friend stopped in a bookstore on the way to a samurai movie. Baker was dramatically illustrating an episode from the samurai movie he had seen the week before. He let out one final imitation karate yowl, and the owner of the bookstore looked up and said calmly, "You should meet Suzuki Roshi."

Shunryu Suzuki had arrived from Japan in 1958 to lead the Japanese-American congregation of Sokoji, the Soto Zen Buddhist Temple in San Francisco's Japantown. He was fifty-three years old, and among his many talents, he had a knack for being in the right place at the right time. The underground Beat intellectuals had already sanctioned Zen for the emerging counterculture. With the revolution gearing up, "Zen" was a trusted password. Idolatrized for its fervid rejection of the material world, it not only pointed to emptiness but was used colloquially in ways that communicated next to nothing. What this indicated to Suzuki Roshi was that, unlike in the Orient, here there were no preconceived ideas about Buddhism—at least not too many—and none of the sectarian judgments and rivalries that had undermined the vitality of the Japanese Zen schools. For Suzuki Roshi, Zen in Japan had become so stultified that he had studied English in high school in hopes of coming to America. Even at that early age he was convinced that only in the West would Zen find fresh minds. He was not to be disappointed. Nor did he deliberately start a Zen center. As Sokoji's high priest, he was responsible to the Japanese-American congregation, who displayed little interest in zazen. There were no outreach programs, public relations, brochures, or announcements. The small master just sat zazen every morning at 5:40.

"So I put away my imaginary sword," recalls Baker. Suzuki Roshi was giving a lecture that evening and plans for the samurai movie were scratched. Baker began attending the lectures regularly and dawn meditation occasionally. About three weeks later, he was walking down the street with one of D. T. Suzuki's books and thinking that he was "not good enough to meditate"; he would attend the lectures but skip the zazen. He stopped, flipped the pages of his book, and read: "It is a form of vanity to think that you are not good enough to meditate." Over the next five years, he rarely missed a sitting period.

In his Santa Fe study Baker sits on the edge of his chair and speaks with an implosive intensity: "From the minute I connected with Suzuki Roshi I had no hesitation or reservation. I took to zazen like a duck. I wasn't very good at it but I was completely comfortable with it. Once I did it I *immediately* believed in it. I knew it was better than psychotherapy, and I knew that it was a good way for me to work with myself, which I knew that I had to do. I had so many complications jammed up in me that I felt relieved after each time I did zazen."

Gesticulating passionately, he pronounces "Suzuki" so fast it sounds like "Suki." He continues, "There were two independent things: one, Suzuki Roshi talked about zazen, and two, I was convinced by doing it. My zazen was in no way independent of Suzuki Roshi because I did my zazen in Suzuki Roshi's mind. I felt I was doing zazen inside him even if he wasn't in the zendo. His mind was bigger than mine. So my mind was expanded by being inside his mind. And I got inside his mind by listening to him lecture." Prone to summing himself up, he concludes: "One: he was what he was talking about. Two: everything he said I agreed with. And three: he was like a Buddhist text come to life. I was reading Huang-Po at the time."

He leans back and clasps his hands behind his head. To his right is a black and white photograph of Suzuki Roshi in exactly the same position, sitting back, hands clasped behind his head. "I loved Suzuki Roshi. And I was in love with him. Not sexually. But just to say I loved him isn't strong enough. I *completely* loved him and would have done anything for him. I had only one desire, which was to be Suzuki Roshi's attendant. I was not studying Buddhism. I was studying Suzuki Roshi. He could have been anything. I was studying him as a person. He was the finest man I ever met. I was also studying Buddhism parallel to studying Suzuki Roshi. It happened they were the same. But that wasn't necessary. I would have continued studying Buddhism if he had been a Hindu because intellectually I was interested in Buddhism.

"Suzuki Roshi once said to me, 'I need people who are already prepared.' He was not going to be alive long enough or live in America long enough to really work with students who were not already prepared. His idea was that New England Transcendentalism—Thoreau, Emerson—was a good preparation for studying Buddhism. And my whole family was immersed in that." Baker was also singularly available. He had developed no career interests, continued to see himself outside the establishment, had no pressing needs to make art or to earn money. For the time being, he was his father's son: academically brilliant, emotionally isolated, sullen, with no direction and no ambition. He says, "My only interest was in understanding things and I wasn't even very good at that."

Three critical experiences in Baker's early studies helped him focus on a direction. A couple of months after his first sitting at Sokoji, he was riding in the back seat of a car, with Suzuki Roshi in the passenger seat and another student driving. "I had been reading the Lankavatara Sutra and asked Suzuki Roshi, 'Do you think that Americans like us can really understand Buddhism? Can we realize Buddhism?' And he turned back to me and said, 'If you try, you can.' For me, that was: okay—that's it."

The second experience occurred when another student said to him, "If we really knew what we were doing, we would devote our lives to Buddhism." Baker recalls that he took this "as a fact, as a completely true piece of information. Later on, that same guy didn't even remember saying that. He was just the agent for me to hear it." And the third experience occurred after he had been practicing for about a year, when Suzuki Roshi stopped speaking to him. "We were still sitting at Bush Street, and every morning Suzuki Roshi would stand outside the exit of the zendo and bow to each student as they came out. And then suddenly one morning he stopped. He bowed but he wouldn't look at me. And then I'd go to his office and he wouldn't look up and I'd leave. This went on for a year. But after about a month I decided: he is my teacher whether he likes it or not, and I don't care how he treats me. It makes no difference. I am going to study with him and I will just study at whatever distance is necessary. He is my teacher. That's it. It wasn't his decision. It was my decision. So I just kept studying. And after about a year he started smiling at me again. And we never mentioned it."

Five years later they were on an airplane together. The tired roshi leaned his head against Richard's big shoulder like he often did on car trips. They were returning from Los Angeles after meeting with Japanese Soto officials who kept asking Richard if he was Suzuki Roshi's disciple. On the plane he asked, "Can I say that I am your disciple?" Without moving, Suzuki Roshi said, "Yes. You can say that."

After beginning his studies with Suzuki Roshi, Baker stopped playing the outsider role and returned to school, studying Oriental history and the history of science and technology at the University of California, Berkeley. At the same time he got a job organizing conferences for the university's letters and science extension. One of his earliest ventures was the first "World Conference on Shell Structures." That was followed by, among others, conferences on "Botanical Histochemistry," "Transportation of Radioactive Materials," "Existentialism and Zen," and "Rock n' Roll," as well as one on "The Problem of Identity" for which he designed a brochure with quotations from Erik Erikson, Saint Paul, Dogen Zenji, and Thoreau. In 1965 he organized the historic Berkeley Poetry Conference that included Robert Creeley, Robert Duncan, Allen Ginsberg, JoAnne Kyger, Charles Olson, and Gary Snyder—most of whom would pass through Zen Center in the years to come. With the conferences, Baker reflected the intellectual renaissance that California was cultivating and that had no home on the East Coast. In New York the poetry scene was isolated; art was distinct from religion, the mystical coalition was still fragmented, and science was confined to the academies. In California a lot of people were beginning to learn a little about a lot of things, which, viewed from the East Coast, seemed superficial and intellectually spurious. But among the eclectic advocates of the New Age were dedicated pragmatists who took the life of the mind seriously. Real work was getting done within a holistic framework, and under Baker's direction Zen Center would become one of California's most lively forums for this work.

In 1962 the American zazen students of Sokoji incorporated themselves into San Francisco Zen Center. Baker was Suzuki Roshi's right-hand man in several ways—and not just for administrative functions or the mechanics of operating in a new land. He has been compared to a walking computer with sensory antennae that reach to the outer limits. An intermediary without equal, he could translate the culture for the teacher and strategically map out an American context for the transmission of the teachings. "Zen Center," he says, "was founded by me, Suzuki Roshi, and the sixties. It's complicated, because everyone who was there feels that they did it. It's like radar. When the United States government made the decision to go ahead on radar, forty people later claimed that they made the decision to go ahead with the research. And in a sense they did. But who made the decision? Suzuki Roshi founded the teachings. He's the one who inspired people. He's the one who gave people the intangible sense of quality and integrity and enlightenment. And that's absolutely the most important. But when you look at the structure of Zen Center, the place, the location, the rules—I did all that. I did it with him. I did not make a single decision without his okaying it, but basically he always agreed with me."

With Suzuki Roshi in residence on Bush Street, students began renting the low-income apartments in the adjacent town houses. By 1962 twenty to thirty people came regularly to dawn zazen and the weekly lecture. Within five years these numbers quadrupled, but with no sweeping vision beyond the fundamental practice of zazen. Students maintained jobs, made art, went to school, spent evenings with their friends and families. Suzuki Roshi favored this. He did not want momentous changes in lifestyle and discouraged students from sitting too much, afraid that they would rush in and overdo it. But the apartments near Sokoji nonetheless became small satellite communities on their own, with residents stipulating that practice at Sokoji was a prerequisite for incoming roommates.

Once students began living together, ideas of working together soon followed. One plan proposed a Buddhist bookstore under the aegis of Zen Center. For the first time, students saw an angry Suzuki Roshi. "This is just a selfish idea," he told them. Anything that would take business away from existing shops was incorrect. Special books should be ordered through local bookstores. They had not thought about others. Recalls Baker, "We were all standing there looking down at the floor. That way of looking at it had never occurred to us. After that I thought he would never agree to doing businesses."

Inevitably the possibility came up for Zen Center to rent the nearby apartments and sublease them. Baker was all for it but not Suzuki Roshi. At various times the master told him: "If you mix family and residential concerns with practice, practice will always lose. If people get involved with spouses and children, those feelings will be stronger than whether they practice or not." Suzuki Roshi left behind grown children when he came to California; two years later he was joined by his wife. He typified Japanese monks, who often married when they left the monastery and took over a temple. He also typified Japanese men, whatever their profession, whose ideas about family and work presented no conflict in their lives. But for most American monks, combining family and practice set off emotional as well as doctrinal conflicts.

With a deep sigh Baker slows down and says, "I did not heed his warnings." Not only did he dismiss his teacher's warnings, but he dismissed them in a big way. In order to build an institution that was going to transform America, he needed people. He also needed to take charge of people and places, to shelter and protect, as he had when he put himself on fire watch at age six.

In *Zen Mind, Beginner's Mind*, a collection of his lectures, Suzuki Roshi said that when one practices, one's spouse practices, whether formally or not. "He certainly felt that a whole family could practice," says Baker, "but his view was—and my view has become—that for *most* people, practice is something they do when they are young, or something they do when there is a crisis. Most people do not make it their whole life. They practice intensely for a while and then they stop. Particularly if there is no career support for it. It's like being an artist. How many people paint *all* their lives whether they sell their paintings or not? And how many people who make art are really artists? And how many are artists in ways that change their lives?"

The answer may be few indeed, but in San Francisco in the early sixties it seemed that everyone under thirty was busy being an artist, breaking through to the other side, intent on transformation at any price. President Kennedy promised to do it for the nation and only America could do it for the world. Meanwhile, in the pedestrian outskirts of Camelot, transformation was increasingly pursued with mind-altering drugs. "You have to understand," says Baker, "the whole question of residency came up when 'flower power' was in full bloom. Everybody was taking acid. Things were a little out of hand. And I felt that we should take more responsibility. The turning point for Suzuki Roshi came when he began to feel that the apartments had become like buildings on the temple grounds; they were part of the temple. At some point his feeling was that Zen Center should accept the responsibility because, in effect, it already had the responsibility. But he always saw common residences as an extension of the temple, not the organization of a community."

Baker himself never took acid, although he organized the first LSD conference in the United States in 1966. Ten years earlier he had tried mescaline and peyote but found their effects not that different from his ordinary state of mind. "By the time the sixties came around, I decided to put all my eggs in the Zen basket. People who had taken acid tended to get into practice faster, but after the initial immersion in practice leveled off, their experience of meditation would remain shaped by the taste of the psychedelic experience in ways that were limiting. Particularly if they believed in the acid experience. But it did allow a lot of people to get into practice."

According to Baker, Suzuki Roshi came away from Japan with no particular regard for monastic practice. "He thought that real Mayahana practice should be done in the streets and with people and in ordinary circumstances. And I accepted that. But I think that after five years he decided that I was the only student who had made a success of this, that I was the only one who had really gotten into Zen practice without any semblance of monastic training. So he decided that we should have a country place where he could have more concentrated contact with students. And I took the job of finding him a place."

That place is the remote Tassajara Hot Springs, 160 miles south of San Francisco. Not unlike the spiritual path itself, the no-exit dirt road to get there inspires fear and awe. The fourteen-mile ride from Jamesburg climbs to 5,000 feet through the uninhabited Los Padres National Forest, then nose-dives into an isolated valley of the Santa Lucia Mountains, thick with maple, sycamore, and a perilous quantity of poison oak. Local Indians ascribed curative powers to the mineral springs that feed the Arroyo Seco River and made pilgrimages there to purify themselves. Later, Spanish settlers gathered to dry their meat in the sun; the Spanish name Tassajara means "drying place."

Baker and his wife, Ginny, first came across Tassajara during a camping trip to Jamesburg, formerly called China Camp for the Chinese laborers who camped there in 1884 while building the stagecoach road into the springs. After the road was built, Tassajara became the most popular resort in Monterey County. An old newspaper clipping reports that the waters were reputed to relieve "rheumatism, gout, dropsy, malaria, paralysis, liver and stomach disorders and make the skin soft and velvety." And the springs were particularly appreciated during the winter months when the sun never hits the bottom of the narrow ravine.

In the midst of negotiating the purchase of Tassajara, which would be the first American Zen monastery, Baker said to his teacher, "We have to do this thing seriously. All the priests cannot be Japanese." His concern addressed the custom at Sokoji of treating Japanese priests with a deference not accorded the Americans. Baker had bridled under the impression that American lay students were categorically denigrated and he pressed his point that Tassajara had to fully recognize American practitioners. Suzuki Roshi replied: "Then you have to be a priest."

"And I said, 'I know.' And I was kind of offering myself. I felt like a sheep." Removing his glasses to wipe away tears, Baker says, "I did not do it for me. I didn't care about being a priest or not. I did it for American Buddhism."

In 1966 anyone with Baker's pragmatism could see the chances of Zen going the way of the last psychedelic hallucination. The volcanic underground had finally blown its top at the Be-in in San Francisco's Golden Gate Park. With LSD and dancing in the streets, the revolution had finally come, freeing America at last from Uncle Sam Greed—or so it seemed in the euphoria of the summer of love. Suzuki Roshi wandered through the park, holding a flower handed to him by a smiling nymphet; Allen Ginsberg chanted the Heart Sutra while Timothy Leary witnessed the astonishing success of his vow to turn on America. But it became apparent all too soon that while drugs could be an extraordinary agent, they weren't an answer. Dozens of answers were in the wind; but without conduits for grounding, they would blow right out to sea—and most of them did. Baker already knew that with no social context for altered states of consciousness, the meaning leaked out. He was beginning to see himself as instrumental in providing a solid vehicle for change. By 1968, in fact, the trusting tribal celebrations of Haight-Ashbury were destroyed by killer-speed drugs, crime, despair, and suicide.

Not all elements of the counterculture bottomed out with the rapid abrasion of the Haight, but few retained the impulse to uplift society. With the Vietnam War galvanizing every level of antiestablishment sentiment, destroying the order became more appealing than trying to elevate its platform. Kathy Fischer, who came to Zen Center in 1972 at the age of twenty and is now a priest at Green Gulch, says, "Some hippies smoked dope and went into computers. Some smoked dope and went into the hills and were never heard from again. Some armed themselves and waited for the revolution. And others came to Zen Center and thought they could transform the world."

Suzuki Roshi performed Baker's ordination at Tassajara the evening before the monastery's opening ceremonies. Baker had his head shaved, wore the robes that Suzuki Roshi had ordered from Japan—which were extremely uncomfortable in the heat of a Tassajara summer—dutifully went through all the ceremonial chants in his teacher's native tongue, and accepted his dharma name, Zentatsu Myoyu. After that he ran around with blue jeans sticking out under his robes and repeated his objections to Japanese formalities. With both true and mock arrogance, he flaunted his disdain for ritual when interviewed for a 1968 *Time* magazine article on Zen Center: "Japanese like huge ceremonies that go on for a week. Now the Roshi will take a two-or-three-day ceremony and cut it down to two hours. Recently I told him that if he doesn't cut it down to half an hour, I won't come."

In 1967 there were two hundred applications for the first three-month training intensive at Tassajara. In July, 120 people attended the first weeklong sesshin. Among the summer residents were half a dozen close friends, including the Bakers, who spent idyllic weekends at a nearby summer house. "It was a group of friends who loved and were in love and had various levels of physical and romantic and platonic love." Whatever emotional commitment Baker begrudgingly made to communalism, it was out of the simple— if naive—desire to recapture this. "For me," he says, "it was that sense of love and friendship that we had, supporting each other emotionally and in practice that was so inspiring. Part of this inspiration was influenced by the sixties. But it did not come from my thinking that 'community' in and of itself was good. The last thing I would ever have done was start a commune. I'm not interested in community and I always said that at Zen Center. It was merely a way to create an opportunity for practice."

Suzuki Roshi had no doubt that Tassajara would accommodate men and women; and no departure from Japanese monasticism was more radical. Summing up the situation with dispatch, Baker says, "Once you have men and women you have fucking, and once you have fucking you have babies, and once you have babies you have residential considerations, and there is no way of stopping it."

Initially, however, the most pressing concerns at Tassajara were financial. When Zen Center purchased Tassajara, there were only forty to fifty regular members and its annual budget was $6,000. With the new property, Zen Center had to pay out $300,000 over a period of seven years. But Tassajara represented a solid foothold in the elusive struggle against established values, and it drew support from people who had no interest in actually doing Zen practice. More than a thousand donors sent in contributions; Gary Snyder, Alan Watts, and Charlotte Selver, among others, did benefit readings and workshops; a "Zenefit" at the Avalon Ballroom featured Big Brother and the Holding Company, the Jefferson Airplane, and the Grateful Dead. Most of the money, however, came through the fund-raising efforts Baker directed toward East Coast Orientalists who had been interested in Krishnamurti and Yogananda and were subsequently introduced to Zen by Nancy Wilson Ross. Explains Baker, "In that generation of wealthy Wasp Americans, there are no families who did not have some of its members involved with Eastern religions."

The first Zen Center business was the Tassajara guest season. From Memorial Day to Labor Day guests who had been enjoying the hot springs for years could continue to use Tassajara as a resort. Suggested by Silas Hoadley, one of Suzuki's first students, the guest season proved to be a gold mine, eventually providing Zen Center with $250,000 net a year. The reservation desk opens in March and within two weeks the season is booked. Guests are welcome to join any part of the monastic schedule. With an epicurean shift that only the state of California could have sustained, the popularity of the resort was not diminished by Zen management. As in the old days, the rustic cabins that line the creek have no electricity, television, or telephones. Unlike the old days, the Zen resort offers no booze, loose women, music, gambling, or all-night dancing. At 4:40 in the morning a hand bell announces dawn zazen. Guests have the option of getting up or going back to sleep. It is, nonetheless, not everyone's idea of vacation. In August, for an average of $500 per couple per weekend, guests can leave their unair-conditioned cabins, stagger down the path in 112 degrees in the shade, and cool off in sulfuric springs with temperatures of 110 and the smell of rotten eggs. In addition to the gourmet meals and the healing power of the waters, what guests derive from Tassajara is some privileged inclusion in the rural peace of monastic life. Or as one cynical New Yorker said of her own annual pilgrimage, "It's a dose of spiritual virtue by osmosis."

Baker's reasons for initially supporting the guest season were not financial: "I thought we should practice in a way that did not exclude the people who had been using Tassajara as a resort for years; they should be able to continue to enjoy the hot springs. And also I thought it would be a way to present Buddhism to a larger population. I thought, gee, business is giving us an excuse to present Buddhism."

Suzuki, who was not particularly interested in using business to present Buddhism, was primarily concerned with providing a way for students to support themselves in a situation conducive to practice, and that included working with dharma friends. Baker says he shared this view but found that the businesses were a "surprisingly effective means for communicating Buddhism. Almost all of our doctors, lawyers, dentists became partly Buddhist through the connection with the community. A large number of people who dined at Greens started coming to the Sunday lecture."

One spring day in 1968 Baker was walking down Bush Street when another student came up and said, "I hear you're going to Japan." That was news to him and he went looking for Suzuki Roshi. The following October the Bakers sailed on the *California Bear* for Kobe, Japan. Except for short visits they did not return until the fall of 1971. "Suzuki Roshi had already told me that he wanted me to be his dharma heir. When he sent me to Japan, he said, 'You have to have the credibility of having been to Japan.' Then he said, 'What will really give you credibility in America is if you have a Japanese student. So in the future, I hope Japanese people come to practice with you.' Unbelievable as it sounds, he also told me that he wanted me to reform Japanese Buddhism. And I said, 'Suzuki Roshi, that's a whole other level, do you really want me to do that?' And in some sense I looked into it. I had offers in Japan to start temples and train Americans. But I didn't care about it, and I told Suzuki Roshi, 'That's the limit! I'm not going to do that.' And I don't even know why he thought I could. He was serious about it. But he also thought I was better than I am. And he always worried that I would do things too much my own way. He didn't know why I was making Zen Center so big. He used to say, 'But my wife thinks it's all right.' "

In Kyoto the Bakers settled into Gary Snyder's house at the north end of the city while Snyder was back in California. Richard and Ginny both studied the Japanese language assiduously, and Sally went to a local Japanese school. Every evening Baker attended zazen at the Rinzai complex Daitokuji. Comparing the two main sects of Japanese Zen, he says: "Rinzai is more aristocratic and artistic than Soto, more clipped and refined and precise. The whole thing has more juice, more sharpness. I don't think it is necessarily better, but in Japanese society it definitely has a higher style than Soto. Rinzai buildings look great and Soto buildings look like barns. In Japan Soto is called 'Farmers' Zen' and Rinzai is called 'Aristocratic Zen.' Suzuki Roshi was Soto but he didn't think of himself as Soto. The Buddhism that interested him was in China before Rinzai and Soto split into two schools. But in Soto there is a very powerful tantric, esoteric tradition that Suzuki Roshi is part of. The Soto school—not everybody in it, but the school itself—got stuck in a certain socioeconomic niche. It's big. It has a wide appeal through its 30,000 temples, which are scattered all over Japan. Through a kind of religious authenticity, Soto disdained the connections to the rich, powerful samurai families associated with Rinzai. That's where the money and aesthetics were. So Soto, out of a kind of purity, got stuck with a pedestrian aesthetic. In its most ideal form, Soto is more generally Buddhist. Rinzai is a more specialized school of Buddhism."

For three months Baker left Kyoto for the Soto training center Eiheiji. Sweeping the grounds with the other monks, he noticed a little pathway off the end of the yard where pine needles had collected over a period of weeks. "So I would go over there and start sweeping. And they would get mad at me because sweeping with everyone was more important, even if it was meaningless work, than doing necessary work independently. So finally I would sweep with everyone else and feel like a fool. I hated samu. For an American, it was one of the hardest things to do."

Baker has called Japanese Buddhism "Big-roofism," a sardonic reference to the innumerable temples that symbolize the materialistic sprawl of religiosity. These temples, which stand above the roofs of every village, are the site of much fine village education and community activity, however, and Baker saw that within this social role—and not independent of it—private religious aspiration was nurtured, and that it, in turn, reverberated back out to society through cultural institutions. Baker was getting ready to return to a society that offered no support for Buddhism on any level, and he was preparing to move out on all fronts.

He claims that he continued to run Zen Center from Japan, and that he knew more in absentia about what was going on than most people who were there. Without Baker's immediate direction, however, the center changed quite a bit—and along expansionist lines, even under Suzuki. In 1969 Suzuki resigned his position at Sokoji to devote the last years of his life to establishing Zen practice for Americans. That same year Zen Center purchased 300 Page Street, formerly the Emanu-el Residence for Jewish Women. Designed in the thirties by Julia Morgan, the red-brick structure incorporates a lovely courtyard but nevertheless rarely succeeds in its attempts to alleviate institutional banality. Suzuki Roshi and his wife moved into Page Street, and the fifty-room residence quickly filled with students. As in the days on Bush Street, members began to occupy the apartments in the immediate vicinity, despite the hazards of living in a high-crime neighborhood. With Page Street right in the heart of the city, practice and residence were no longer solely associated with the monastic routine of Tassajara.

With the publication of *The Tassajara Bread Book* in 1970 came another major expansion. Under head cook Edward Espe Brown, the Tassajara kitchens baked extra loaves of bread during guest seasons for purchase by departing guests. Requests for the recipes soon followed and the cookbook ensued. To date, it is one of the best-selling bread books in the world, putting Zen in the kitchens of the unconverted and allying Tassajara with wholesome living. The cookbook then led to the Tassajara Bread Bakery, a retail bakery and coffee shop on the corner of Cole and Laguna streets that opened in 1973. Suzuki Roshi did not endorse a bakery as Zen practice anymore than he did communal living. His approval for the bakery was a response to an existing situation, and he thought it would benefit students to work in places where business ethics supported Zen training.

Several Japanese teachers came to the United States to assist Suzuki Roshi, but the most decisive influence on Zen Center was Tatsugami Roshi. An ex-sumo wrestler, Tatsugami had spent the previous twelve years as practice leader at Eiheiji before coming to California in 1970. At Tassajara he whipped the troops into shape with the same militaristic zeal he had unleashed on his Japanese novices. He demanded perfect sitting and walking posture, taught the details of Buddhist services, enforced hierarchical distinctions based on seniority, and introduced the Japanese words for ceremonies, positions, instruments, and vestments—all of which have stayed in use.

A senior monk at Zen Center today says of Tatsugami's rule: "As Americans, there was a kind of insecurity in embarking on the Zen path. It was an intimidating undertaking and the perfection that Tatsugami Roshi offered provided a security that we wanted." The athletic demands of zazen lend themselves to perfectionism under any circumstances, but unlike the monks at Eiheiji, many Americans besides Baker were using Zen to trade in past cultural identities for new ones. Zen form became a new identity. Implicit was the belief that the perfection of form embodied the spirit; and if that wasn't exactly true, with Suzuki Roshi around no one worried that the practice might be too true to the letter.

Philip Whalen's first trip to Tassajara reminded him of being back in the army. "It took me several training periods to see that they weren't trying to kill you. All you had to do was follow the schedule and you wouldn't have to argue with anybody, not even yourself." As a current zendo monitor remembers it, "Suzuki Roshi did one of these great routines. He got this tough cop in and he played nice guy." But the rigidities lasted long after Tatsugami left, contributing to Zen Center's reputation for "holy style" practice, somewhat stiff and picky. And despite Baker's early refutation of Japanese Zen formalities, he was the one who maintained them.

In December 1970 Suzuki Roshi, dying of liver cancer, made a brief trip to Japan. At his former temple, Rinso-in, he formally transmitted the dharma to Richard Baker, making him his dharma heir. Suzuki Roshi was dying faster than he had expected. According to Reb Anderson, his main attendant while Baker was in Japan, he had only six months when he thought he had two years. The following fall, with Suzuki Roshi gravely ill, the Bakers returned to Page Street. When Baker went to see his teacher, Suzuki Roshi said: "I am so sorry for what I am about to do to you."

"He started to cry," says Baker. "He understood that Zen Center was going to take over my life. I heard what he said. It didn't discourage me or daunt me because once I decide to do something, I'm just going to do it and not worry about the consequences."

In November 1971 Suzuki Roshi, too sick to stand alone, installed Baker as abbot of Zen Center in the service hall of Page Street. Two weeks later, on December 4th, Baker Roshi performed his first major ceremony as abbot of Zen Center: Suzuki Roshi's funeral.

When pressed, Suzuki Roshi had said that he personally knew nothing about enlightenment, but no one believed him. Certainly, in keeping with his Soto tradition, he wanted to unhook his students from a materialistic desire to "get" enlightened. Once he said, "What do you want to get enlightened for? You may not like it."

In addition to who he was, Suzuki Roshi was also who he was supposed to be, fulfilling the American preconceptions of an inscrutable, old Oriental Zen master. That his personality remained largely unknown was not because he didn't have one. Nor is it correct to say that all his life he manifested only realized enlightenment. If he didn't make himself clear to Americans, it was by default, not design. The most pervasive American myth about enlightenment is that it eradicates any trace of personality. This derives partly from early Western writings on Buddhism and translations in which "personality" and "ego" were used interchangeably; "dropping the ego"—the prime guideline for Buddhist practice—became synonymous with having no personality. In Buddhism "personality" may have more to do with the doctrine of karma than psychoanalytic theory, but neither view leaves anyone independent of inclinations, talents, and characteristics. Roughly speaking, the extent to which one gets attached to one's personality and allows those attachments to control one's identity and predetermine one's actions is a matter of ego. According to Buddhist teachings, personality is not where the juncture between teacher and student resides, and any attempt to locate perfection in personality will result in disappointment. Of all the Buddhist schools, Zen in particular has not fostered anything comparable to the Christian ideal of living saints. The continuation of the teachings has relied on the *role* of the master. Suzuki Roshi's role as teacher was totally accepted by his American students, but not necessarily because Americans had an understanding of roles or accepted the inevitable limitations of personality. His enigmatic Oriental qualities worked beneficially, postponing the encounter between the American preoccupation with personality and the Buddhist reliance on role. That would come soon enough with American teachers. And if, in Baker Roshi's case, this turned out to be a time bomb, the transition has not been easy for any American lineage holder who inherited students from an Oriental teacher.

After Suzuki Roshi's death dozens of new students faced an abbot they didn't know. Older students faced an abbot about whom they had serious reservations, for the late master was not alone in his qualms about Baker doing things too much his own way. Among senior students there was a pervasive anxiety that with the passing of Suzuki Roshi, Zen Center would be devoured by Richard Baker, for he had, as one student said, "more energy than the rest of the community put together." By Baker's own admission there was no one who didn't have some difficulty with him. Nor was anyone surprised that he would lead Zen Center. He was the right man for the job; by most accounts, including his own, he was the only one. Still, for too many people at Zen Center, if he wasn't quite Suzuki Roshi, he was supposed to be—not only because he had inherited the abbacy but because he had received dharma transmission.

Once in a public meeting someone asked Suzuki Roshi, "What is dharma transmission?" "You shouldn't ask," he replied. In response to another question, he had once said, "Everyone's enlightenment is different." But since transmission was not a subject for public discourse, the myth of dharma heir as some kind of spiritual clone was in circulation, even before Baker became abbot. Also taken for granted—by almost everyone except Baker—was an intrinsic connection between the abbotship and dharma transmission. Both *seemed* to affirm spiritual authority. As far as Baker is concerned, "If Suzuki Roshi had not given me the lineage, had not done the transmission ceremony, I still would have been head of Zen Center. Receiving dharma transmission was a personal thing between me and Suzuki Roshi, and for me it had almost nothing to do with Zen Center. Zen Center was designed around the upper limits of my particular abilities. It could not survive without me."

In 1971 the new abbot assumed that his role was granted by the fact that he had the most energy for organizing the center, that he was the most willing to do everything, that he did it better than anyone else. His authority, therefore, was not ephemeral and not based on the mysteries of transmission but concrete and measurable. He presented himself as more sophisticated, better educated, and more aesthetically evolved than his students. Few disagreed and no one challenged his judgments. "I had the authority because I was the founder of virtually everything at Zen Center. Look at where the Buddha came from, the rug, the wall color, where the buildings came from. It was amazing what I did." And from the perspective of New Mexico 1987, he adds, "And it was probably wrong. It was a mistake because it made it too much mine. It didn't allow other people to participate. And I didn't make strategic accommodations to the problems that it caused. It was not thoughtful to the students. But I just didn't know. If we needed a Buddha, I went out and got one. It wouldn't have gotten done without me, but it also caused problems.

"Suzuki Roshi created the teaching and I created Zen Center. I don't care what other people think, it is correct to say that I may have created the illusion that Suzuki Roshi created Zen Center but basically, I did. Nothing like Zen Center would have existed if I hadn't been there to 'translate,' to make him accessible. And I overdid it. I created too much structure so that anything the students heard they thought was a teaching. But for me a good part of the teaching was creating the arms, the structure that allows a person to hear the teachings. When I came back from Japan, I knew why those people were there and how they got there. I orchestrated it. I was Suzuki Roshi's agent in a sense as well as his disciple. And I did all that because I felt that Zen Buddhism was going to be an enormously powerful, formative influence in the United States in the next decade."

One of the biggest dilemmas that Baker set up for himself was that by denying the spiritual authority invested in him he did not take responsibility for it. According to Baker, "Because of my complex and intimate relationship to Suzuki Roshi, I did not feel that those students were just Suzuki Roshi's students. They didn't realize how much they were my students. But I had been supplying the context that allowed them to study. And I already knew the kind of personal authority I had with people. I did not know if I would have the same teaching authority. But I knew that personal authority would go a long way."

Eventually there was total confusion between spiritual authority and the superior talents of community leadership. As far as the students were concerned, they were certainly, in theory, not submitting their lives to Baker's personal authority. Their trust was not based on his aestheticism or his talent for real-estate ventures or his energy for getting things done. But Baker was right. His personal authority did go a long way. Within a couple of years his teaching authority was accepted by most of the old Suzuki Roshi students, but it was his domineering personality that controlled Zen Center and affirmed his entitlement. He says, "If I had thought my authority to run Zen Center rested on something as personal as dharma transmission, I would have thought that was stupid. I wouldn't have accepted authority on those terms. I am not interested in 'spiritual' anything. I don't even know what spiritual authority is."

Before he died Suzuki Roshi spoke of one more expansion. The city center worked well for single people, but he thought families would fare better in a rural setting organized along secular, not monastic, lines. In 1972 Baker Roshi proposed buying the 115-acre Green Gulch Farm for $200,000, a price that represents a donation on the part of the owner, the property being worth several times that on the open market. The summers were chilly and foggy and the winters chilly and rainy; still, it was spectacular beach-front farmland half an hour from San Francisco. For senior members the proposal came too soon after Suzuki Roshi's death. Baker says, "My intuition was just the opposite. Take on a big project when things are shaky and everyone's shakiness goes into making it work and it's inspiring. Also, two spaces are claustrophobic. You're either here or there. It is ab and ba. With three spaces, you get ab, ba, ca, ba, cb, etc. Three spaces, you lose your balance."

The board of directors opposed the purchase, and Baker threatened to leave. If Baker left, he would take the lineage with him, severing Zen Center from its formal link to Suzuki Roshi. Whatever this mysterious dharma transmission entailed, the board communicated that Baker had it and they did not; the board acquiesced. The showdown over buying Green Gulch marks the start of what came to be vilified as Baker's manipulative use of his role. But in the immediate aftermath, Green Gulch became a huge hit. From this confrontation another important message was soon delivered to the new abbot: he could see what people wanted, needed, and would appreciate even if they could not.

Green Gulch's success reflected Baker's continued ability to keep pace with the times. For newcomers in their early twenties ripe for the back-to-the-land movement, Green Gulch was an Aquarian Eden where every 1970s organic bioexperiment had its day in the sun. Originally, it was operated as an egg farm and grew produce in hand- and horse-cultivated fields. Alternative energy systems were installed along with a biodynamic garden started by the English gardener Alan Chadwick. Today, with sixteen acres under cultivation, the flower gardens alone resemble the estates of titled Europeans. The vegetables supply the community kitchens and are marketed at health-food stores and restaurants throughout the Bay Area as well as at the Green Gulch Greengrocer, a Zen Center neighborhood store kitty-corner to 300 Page Street. A swimming pool and an enormous barn, which was subsequently converted to a zendo, came with the property. Public buildings of exquisite craftsmanship were later added. Visitors stop by on their way to Muir Beach or Mount Tamalpais. A San Francisco writer recalls that, "It was a comfortable place for someone who wanted to think of themselves as a radical humanist-atheist-to-be." Shaved monks ploughed the fields while children played on the grass and cows and horses grazed in the pasture. The work was hard and the days were long, starting at 3:40 A.M. with two periods of zazen, but that didn't daunt New Age idealists. The concept of freedom taught in American grade school was only a chauvinistic rally to power politics; their doors of perception would be truly cleansed, their liberation capable of transforming the superfluities of civilization. And the optimism inspired by Green Gulch conquered most of the lingering doubts about the new abbot. His role was affirmed by superhuman energy and an ingenious ability to make things happen.

Yet Baker's strategy contradicted Suzuki Roshi's original intention. He explains: "Suzuki Roshi didn't want a monastic practice at Green Gulch in which people felt that in order to be serious Zen students they had to follow a monastic routine. His idea was to create a community dimension to the practice, to help protect the integrity of the practice—but not to make it central to the practice. He expected a Zen farm commune to be peripheral to the community as a whole, and I made it central."

Making it central subjected it to monastic standards. Initially Green Gulch (and Tassajara) reverted to conventionally gendered activities. "The big boys got to drive the trucks," says Phil Whalen. While feminism was on the rise in the cities, country mothers stayed home with the children and in the kitchens. At Green Gulch, in accordance with the hierarchy of role-related activity, husbands were in the zendo more frequently than wives. But for parents—men or women, ordained or not—the schedule offered continual conflicts. Lectures, meetings, guest speakers, and so on, demanded a choice between practice and family, between attaining "the mind that abides no-where" and grounding security for their households.

Even in the early days the mood behind the scenes was not serene. An exacting administrator-in-chief, Baker was brilliant, impatient, and critical. Those working in close contact with him were enchanted, intimidated, and exhausted. Reb Anderson obeyed Suzuki Roshi's request to remain at Zen Center and help Baker Roshi. Now in his mid-forties, he long ago earned the reputation of being Zen Center's model student through his calm reserve and ascetic devotions. In a ceremony in the winter of 1983, Anderson was acknowledged as Baker's first dharma heir, but their relationship soon deteriorated. Even though Baker has since cast aspersions on Anderson's transmission, Zen Center continues to acknowledge him as the lineage holder. Anderson recalls that when Baker returned from Japan in 1970, "I told him, 'We don't have to make everything so big with so much property and so much money.' But soon I got caught in the hysteria. He convinced us that we were Bodhisattvas by making this historical contribution to America. And in order to be historical, we had to expand, we had to keep busy, and we had to keep the pace real fast."

The integration of all three locations, as well as the businesses and the membership, was entirely held together by Baker. He alone was the centrifugal force, the creator and destroyer of all Zen Center reality. "He functioned as the mind of everyone," says Sarah Grayson, who followed Baker to Santa Fe and has advocated his return to Zen Center. "Everyone was part of him and he was part of everyone and that's why people are still so attached to him. That's where the glue was. The glue was his mind. His big mind, not his intellectual mind."

Page Street functioned as the bureaucratic and academic wing of the center. In 1973 it inaugurated the Shunryu Suzuki Study Center, which offered classes on Buddhist texts and Oriental religious and cultural history. Within the first year visiting lecturers included Trungpa Rinpoche, Aitken Roshi, Nancy Wilson Ross, Houston Smith (current board member of the Dharma

Sangha), Edward Conze, Masao Abe, and Thomas Cleary. And that was only the beginning. Public programs operated as an avant-garde clearing house for poets, dancers, artists, social activists, and sensory-awareness therapists.

The following year Page Street organized the Neighborhood Foundation, a liaison between students and the existing Page-Laguna Neighborhood Association, to upgrade the surrounding twenty-block area. Within the next three years Zen Center would own several buildings on Page Street, including a twenty-unit apartment building, a Victorian guest house, and a town house residence for the Baker family.

Despite Baker's early objections to the priesthood, he reinstated the Zen convention of monastic supremacy. Zen Center monastics did not refrain from sex, alcohol, or family life, but commitment to practice was the unequivocal priority. The ideal version of Zen Center presented spiritual and political equality between secular and ordained modes and between residents and nonresidents. The real version saw committed students as ordained residents working full-time for Zen Center. Baker ordained more than sixty students and openly urged people to make the community their first priority: "Taking care of the temple *is* the practice." All of Zen Center was the temple; he made every effort to accommodate residents and to find jobs conducive to individual needs. Most of the Page Street residents worked in the administration or in the community-owned businesses that by 1974 included the bakery, the Green Gulch Greengrocer, and the Alaya Storehouse, a factory and retail shop for comfortable clothing and meditation mats and cushions.

Tassajara was where it all came together. It was not immune from elements that were later to become problematic, but within the traditional monastic routine people identified themselves as Zen students, and from that base Zen Center made sense. Students still boggled by Baker's departure and by what he calls "ZCM"—Zen Center Mess—have concluded, "You had to know Baker Roshi at Tassajara." Dissidents who wanted his resignation in 1983 still recall specific periods of zazen fifteen years ago when, seated next to him in the big wooden zendo, they could feel the concentration of his zazen. Sarah Grayson came to California from Mississippi, earned a degree in sociology from the University of California, and then opened Petrouchka, a prosperous Russian vegetarian restaurant in Berkeley. A stately woman in her mid-forties, she has confronted Baker with her criticisms in no uncertain terms, but nothing undercuts her experiences at Tassajara: "In the intensity of the kind of practice that Tassajara offers, you're operating with a spiritual mind within a spiritual bond. It's removed from his emotional life and from my emotional life—from anybody's. It's not about personality, it's not about ego. If people haven't had that experience with Baker Roshi they don't know him as a nonego being. His ego is so overwhelming that when it's in operation it can blast you away. But when he's operating in the context of the monastery and in dokusan and in sitting practice, then you are dealing with someone else totally. I am only concerned with him in a practice relationship and he can be extraordinary in that context. When he really sits, it's utterly amazing. All the other things became problems. He's very powerful. A lot of people got a hit off his power and stayed stuck to that. But when he's extraordinary he's extraordinary, and what made the community work was his practice relationships."

Baker Roshi saw students privately at all three locations, but dokusan, like other aspects of practice, was intensified at Tassajara. Traditionally the Zen master displays no interest in personal history, dramas, or any kind of descriptive data. He is ideally a mind reader in the sense of reading the nature of mind itself, of seeing where the flow of the small mind to the infinity of no-mind is blocked, stuck, or cannot let go. Baker Roshi functioned this way for some. But most Americans have confused dokusan with culture-bound concepts of intimacy in which sharing private, secret, or painful personal details defines the terms of intimacy. There is no consistency among American teachers trained by Japanese Zen masters on how to address fundamental differences in the ways Japanese and Americans think about themselves. And very few have figured out how to draw the line between Zen teacher and life counselor.

At Zen Center, dokusan became the place where students discussed their marital problems, affairs, unwanted pregnancies, alcoholic parents, abused childhoods, and so on. The disclosure of personal details is not where the intimacy of Zen practice resides, but Baker got caught in the entanglements of giving advice, making suggestions, and often telling people what to do. "I can have something to say on almost any topic. And if people ask me something, I just answer. It was just advice. But it was hard to make it *just* advice."

Where Baker lacked the confidence required to define the parameters of his teaching qualifications, the students willingly filled in the blanks. It was advice from one who supposedly knew them better than they knew themselves and was capable of getting himself out of the picture enough to advise wholly on their behalf. Baker was told things that people didn't tell each other, contributing to psychological dependencies that he was not trained to handle. He became the sole arbitrator of personal decisions and what actions did or did not hurt others or the community. Case by case this may have had its merits, but as a strategy for community harmony it became a disaster. In addition to spiritual omniscience and paternalistic jurisdiction, it also invested him with the very potent power of private information. This blocked open communication, making it less accessible by placing Baker on an ever-higher pedestal. The more students invested in him, the more perfect he had to be in their eyes to justify that investment.

The community was not oriented toward psychological awareness. On the contrary, a subtle repression of emotional matter persisted. A 1972 newspaper article on the peace and quiet of Tassajara quoted a senior monk saying, "Anything one talks about in public isn't very important," a paraphrase of a Zen virtue passed down from China to Japan. Imposed at Tassajara, the virtue of silence was misconstrued in a way that retarded emotional and psychological expression. At Tassajara the conformist militarism of heroic practice discouraged personal reflections in public as petty and self-centered. Criticism was dismissed as personal resistance. Ultimately this ethic played a big role in the conspiracy of silence that allowed mistrust to fester and that created a duplicitous schism between private doubt and public affirmation. That silence had been idealized as a Zen virtue made its misuse all the more pernicious. It also prescribed what Baker now calls "the official discourse" in which everything was couched in Buddhist terms. For example, no one could say they wanted to leave Tassajara for any reason other than "It would be good for my practice." It also meant that requests to the abbot for job or residence changes were too often phrased in obsequious flattery, appealing to his compassion rather than risking rejection. In general, the social organization of the community was informed by "official Buddhism," a style that came to be faulted for its self-conscious preoccupations. Then again, a Zen center in America in the 1970s didn't have too many other options.

Hakuin Zenji, Japan's great Zen master of the eighteenth century, said that a Zen teacher has three obligations: to the laity, to monks, and to leaders. "To leaders," explains Baker, "because they affect a lot of people. And Zen Center had that connection more than any other group." During Jerry Brown's governorship of California, from 1974 to 1982, Zen Center had a direct line to Sacramento. Baker estimates that by 1980 thirty percent of the governor's staff had gotten to the state capital directly or indirectly through Zen Center. Gary Snyder, Bob Gnaizda, Stewart Brand, Peter Coyote, Gregory Bateson, and Sym Van der Ryn all held official state positions. In addition, unofficial advisers like Brother David Steindl-Rast, Mike Murphy, and Alan Chadwick were familiar faces at Zen Center. For public-interest visionaries of the New Age, progress in the seventies rested with institutionalizing the idealism of the sixties. But for Richard Baker to have served Governor Brown formally would have been a step down. He already had direct access to Brown and everyone else in the administration. To the American Bodhisattvas at Zen Center, their historical contribution never looked more promising. Proximity to legislative power reinforced their resolve to make the future, not choose it. And Brown's election escalated the potential for Zen Center to function as a resource for the larger society.

In 1979, after two years of preparation, Zen Center and Baker took a giant step into the public arena with the opening of the restaurant Greens. An old warehouse at Fort Mason on the city's waterfront was converted into a palatial interior, overlooking San Francisco Bay and beyond to the Golden Gate Bridge. When Baker argued for establishing Greens at this former World War II naval station, it was dreary and isolated. But the restaurant's view, its interior, and its whole new approach to vegetarian cooking has made it one of the most highly rated restaurants in the country. Until Greens, vegetarian restaurants were associated with brown rice, aduki beans, serve-yourself green tea, burlap curtains, and macrame plant holders. Greens filled its space with huge abstract paintings by Edward Avedisian and served meals that appealed to gourmets. As always, Baker controlled the look, selecting the paintings, menus, napkins, plates, glassware. Wine lists accompanied the menus, but only after Baker discussed the ethics of serving liquor in a Buddhist-owned establishment with Tibet's Dalai Lama. There were objections to Greens as there had been objections to Green Gulch, but again Baker prevailed. While Green Gulch absorbed the ideals of back-to-the-land hippies, Greens combined high-definition aesthetics with homegrown vegetables to make it the perfect enterprise for the yuppie decade.

Its press coverage alone glorified Zen even for established San Francisco conservatives. It made Zen Center acceptable, and that sanctioned Zen practice. Baker had deliberately kept the media out of Zen Center, turning down innumerable requests for television documentaries and magazine articles. "Greens was the kind of statement I was willing to make," he says. "As a practice place, it interested me more from a customer's point of view than from the employee's. We got ourselves out there in a visible way. I didn't want waiters wearing robes. I wanted it to be invisibly Buddhist. And except for being vegetarian, it was. We emphasized service. I wanted businesses that required contact with people. And I think people did feel different in the bakery and at the restaurant than they did in other places. There's a Buddhist expression that says if one person is practicing it affects fifty others—mother, father, shopkeepers, guests. It's true. So with the bakery and with Greens people could actually feel your perception of them. They were not just a customer or a means to make money; they were related in a direct, human way."

At Greens, Baker was another fashionable diner, arriving with scores of glamorous cronies, fast-lane movers and shakers whose company he appeared to enjoy much more than that of his students. Like other wheeling mavericks, he often mixed pleasure and business, discussing with the building commissioner ways of circumventing codes for the construction of the traditional Japanese teahouse or giving opinions on civic projects to municipal officials. His lifestyle did not change with the opening of Greens, but it was exposed in ways that few students had previously witnessed—and the platform from which Baker's Buddhism was to transform society suddenly seemed to require a score of indentured serfs.

Lou Hartman, who at seventy-two is Zen Center's most senior monk, was once assigned to clean up the liquor bottles the morning after one of Governor Brown's private parties at Green Gulch. He obediently went about his job, but it reenforced his sense that within Zen Center there was a kind of elitist skull-and-bones society where all the important work was going on. Mike Murphy, Stewart Brand, Jerry Brown, and Richard Baker became identified as a club of Californian golden boys who traded favors and used each other's assistants, ideas, and resources. Students were both proud and perplexed by Baker's high-flying social life; they basked in the glory of his connections, but also felt neglected. He alone was the adventurer, courting exclusive realms that most could only enter on his coattails. Like good wives, they were relegated to vicarious triumphs and expected to accept their station. As Yvonne Rand, who became Suzuki's secretary in 1966 and has since held every administrative position at Zen Center, says in retrospect, "With Greens, Dick left the community behind. We all hung together because we believed in the dream. He needed people to do the work—although maybe it would have been better for them to wander around."

According to Baker, the abbot's role demanded private and public entertaining: "Ninety-nine percent of what I did was for the sake of Zen Center. I needed to create the kinds of connections that enabled me to support Zen Center and to create a social network for Zen Center to be a resource. If I spent $6,000 a year taking people out to dinner, I could get that with a phone call. But the students don't think of it that way. They're thinking, 'I don't have enough money to go to the movies.' But I can't fund-raise for them to go to the movies. I felt that I was producing enough income for Zen Center to justify the money I was spending. Everyone thought I was spending their money. Of course I created the money I was spending. I saw the platform as a way of presenting Buddhism, not myself. And it is true that I used the students as part of that platform. But I did not think I was using them for personal gain, and I thought they shared my goal."

Many did. But he managed to convince no one, not even his fans, that his pursuits of the rich and famous were altruistic sacrifices for Buddhism in America. A supporter who today advocates his return to Zen Center says, "He thinks he's capable of making the jump from a deep concentrated presence to media star with no loss of spiritual quality. That's the side of him that is wall-to-wall hype." Increasingly, Baker was perceived as being corrupted by fame and fortune, choosing people and places that gratified his seductive intellect over the ego-killing practice of zazen.

With the addition of Greens, students felt more overworked and underpaid than ever. Twenty to thirty years old in 1970, many now had children in school and teenagers ready for college. Zen Center gave Baker Roshi an additional $10,000 for each year that his elder daughter was at Brown University, but no such monies were available for other children. The more practical reasons for traditional celibacy were becoming all too obvious. The more Zen Center and its abbot acquired worldly status, the less appealing the monk's path of utmost simplicity looked to the work force. By 1980, despite the success of Greens, Zen businesses were fast becoming an oxymoron for their staffs. On the one hand, the businesses were not "Zen-like" enough, and on the other, stipends weren't high enough to cover secular lifestyles.

Then came the infamous white BMW, the car that Baker bought in 1980 for $21,000 and that became the ultimate symbol of self-aggrandizement and poor judgment. "What Baker transmitted," said a senior priest, "was power and arrogance and an attitude that 'I have it and you don't.' " However ethereal this "it" had been in the past, a white BMW suddenly became its insignia. He was accused retroactively of having flaunted power by the way he walked into a room, by the way he preferred to talk rather than listen, and by the high-handed way that, as he admitted himself, he treated others. Gestures, glances, and tone of voice had inhibited criticism and too often left people hurt and angry. But unlike the car, gestures were too elusive to confront. And in the grand scheme of things, the complaints sounded trivial—to Baker and the students; yet something in the irksome presence of this white BMW got under the student's skin, and the irritation would not go away.

Continuing to combine the roles of benevolent ruler and spiritual master, by 1980 Baker involved himself in the antinuclear movement. He was convinced that without immediate Herculean efforts there would be a nuclear disaster, if not by intention then by accident, within ten years. In 1981 he went to Russia with Mike Murphy as part of a track-two diplomacy program sponsored by Esalen Institute in which their meetings circumvented organized political channels. The platform had gone international. Despite widespread support, the antinuclear movement was still another sphere that took Baker away from the community; but as a woman who has been at Zen Center for twenty years says, "How much could we bitch about a car when he was driving off to the airport to save the world from the nuclear holocaust?"

On April 8, 1983, the Zen Center mess began brewing in earnest. Baker Roshi was leading a retreat at Tassajara and students at Green Gulch were busy preparing for a peace vigil they had organized at the main plaza in Mill Valley. While Buddhists throughout Japan as well as the United States were celebrating the birthday of Gautama Shakyamuni, the directors of San Francisco Zen Center called a board meeting at Page Street. Three senior priests announced that Baker Roshi was romantically involved with Anna Hawken, a married woman who had been living at Green Gulch. Baker Roshi had often referred to her husband, Paul Hawken, as his best friend, and in fact the couple and their children had moved to Green Gulch with special residential provisos provided by the abbot. Paul Hawken, who had been personally informed of the romance by Baker, was now threatening to commit suicide—but not before going public with the affair.

Dozens of students knew about several previous affairs and also knew that Ginny Baker had not been caught off guard, that she and her husband had arrived at a private understanding some time before. Many students suspected as much but preferred not to know for sure. Of the several hundred students living in or near Zen Center, most—including some of Baker's personal attendants—never suspected anything of the sort. But for the first time, an angry man was involved; not coincidentally, it was the first time Baker's conduct was used by an adversary to solicit sympathy from senior male priests. And it was the first time that anyone had threatened to expose Baker in ways intended to hurt Zen Center. The sixteen-member board made two decisions: they would confront Baker Roshi and they would proceed calmly to inform community members about what had happened.

All hell then broke loose with a bitterness that facts alone cannot explain. The news hit like a seismic bolt that blasted out from the undercurrents every trace element of rage. The long absence of any open dialogue finally took its toll with a vengeance. There was no component of the official discourse, nor any inarticulated myth that bonded the community, that had not contributed to a communication blockage that was dying to burst. For many contemporaries outside Zen Center, Buddhists and not, the community's response has always been somewhat mystifying. After all, this was California 1983, and Zen Center had responded with the hellfire damnation of the Puritan Fathers.

By all accounts—except Baker's—public disclosure of adultery was the straw that broke the camel's back. In Baker's view alone, the Zen Center mess was catalyzed by the irate husband—the Machiavellian magician who overnight turned positive projections negative. For students, Paul Hawken was a timely catalyst, but from an overall view neither he nor the affair itself played a prominent role in what happened at Zen Center. They simply sparked off a seizure of madness. In the contagion of fury, isolated acts of betrayal were thrown onto the communal bonfire to both exorcise and illume Baker at his worst. The disclosure of adultery triggered memories of the time he didn't say hello in the hallway, the time he criticized someone publicly at

Greens, the time he bought a $2,000 end table. Public airing of grievances was long overdue. The conflagration took on a militant life of its own—and it was coming straight for the abbot.

The pervasive understanding that adultery was off limits came directly from Baker Roshi. If there was a puritanical edge to Zen Center, it was mainly because the abbot himself encouraged it. He was therefore accused of operating a double standard, which for most students was more incriminating than adultery. In the wake of national scandals like Watergate, the cover-up became the object of mistrust more than the event itself. According to Baker, there was no ethic about adultery per se. In his talk at the Lindisfarne conference in 1974 he had said: "The two most important rules of the Sangha community are 'do not hurt others' and 'do not deceive others.' These are especially important in guiding members of the community in love and sexual relationships. When these two commonsense rules are honestly and carefully observed, almost all of the sexual problems that beset and in fact often destroy most communities are avoided or solved. But you must be able to find the general community's good—the priority, ethics, and ethos of everyone finding a way to live together—above your own particular satisfactions. In a community it usually becomes very clear that when the price of personal satisfaction is deception and pain, it is not worth it."

"The double standard came up around the question of hurting others," says Baker. "I took the mode that if you weren't disturbing the community, you could operate any way you wanted. At the level of not disturbing the community, it looked like I had a relationship with Ginny that was *completely* intact. Not true. But *fundamentally* it was intact and still is."

Sex became another sphere in which Baker seemed to set himself above the community. Like the BMW, as opposed to all the nebulous, private inklings that had reluctantly added up to a reevaluation, adultery was a public target. This time Zen Center would not hedge on its communication. "If we had swallowed our silent screams one more time," said a former attendant, "we would have choked to death."

What remains more ambiguous is the allegation that Baker randomly slept with students. Several relationships, including the one that precipitated the Zen Center mess, grew out of social friendships that had not been defined by either the hierarchical or spiritual qualities of the teacher-student dynamic. Baker's affairs had been heartfelt and long-lasting, not capricious. He says he stopped the affair with Anna Hawken in an effort to hold Zen Center together, a decision he has since regretted, having openly claimed that she was the love of his life. But he has denied that he abused his role to seduce female students or that extramarital sex was one of the perks of his job. "The accusation of a teacher sleeping with students," said Baker, "is generally meant to imply someone who is using his power with women who are very young or where there is a misuse of his authority. I have not done that."

Even though rumors regarding Baker's affairs got way out of hand, the basic issue of trust remained. In the past, discontent and criticism had been expressed only in one-on-one dialogues in which Baker's reality had dominated. Now, with the tables turned, and within a climate of extreme confusion and disappointment, it was doubtful whether rebuilding that trust was possible.

The meeting at which Baker was confronted left most board members with the impression that the abbot did not comprehend the mood. Zen Center had never been out of his control. He was asked not to lead services or give talks. By the end of April 1983 he asked for a leave of absence for one year. His expense accounts were stopped and his stipend limited. It was then that Baker announced that he wanted to walk alone from Page Street to Tassajara, a distance of 175 miles. His students enthusiastically interpreted this as an act of penance, but Baker said that was never his intention. In any event during this "walk" he showed up in New York and Palm Springs, was rumored to be visiting Linda Ronstadt in Los Angeles, and eventually arrived in France, where he visited the Vietnamese monk Thich Nhat Hanh. In short, intentionally or not, he added insult to injury. From France he sent a letter to the sangha apologizing for the suffering he had caused. The letter was interpreted as perfunctory and insincere. They wanted him to understand the problems on their terms, to see himself as they saw him, and to acknowledge moral wrongdoing that to this day he adamantly disclaims: "The only scandalous thing that happened at Zen Center is how I was treated."

Having remained immune to the growing discontent and deafened by the attack itself, Baker could not hear the complaints. They remain the accumulated debris of what Baker calls "the irrational surge"; he still does not acknowledge the psychological buildup that aggravated the circumstances. From his perspective, things went from good to bad overnight—and it was a nightmare. "They didn't want me to apologize," he says. "They wanted me to *submit* to them and I wouldn't do that."

Baker was accused of using people's weaknesses against themselves for his personal and political benefit. This was a particular sore point with women as the attributes of the obedient Zen student had played on classic female stereotypes in a male-dominated society: acquiescence, dependency, desire to please, low self-esteem. In his determination to make Zen Center the biggest and the best, he had satisfied the growing membership with housing, jobs, braces for children, hearing aids for the elderly. Materially, he had tried hard to please everyone; but in his devotion to the institution, he had not paid enough attention to human needs. Not long ago, a former student said to him, "You are so naive about people." "I'm just beginning to see that now," says Baker.

The opposition to Baker was led by senior board members, who championed "the Suzuki Roshi revival," a tactic in which the late master was used as a weapon against Baker. From a conservative perspective, not trusting the teacher is not trusting *his* teacher. This put Zen Center in direct confrontation with Suzuki Roshi, dead or alive, and in order to deny Baker they had, strictly speaking, to abrogate Suzuki Roshi's authority. Instead, in the wake of overt contradictions to the teachings of lineage, they created an idealized Suzuki Roshi against whom to measure Baker. Recently, at his home in Green Gulch, Reb Anderson said, "There are people here today who hardly knew Suzuki Roshi and some who didn't even like him that much. Today they love him. He's the one who can do no wrong."

The Suzuki Roshi revival—and subsequent deification—was used to deny Baker's contribution to Zen Center. Suddenly the dead master was the immediate predecessor of the students, with no one in between, and they, the Suzuki Roshi students, claimed they had never believed in Baker Roshi anyway. Circumventing Baker strengthened their direct descent from Suzuki. Baker has said that despite initial resistance to him, all of the seniors came to believe in him as a Zen teacher—with the exception of Mel Weitzman, now abbot of the Berkeley Zendo, which Weitzman and others have confirmed. "Mel never bought into me as a teacher," says Baker with a chuckle, "and I always kind of respected him for it."

The reaction to the crisis seemed to divide along gender lines: women were angry about sex and men were angry about money. Neither issue had much force alone, but together they were evidence of an authority and power that had grown oppressive. Baker was abbot, teacher, leader, administrator-in-chief, mayor, landlord, employer, marriage counselor, psychologist. "I held too much power," says Baker now. "I disempowered my students. I didn't see that. They were disempowered because of my lack of insight. I am fairly astute about society and community. But I didn't make a simple observation. There is a certain passage to adulthood in our society that everyone has to go through or they feel defeated, and I interfered with that rite of passage."

In the Lindisfarne address, Baker had said, "A community can help us become free from viewing our lives as dramas of success or failure requiring a leading actor and a series of emotional scenes." If this was true, then the madness itself so violently contradicted the official discourse that it became almost as devastating as the events that created it. Baker was called the emperor with no clothes; by the time the fireworks faded, he was not standing naked alone. All the affectations of Buddhism peeled off. For twenty years, Zen Center students thought they had an edge on samsara. Now, in the main meeting room of the empire, a priest ordained by the abbot called him a "pile of shit." Burning the images of Buddhism has a glorious history in Zen and in the long run may prove beneficial for Zen Center. But in the immediacy of the heat, people suddenly looked monstrous to each other and to themselves, and it was terrifying. That spring of 1983 has been repeatedly described as the time when Zen Center went crazy. However large and amorphous Zen Center had become, it responded to the crisis as though it were a traumatized nuclear family. There is still no one version, no bottom line to fall back on.

What is certain is that the Zen Center mess radically undermined the membership's sense of its identity. "American Buddhism emerged as just 'American,'" said Kathy Fischer. "We unraveled into nothing but greed, hatred, and delusion. We weren't just disappointed in Baker Roshi. We were disappointed in ourselves. We were enraged by the inequities that we had permitted and projected wildly onto him."

During the summer and fall of 1983, Zen Center organized small affinity groups and paid professional facilitators to help members sort out their doubts, disillusionments, and disappointments. "We spent $5,000 for someone to come to Zen Center and teach us how to talk to each other," re-

calls Katherine Thanas, a down-to-earth priest of sixty who has been direct-
ing Tassajara for the last several years. "Because everybody's primary relationship was with the abbot, the bonds of community were not developed."
In the past there had been no space for criticism. If you didn't like Zen Center,
you were free to leave, a policy that has since been called "the totalitarianism
of democracy."

The board of directors never asked Baker to resign. Ed Brown, then co-
director of Greens and chairman of the board, took his prerogative as an individual to write a passionate public letter begging Baker to resign. Baker
submitted his letter of resignation on December 8, 1983. The most disturbing episode in the history of Zen in America, which had begun on Shakyamuni Buddha's birthday, now ended on Bodhi Day, the day that commemorates the Buddha's enlightenment. At Zen Center, however, there was little
to celebrate. The resignation itself hardly resolved the issues that had been
raised, nor could it restore stability to a shattered community. Some saw
Baker's resignation as an inevitable conclusion, coming just short of im-
peachment. Others estimate that Baker had enough support to weather the
storm but had stumbled too hard to keep going. "I was in love," he said, "and
vulnerable and deeply wounded."

The resignation cast its own very long shadow as an admission of slow defeat. Baker says, "I could not be true to Suzuki Roshi's teachings and stay. At
the same time, I had made a commitment to Suzuki Roshi to take care of Zen
Center for the rest of my life. And that vow is still a problem for me. But in a
bigger sense, to be true to Suzuki Roshi and teach the way he wanted me to
and experiment with the teachings the way he wanted me to, I had to leave."

With Baker's departure Zen Center was congratulated by humanist sa-
maritans, feminist Buddhists, Zen students disillusioned with other teachers, ideologues of democracy, and California anarchists for "stopping the
teacher." But since 1983 Zen Center has discovered that "stopping the
teacher" may be easier than figuring out the next step. Five years later Katherine Thanas said, "We tried to get rid of the problems by getting rid of him.
Until we face the problems of trust and confidence in ourselves we will keep
blaming him and won't be able to go forward."

Many of those who left Zen Center angry have stayed angry. But those
who stayed on, like Thanas, have tried to accept their responsibility for their
own participation in the history of the community. According to theories of

codependency, Zen Center has been defined as a family in which everyone participated in the problems. Thanas explains that "you cannot process what happened without confronting your own collusion in the events. We are all responsible, and those people who cannot acknowledge this, who continue to target Richard Baker as victimizer, cannot get on with it."

Five years after the Zen Center mess, Yvonne Rand, who for her identification with the community has been called "Mrs. Zen Center," has reached similar conclusions. There was no counterpart to Baker, but Rand came as close as the structure tolerated. For years she was the token female of an inside core called "Yvonne and the boys." The same age as Baker and almost as tall, she has a physical presence every bit as powerful as his and used it effectively against him. But Rand, too, stopped looking in Baker's direction for answers. Suzuki Roshi had told her never to leave Zen Center. Following his death, she was in ill health for ten years. There had been, in rapid sequence, pneumonia, a car accident, bronchitis, leukemia. With the help of a therapist, she came to attribute her illnesses to a disparity between her ideals and her own experiences. "I had to learn to trust myself. I gave my authority to Dick. I believed his version of what was safe, healthy, appropriate." By abdicating her own experience, she protected Baker and at the same time protected what was most familiar from her childhood. "I recreated the dysfunctional relationships I had with my family. The patterns were to learn to keep secrets, to become skillful at denial, and to have a low threshold for overt truth telling." Rand, who was a member of Adult Children of Alcoholics, concluded that it was a pattern of learned helplessness based on a system of collusion, protection, and avoidance. "Dick invited my dependency. I had a tremendous investment in Dick's being perfect and in believing his vision. And I did him a disservice. Each one of us had too much invested in him to see him clearly."

Arnie Kotler, who had been Baker's attendant through the early eighties, left with Baker to start the Mariposa Street center. But he stayed in California when Baker moved to New Mexico and now runs Parallax Press. Sitting in the garden of his house in Berkeley, Kotler says, "The myth of transmission was so strong that it did not allow many of us to trust our own perceptions. We deferred our own sense of things to this mysterious authority and construed everything presented by Roshi as the dharma. It's very liberating to discover your teacher's fallibility and to begin to trust yourself. I stopped turning to Roshi for everything and this shift has allowed our relationship to mature.

"What Zen Center saw as 'coming to grips with the situation,' I saw as a pathology. We did not make the best of a bad situation. Really trying to find a solution had to take into account all the complexities, including Roshi's inability to understand our sense of what the problems were. The community's idea of 'solution' was to ask him to make changes that simply did not make any sense to him. Where is the compassion in that?"

Baker still cannot fathom the degree of hostility generated by his own behavior, but he is not alone in identifying political factions and personal power plays among seniors. He came up against newborn power brokers whose stakes seemed just as proprietary. "I suddenly understood Greek mythology," said Anderson. "What it felt like to the mortals when the Olympian gods were fighting it out." Because of all of the political infighting the crisis unleashed, Zen Center was described as a combat zone long after Baker left.

Several of the seniors who most wanted Baker out left shortly after he did. The residency has been reduced by more than half. Leadership has been tested by councils and appointed abbotships. Baker's energy has not been replaced. There is no one to advance a rigorous cause, and Zen communalism without a strong teacher has been losing the interest of many seniors who have stayed on. But with the benefits of meditation increasingly acknowledged in the society at large, there has been a resurgence of public interest in zazen. Without Baker's charismatic leadership and particular sense of purpose, many people who formerly felt estranged by the dynamics of the community now feel permission to investigate Zen on more personal terms, independent of the biases of community participation. Shared leadership, though certainly not as inspired or visionary as Baker's, has provided ample guidance for new students in their twenties as well as for older people, and Zen Center's programs have continued to cultivate serious commitments to meditation practice. Norman Fischer, a poet and senior priest who has been the practice leader at Green Gulch, says, "Now we've got a student-centered practice where before we were teacher-centered. It's not as flashy, but in the long run I think it's more solid. And the odd thing is—or maybe not so odd— the present circumstance is a natural outgrowth of what Baker Roshi taught us: trust yourself as he, in his crazy way, trusted himself and still does. I have often reflected over the last five years that, strangely enough, things have worked out perfectly. As stubborn as he is, there was probably no other way. And what he created continues. Despite the ruptures that the community suffered, our practice is very solid and we owe that to him."

Fischer, who has consistently been a friend and supporter of Baker Roshi's while remaining at Zen Center, clarified his use of "student-centered," a term that has become identified with antiteacher sentiment: "It doesn't mean that students call the shots or elect the roshi. It means that the student is closely observed by the teacher and that what the teacher uses to turn the wheel of dharma is the student's experience—not his own creative urge. It means teaching by looking at the student deeply rather than looking at the dharma without noticing the student, as Baker Roshi did. It was, I think, an honest mistake, backed by tradition. In Japanese Zen it was considered that the teacher *is* the temple. The students, grounds, food preparations, etc., are expressions of the teacher. This teacher-centered training accorded itself perfectly with Baker Roshi's own karmic predilections. It's a notion that may work well in the hierarchical stratifications of Japanese society, but here it robs people of growing up."

While the term "student-centered" has become associated with political efforts to tailor the un-American autocracy of the Japanese roshi, the way Fischer situates the student in relation to the teacher and the dharma is, he says, "what enables us to walk the edge between the extremes of authoritarianism and democracy—neither of which has worked well at Zen Center."

There are students at Zen Center today who believe that Richard Baker is still a Zen teacher. Some see "Zen teacher" as a legalistic term that has no more to do with personality than "lawyer," "violinist," "electrician." For others, Baker earned the title on his own merits. But most of those same people do not want him back as abbot, drawing a distinction that Reb Anderson outlined: "Zen masters do not have to know others' subjectivities and feelings. Abbots do. Zen masters are not necessarily leaders of spiritual communities. Abbots are. So abbots have to understand the hearts and minds of the community. They must learn to see through the eyes of the community and hear through the ears of the community. Abbots are a subset among Zen masters. A Zen master doesn't have to be an exemplary model for a community. An abbot does. A Zen master can be quite eccentric. An abbot cannot."

Philip Whalen said that the most interesting thing about the Zen Center mess was the $25 million asset. Buddhists with a conservative regard for lineage felt that if a hundred percent of the membership no longer wanted to study with Baker Roshi, then a hundred percent of the membership should have left. But as Whalen points out, however correct this position may be with regard to conservative attitudes toward lineage, at Zen Center it was undermined by a preoccupation with the enormous assets of the organization. Baker had never played by the rules, but that same outsider perspective enabled him to realize a venture few ever dream of starting. From the perspective of his supporters, only after the empire was in sufficient order did his foes claim it as their own, faulting him for the same characteristics that secured the goods to which they were now the ungrateful beneficiaries.

In Japan a priest of twenty years standing would be running his own temple. "Big-roofism" perpetuated clerical careers. In the United States this is not even on the horizon for Buddhist clergy, which leaves the priesthood limited to the dependent role of child-student. Within Zen Center the only adulthood offered was in terms of community administration, but that was devalued by the hierarchy of monasticism. "For the first five, seven, eight years, people went around saying, 'Isn't it remarkable how he can get things done,'" says Baker. "But after ten or twelve years, this same appreciation soured through feelings of inferiority. At age twenty, students were still willing to feel inferior, but adults nearing forty were not. I represented a bottleneck. A lot of people felt empowered by what happened. And I think that's positive. And another positive aspect is that it also empowered me. It has given me permission to teach just as I bloody well want, which I didn't do before. I used to worry too much about *presenting* Buddhism. I thought that was my responsibility. I feel complete permission to do what I want now. And to teach Buddhism exactly as I want to teach it. I didn't feel that way at Zen Center. I participated in the image too much. I stopped dancing the whole time I was there."

By the time Baker left Zen Center, his schedule was so overloaded that the kind of intimate study sessions that he now holds in Santa Fe had become a distant memory. One of the few times that students could even lay eyes on him were his public Sunday lectures. "When I was at Zen Center three to four hundred people would attend my lectures at Green Gulch. They had the sensation of learning. I had the ability to create that sensation, but I learned that I wasn't getting much across. Now I am only interested in taking students whom I can spend a lot of time with. I am taking responsibility for the students and for whom I'll say I'll practice with. I didn't do that before. Anyone was welcome. I never said no. The contract was not clear. I try a lot harder now to be a good teacher. I don't think I am any more successful but I try harder. I try to get more across and I try to find out if people understand what I'm talking about."

In his teaching, Baker seems most compelled by the possibilities for Buddhism to affect the conceptual level of society. "From my point of view, Buddhism is the most sophisticated man-made explanation for what is going on. It is a language. It's not the only language. It's not the only way, but in my opinion it is the most sophisticated language that man has developed that isn't a revealed teaching, that isn't a rule book. In order to integrate Buddhism into the society, you need a critical mass. Biology, physics, psychology, sociology, logic have all become disguised forms for teaching Buddhism in our society. Economics and politics have not. Those ideas in the society make it possible for people to practice. If you don't have a conceptual support within the society, it's real hard to practice. The problems of momentum and inertia can become overwhelming."

From the start Baker's pursuit of Buddhism was so integrated with scientific and sociological phenomena that even he has difficulty identifying himself as a "Buddhist." Within a postmodern planetary view, the term implies limitations, and he identifies more with an international community of social healers who share a "civilizational vision." Unlike other members of this intellectual metasociety, he has had unique testing grounds at his disposal. He has defined himself "as more of a scientist than anything else. I am the test tube and I put things in the test tube to see what will happen. Zen Center was a big social experiment for me."

A small nonresidential center in Santa Fe in the 1980s, however, cannot simulate the laboratory that San Francisco Zen Center in the 1960s provided. Although Baker has described Santa Fe as the only place left where teenagers still aspire to be hippies, the prevailing winds are hardly billowing the sails of social change. Members of the Dharma Sangha new to Zen, moreover, are closer to age forty than age twenty. But none of this has prevented Baker from trying to develop "Buddhist thinking."

From his earliest studies to the present, his question has been, "What does it mean to be a Buddhist?" No text, sutra, or great religious genius has provided answers that he takes for granted. He has suggested that a modern American investigation comes closer to the intelligence of the scientist or the artist than adherence to the traditions of monkhood, and his urbane talks are illustrated with references to Brueghel, Cézanne, and masters of obscure inventions. "Contrary to popular opinion," he says, "although enlightenment is not intellectually attainable, Zen is intellectually comprehensible."

Talking about Baker, Mike Murphy says of his close friend, "He is the most creative Buddhist I know. And part of being creative is to break set. Maybe the model for Dick is more like the belly-laughing Taoist monk than the dour guardian of holy scripture. Certainly he offended the fundamentalist wing of American Buddhism. But he has remained constant in his devotion to the founding principles of Zen. What happened at Zen Center forced him to shed the constraints of religiosity. Anyone who has known Dick as long as I have can see how beneficial this has been. Life is making him more like himself." Murphy also points out that in the two-hundred-year history of American communes, few have lasted as long as Zen Center, and the only residential communities that have stood the test of time are celibate, monastic orders.

"In Japan," says Baker, "all a Zen student is interested in is the teacher's role as teacher, not his personality. All in all he doesn't care what his teacher does in his other roles. He only cares what he does in his role as teacher. If the teacher can be an agent for his enlightenment, he can drink or womanize or whatever. In Japan, if a person has the energy of four or five people, he's allowed to have four or five lives, five houses, five wives, whatever comes with the territory of that energy. We don't have that feeling. We're anti-intellectual and we want to make everything alike."

In 1987 Arnie Kotler's Parallax Press published Thich Nhat Hanh's book *Being Peace.* The Vietnamese monk, whose teachings and international peace work were popularized in the United States by Richard Baker, writes:

Something has happened in some meditation centers. A number of young people found themselves ill at ease with society, so they left in order to come to a meditation center. They ignored the reality that they did not come to a meditation center as an individual. Coming together in a meditation center, they formed another kind of a society. As a society, it has problems like other societies. Before entering the meditation center, they had hoped that they could find peace in meditation. Now, practicing and forming another kind of society, they discover that this society is even more difficult than the larger society. It is composed of alienated people. After some years, they feel frustrated, worse than before coming to the meditation center. This is because we misunderstand meditation, we misunderstand the purpose of meditation. Meditation is for everyone and not just for the person who meditates.

In the early days Baker applied the persuasive American dream of "everything for all" to the attainment of realization. From a belief in the democracy of enlightenment, he arrived at a more traditional distinction between "transmission" and "mercy" Buddhism. The former refers to the yogic path of nonbeing, which only a few adepts will pursue, and the latter refers to a sense of well-being available to large numbers through meditation. Mercy Buddhism creates the context for transmission Buddhism, and in Japan it is the religion of Zen. In the United States conventional religion was so disparaged by the counterculture that Zen practitioners automatically aligned themselves with the mystical path of the adepts. But a generation later, practitioners have had to reckon with the nature of their own aspirations.

Baker explains: "Transmission Buddhism and interaction with the society have always been the most important to me. Mercy Buddhism is the religious area that I am less interested in and less qualified for. It is not necessarily the least important, but it is not where I'm at. It is also the basis for the other two. [The third dimension is the effect of Buddhism on the culture, "the way we structure our sentences and possibilities."] It creates the opportunity for both adept practice and a source for Buddhist thinking for the larger culture. My sense of sangha is a sense of secret language—a dharmic language of emptiness—and of the possibilities of being and nonbeing that permeate our society through ideas, language, and so forth. That is real community for me. My emotional interest in Zen Center and my love for the people in the community, which is still very tangible and real, is not even in the running with my sense of practice and myself as a scientist in practice. But you need to have a certain critical mass around a teacher—unless you're talking about a religious genius—to create support for individual practice, which allows realization practice to occur within mutual confirmation. In that sense, practice needs some kind of community, but it doesn't have to be residential. Then you have the friends of the community—doctors, lawyers, roadworkers, carpenters—people who are influenced by those practicing Buddhism. Those two levels create the synapse that allows society to be affected by Buddhism. And the teacher is at the juncture of those two. Whether or not a residential center develops through that, or will tend to, is something else. Right now, I don't want that."

The continued lack of resolution between Baker and Zen Center sits well with no one. Buddhist teachers, American and Oriental, have stepped in to urge reconciliation. But while talk of reconciliation flies back and forth between New Mexico and California, no plausible form has yet emerged.

"I genuinely don't know," says Baker, "if I am a manifestation of the teachings or not, and in some ways I don't care. I know that I am in a position to try—it's worth a try. I appreciate Suzuki Roshi because he left me on my own. Whether or not what I do is Buddhism I don't know. But I have the authority and willingness to try. And I am still sitting in Suzuki Roshi's mind. When I say I cofounded Zen Center, it's just silly compared to what Suzuki did, who he was. I was his handmaiden. That's all. But I still feel like I belong there, emotionally. And with no good reason. It's just where I belong."

While the American Buddhist community has not reinstated Baker to the status he enjoyed as abbot of San Francisco Zen Center, he is currently a popular figure on what has been called Europe's white-light circuit—a route of urban centers responsive to New Age planetary advocates. Baker has discouraged Europeans from considering residency at Santa Fe, but he welcomes guests. In 1987, for example, an English scientist turned folksinger, a German biologist, and a Swiss couple, both doctors, spent a lengthy part of the summer at Baker's house. All in their late twenties to mid-thirties, they shared an ambiguous relationship to their host: he was a Zen teacher, not quite *their* Zen teacher, sometimes more like a friend, a great guy, and a lot of fun to hang out with. They gathered for meals with Baker, who took his usual place at the head of the table, with Whalen to his left. "This is what it used to be like at my house on Page Street," Baker said with obvious pleasure. "Only multiplied threefold."

The following fall the Europeans hosted Baker during a ten-day tour organized around a conference at the Proteus Institute in Zurich. The night before leaving, Baker announced that his 8:30 A.M. flight out of Albuquerque required his leaving the house by 6:40. It was 7:30 when he eased his Mazda onto the Old Santa Fe Trail leading to the state highway. Picking up considerable speed, he placed on the dash an electronic device that beeps within ticketing distance of radar-patrol cars. With each roadside mileage sign, he looked at the digital odometer and with supreme confidence announced how many more minutes it would take to reach the airport. He did not miss his plane; he arrived a full six minutes before takeoff. But he had forgotten his ticket. "Oh well," he said, "another day, another dharma," and ran off to purchase another ticket for Zurich, via Dallas and New York.

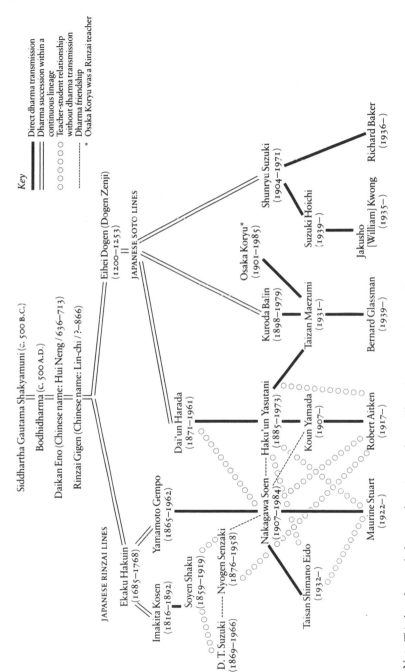

Key

‖ Direct dharma transmission

⫴ Dharma succession within a continuous lineage

○○○○○ Teacher-student relationship without dharma transmission

········· Dharma friendship

* Osaka Koryu was a Rinzai teacher

Siddhartha Gautama Shakyamuni (c. 500 B.C.)

Bodhidharma (c. 500 A.D.)

Daikan Eno (Chinese name: Hui Neng / 636–713)

Rinzai Gigen (Chinese name: Lin-chi / ?–866)

Eihei Dogen (Dogen Zenji) (1200–1253)

JAPANESE RINZAI LINES

JAPANESE SOTO LINES

Ekaku Hakuin (1685–1768)

Yamamoto Gempo (1865–1962)

Imakita Kosen (1816–1892)

Soyen Shaku (1859–1919)

Nyogen Senzaki (1876–1958)

D. T. Suzuki (1869–1966)

Dai'un Harada (1871–1961)

Haku'un Yasutani (1885–1973)

Nakagawa Soen (1907–1984)

Koun Yamada (1907–)

Robert Aitken (1917–)

Taisan Shimano Eido (1932–)

Maurine Stuart (1922–)

Kuroda Baian (1898–1979)

Osaka Koryu* (1901–1985)

Taizan Maezumi (1931–)

Bernard Glassman (1939–)

Shunryu Suzuki (1904–1971)

Suzuki Hoichi (1939–)

Jakusho [William] Kwong (1935–)

Richard Baker (1936–)

Note: This chart shows only those people pertinent to the text. Throughout Japanese names reflect common usage in the United States, even when that usage is contrary to formal Japanese practice, which gives the surname first; the last name listed here is the one commonly identified with the title roshi. Macrons and diacritics have been deleted from Japanese names and nouns throughout this book.

AFTERWORD

One hundred years have passed since Soyen Shaku's address to the Parliament of World Religions. If transplanting a Zen seed to the West was the essence of his mission, then he succeeded unequivocally. Yet in the last ten years Americans have so fiercely wrestled with the forms of the Japanese Zen tradition, that by the end of this century Zen in this country may no longer be anything that Soyen himself might recognize.

When I began this book in 1983, seven American Zen teachers had received teaching authority from Japanese teachers and, at that point, had independent centers. (The two who did not wish to be included in this book were Philip Kapleau Roshi and Walter Norwick Roshi.) Sadly, Stuart Roshi died of cancer on February 26, 1990. She taught to the very end, even after entering the hospital for the last time. Days after the doctors knew that she would not be leaving, she spoke enthusiastically about the coming retreat she planned to conduct at the Cambridge Buddhist Association. She left behind no dharma heirs; how she felt about this remains unknown. Today, her students are scattered. Some have returned to the Cambridge Buddhist Association to study with George Bowman, a dharma heir of the Korean Zen Master Seung Sahn, and a student of the Japanese Rinzai master Joshu Sasaki. Stuart Roshi's death remains a keen loss particularly for women, who continue to struggle against the ancestral patriarchy of the Zen tradition.

At Sonoma Mountain Zen Center, people in their teens and early twenties are coming to investigate Zen practice for the first time in more than a decade. "There is not much in the world for them to look forward to," explains Kwong Roshi.

"They feel despair when they look out into the world." And so after the long dry spell of the 1980s, middle-aged practitioners are being joined by a younger generation.

Aitken Roshi's Palolo Zen Center in Hawaii continues to grow as do his affiliate centers in California, Washington, Texas, Argentina, Germany, and Australia. He has formally transmitted the dharma to four men, and another five men currently hold the title of "apprentice teacher." His choice of successor for Koko An is Nelson Foster, who now leads the Ring of Bones Zendo in North San Juan, California. Aitken Roshi envisions phasing himself out as Foster takes on more responsibility—although when he started the Maui Center in 1969, it was in a house that he and Anne Aitken had purchased for their retirement.

In 1988, the Greyston Seminary in Riverdale was sold and the residents of the Zen Community of New York moved north to a deteriorated section of Yonkers near the site of the Greystone Bakery. In 1991, the Greyston Family Inn opened its first building for homeless families, a formerly derelict nineteen-unit apartment building. The ground floor houses a childcare center that can accommodate ten infants, fifty preschoolers, and an after-school program. Currently under development is the conversion of a Catholic convent into a thirty-five-unit residential center for homeless people with HIV/AIDS. The Greyston Bakery has continued to expand successfully, and is now staffed by members of the job training programs affiliated with the Greyston Family Inn. To date, Glassman Sensei has formally transmitted the dharma to Yuho Harkapsi, Peter Matthiessen, and Robert Kennedy, a Catholic priest.

Still ostracized by most of the new American Buddhist communities, Richard Baker Roshi confines his teaching in the United States to Crestone, Colorado. He is rarely invited to teach at other centers, give talks, or participate in conferences, even those organized specifically for Buddhist teachers. But he spends half the year in Europe, where enthusiastic students either do not know about the Zen Center "mess," or view it as an expression of an immature and sexually uptight society. In addition to the poet Philip Whalen, the only other dharma heir that Baker Roshi recognizes today is the late Issan Dorsey.

Many other American men and women have been sanctioned to teach Zen by such American and Japanese teachers as Eido Roshi, Maezumi Roshi, Philip Kapleau Roshi, and the late Katagiri Roshi. And even more are teaching who have received no sanction at all.

Today, no single selection of five Zen teachers would represent all the different currents of Zen in the United States. Even in cases of "official sanction" the ideals of realization have often been abandoned, and students who have had no personal experience of seeing directly into their own true nature have been elevated to the status of "teacher." Some who are now teaching have broken off long-term apprenticeships with male teachers whose ethical behavior became too problematic for them to support. Cut off from the face-to-face intimacy considered critical to the traditional ideal of transmission, they subsequently sought accreditation from other teachers, who, in certain cases, were outside their own lineages. Within the Zen centers, no scandal has reached the same proportions as Richard Baker's fall from favor, but other teachers have been publicly criticized for having sex with students, as well as for excessive drinking and misuse of funds. On the one hand, teachers with proper credentials have been publicly criticized for unethical actions. On the other, teachers with no formal certificates have attained respect for their virtuous, if unenlightened, behavior. To Americans new to Zen, it appears that dharma transmission, ethical behavior, and some discernible sign of awakened mind have nothing to do with each other.

Historically, face-to-face transmission has been the life blood of the Zen teachings for each new generation. The system was designed to encourage an experiential embodiment of the teachings and to counter the natural propensity of spiritual vigor to stagnate. At this point in the United States, the widespread disregard for the traditional values of dharma transmission—in addition to the libertine antagonism that Americans display for authority—has left the Japanese lineages of Zen without a coherent system of assigning teaching authority. With their increasingly ubiquitous use, titles such as reverend, sensei, roshi, even abbot, often sound whimsical, hollow, and opportunistic. Yet, the fact that even asking if there is a problem seems irrelevant to many Zen practitioners may be the gravest indictment of the failure of dharma transmission to function as a guideline for authenticity in Zen teachings.

The Zen system of dharma transmission remains unique. There are dozens of Buddhist sects in which the priests, meditation instructors, and lineage holders arrive at their positions through systematic levels of study in ways not dissimilar from advancing to college from high school, or from graduate to postgraduate studies. In some traditions leadership is passed from father to son; Tibetan lineages often employ reincarnation to confer spiritual status. In the Zen ideal, "transmission" does not refer to something given and received, but to the recognition of one enlightened mind by another. Even in its more prosaic implications of authority conferred, transmission addressed the issue of awakening and affirmed the value of enlightenment. Yet enlightenment—oddly enough—has become all but a dirty word among many American Zennists. Not surprisingly, the devaluation of dharma transmission coincides with a devaluation of enlightenment itself.

Many of today's American practitioners speak of enlightenment and ethics as separate and contradictory concerns. The quest for enlightenment has been derided of late as the romantic and mythic aspiration of antiquated patriarchal monasticism, while ethics has become the rallying vision of householder Zen. To pursue the unknowable state of enlightenment is now often regarded as an obstacle to a practice that emphasizes "everyday Zen," a state of mindful attention in the midst of ordinary life.

The archetypal debate between Rinzai and Soto teachings— or between those who urge the importance of a specific, sudden enlightenment experience and those who emphasize the gradual growth of clear awareness in daily activity—has historically defined the two main schools of Japanese Zen. Yet the debate shifts considerably when it enters a society whose mainstream fails to recognize or validate the enlightenment experience. To apprehend that all phenomena is impermanent, essentially empty, without a fixed identity; to experience the false fabricated sense of self as a delusion; to allow the boundaries that imprison the ego-centered "I" to dissolve; and to cultivate a view that does not judge, compare, compete, and criticize are not goals prized by normative American social values. Further, in the United States there is still no cultivation of the traditional monastic environment in which both the Soto and Rinzai Zen schools flourished. In Japan, these sectarian differences reflected variations in emphasis, style, and methodology, yet occurred within the common parameters of monastic life and within an ideological framework in which the virtues of the "falling away of body and mind"—to use Zen Master Dogen's description of his enlightenment experience—were valued. Novices who believed that such an experience—known as kensho or satori—defined the ultimate target of Zen practice were cautioned by masters that it was only the first step. Zen's reputation for eccentricity is based both on its use of harsh and unusual methods for priming the experience of emptiness, and on its use of harsh and unusual methods for disabusing disciples of an attachment to emptiness. In Zen the main obstacles to clarity are not so much in the actual experience, negative or positive, as in the attitude and attachment that attends the experience.

Contemporary advocates for everyday Zen affirm classic Soto teachings; but its focus on awareness in the midst of activity supported a consistent awakened state and was not used to denigrate enlightenment. Also, the Soto emphasis on mindful activity cautioned against confusing a momentary flash of insight—or even a deep experience of emptiness—with the mature and seasoned understanding that qualifies an awakened mind.

Recently an American Zen teacher said to me, "I don't give a shit about enlightenment." His language may have resembled that of the old Zen masters, who often employed shock value to scramble habitual mind-set, especially when it came to "ideas about" enlightenment. But, the old masters' and the new American versions only appear similar.

But perhaps the American has in fact scrambled basic Zen stages of understanding: first, that mountains are mountains and rivers are rivers; next, that mountains are not mountains and rivers are not rivers; and finally, that mountains are mountains and rivers are rivers. The second stage concentrates on the essential emptiness of all phenomena, on the "isness" of a mountain empty of language and description, of function, history, context, and aesthetics. In this stage, emptiness is distinct from form; in the third stage, form and emptiness are one, not two; but the experience of the second stage is what mediates the difference between the ordinariness of the first and third stages. To eliminate this distinction, to misuse the profound teachings of everyday Zen, to imply that the first and the third stages are the same, or to forfeit the third stage in favor of the first, accounts for a kind of Zen—if it can still be called Zen at all—that Soyen Shaku would not recognize.

In Zen literature dozens of teaching stories depict awakened masters trying to ground a disciple's ambitious quest for enlightenment in the daily activities of washing one's eating bowls, folding one's robes, cleaning the toilet. The old masters themselves often employed shock to scramble their disciples' ideas, concepts, hopes, and desires for and about enlightenment. Yet to exploit this as license to denigrate enlightenment seems a grievous and perhaps peculiarly American misinterpretation.

In traditional monastic settings, the attachment to emptiness among Zen monks occurred so frequently that it became a well-known phenomenon—the legendary Achilles' heel of Zen and the catalyst throughout Zen history for voluminous attacks on the attachment to enlightenment. But then, criticism lay in the domain of the masters, *enlightened* masters who had stepped off the hundred-foot pole, who had come down from the metaphorical mountaintop to enter the marketplace. Enlightenment disparaged by practitioners, students or teachers, who have not viewed reality from the top of the hundred-foot pole, who have had no personal experience of an awakened mind, is something else altogether.

In the absence of any widespread interest in monasticism, the thrust in American centers of Japanese-derived Zen is toward accommodating lay practitioners. In theory, this does not diminish the supreme place that enlightenment has held in the Zen tradition, but in actuality it does. Everything about the Zen sense of an enlightened mind—the concept, the language, the path, the view—is on shaky ground in a society which considers silence, emptiness, and sitting still ("doing nothing") worthless. This does not make lay practice impossible, but it does make it extremely difficult; and the attempt to fit Zen into the conventions of our society endangers its essence. While the old masters agreed that getting stuck in emptiness was a kind of "Zen sickness," the literature also makes it clear that the path of uncovering one's own original enlightenment is an all-consuming affair, rife with ego-obstacles, extreme mental anguish, and truths that hurt and blind. This is not the quest for mental and physical comfort that characterizes the American way of life.

"Buddha" means awakened one. When Zen practice was first offered in this country, waking up looked like a vital alternative to the bureaucratic clergy and dead rituals familiar to many American childhoods. However naively and ignorantly, Americans pursued enlightenment with good intentions; D. T. Suzuki introduced a somewhat romantic version of satori and Shunryu Suzuki Roshi, founder of the San Francisco Zen Center, never spoke about it—and encouraged his students to follow his example. Soen Roshi despised "the stink of Zen," which could permeate the robes of a monk drunk on his attachment to enlightenment. The consistent message of all Zen teachers however, which was taken very seriously by idealistic, democratic Americans, reiterated Shakyamuni Buddha's good news: that realization of one's own true nature is the birthright of every human being. Yet in the specific domain of Zen training, the methods for cultivating a realized mind evolved in and were tailored for a monastic setting. Since Americans were apparently not yet ready to live by the traditional monastic rules, which included abstinence from drugs, alcohol, and sex, Ameican Zen in the sixties combined monastic ideals with communes. The activities of daily life, common to both households and monastics, of cooking, washing dishes, working in the garden, changing flat tires were—theoretically—accomplished with meditative attention.

In Zen Master Dogen's teachings on "practice-enlightenment," attention to details and meditative mindfulness in action manifest emptiness particularized. In particularity, vastness is known; total attention requires a mind emptied of distraction, habitual patterns, and self-preoccupation. But in the actual life of American communities throughout the 1970s nothing in fact replaced the focus on enlightenment or formal meditation. Attempts to "democratize" Zen practice did not prove successful; the activity, however mindful, of raising children, working in a bakery, or tending the gardens, never achieved the same status as zazen, and despite a certain amount of lip service, zazen alone remained identified with realization. Try as they might, Zen teachers could not disabuse American students from an attachment to zazen as both the surest expression of, and route to, enlightenment.

Throughout the 1980s students got unhooked from an attachment to zazen and to enlightenment, but mostly through anger and negativity, not by stepping off the hundred-foot pole. If teachers helped at all, it was by default. In the midst of sexual scandals and abuses of power, realization itself became disparaged. In this climate the quest for enlightenment began to lose its value, and trust in the dharma was more and more frequently abandoned in favor of psychotherapeutic approaches to problem solving. With the behavior of teachers at the center of concern, ethical probity and the psychological attributes became the standards by which to measure a teacher's capacity to transmit the dharma.

However satisfying to the linear mind of the Western practitioner, a simple shift from an awakened mind to ethical or personality norms don't add up. Ethical behavior may or may not be born of fundamental insight into the nature of reality, and it may or may not be released through the compassion inherent in one's own Buddha-nature. And if the essential emptiness of one's own Buddha-nature is not plumbed as the source for ethical action and compassion, and if ethics is separated from realization, then what is called "Buddhist ethics" offers nothing new to a predominantly Christian society.

In the United States, when Zen centers were starting up in the 1960s, what compelled Americans was not just a polite, antiseptic, prettied-up addition to religious plurality, replete with elitist aesthetics. Zen challenged entire paradigms of Western thought, of Western psychology, even the very beliefs that individuals cherished about their own identities. It was precisely its marginality that imbued Zen with a moral vigor that was so lacking in established religions.

With time the baby-boomer, almost all-white Zen sangha grew up, got married, had kids, and worried about money. During the 1980s, Western Buddhist centers attracted so few young people it seemed American Zen might suffer death by attrition, but physically the centers grew anyway. Supported by the wealth of young rebels grown into good citizens, temples were built, country centers purchased, and factories converted to meditation halls. The middle way became solidly middle-class.

The householder life has long been lauded as an exemplary way to practice Zen. But today the householder discourse is too often used to justify having one's cake and eating it too—one can have sex, make babies, hold a job, develop a career, keep house and use each of these activities as an opportunity to practice without missing a beat in terms of spiritual aspiration. To abandon monasticism in favor of householder activities, or to favor ethical behavior over enlightenment demands, at the very least, new structures, new methods, new practices. But that has not happened, and the recent focus on ethical behavior complies nicely, if not somewhat self-righteously, with the dualistic moral considerations necessary to the householder lifestyle. Furthermore, Buddhist laity were traditionally as dependent on community as was monasticism itself. In North America, aside from a handful of residential centers, "the community" for Zen lay practitioners is defined by—job, race, sex, neighborhood—and by the culture-bound values with which they are inbued. Yet it is not simply a historic accident that Buddhism begins with a person walking away from a life of luxury, from a palace, a family, arts, from security and every comfort. Nor is it an accident that Zen was nourished in a monastic setting, by students and teachers who chose to abandon their worldly existence.

The most compelling question today is whether the Americanization of Zen now underway is a necessary process of cultural adaptation or if what we have confidently called "Americanization" has become a justification for the co-optation of Zen by secular materialists. In the 1960s and 1970s, American practitioners were arrogant about Zen, proud of their engagement in an enlightenment tradition that employed personal experience as opposed to blind faith or the devotional, or community practices, of their childhoods—or of other sects of Buddhism. Zen engaged its American adherents in such a radical alternative to common encounters with religion that it became embarrassing for long-time practitioners to even entertain the idea that perhaps conventional congregational worship was what one wanted or needed most from a religion. Perhaps deep down many Americans are concluding that community is more important than personal insight; perhaps sitting quietly and calming the mind provides psychological benefits without offering the inspiration to go further. Perhaps after twenty years of zazen with no remarkable experiences to report, they feel betrayed by false seductions. In short, rather than say, "I'm not so interested in getting enlightened"—or, "I am not so interested any more," or "I no longer believe in the efficacy of enlightenment," Zen practitioners are beginning to disparage enlightenment itself. Again, when a great Zen master knocks enlightenment, it is one thing; but the denigration voiced by many Americans has been too often accompanied by an unacknowledged lack of aspiration, an appeal for approval from the dominant Christian culture, an attachment to personal comfort, and an indulgent lifestyle. The point here is not to argue in favor of an enlightenment tradition over other forms of religious endeavor—either within or outside of Buddhism—but to relocate enlightenment at the center of the Zen tradition.

The replacement of enlightenment by the ethical standards favored by many of today's Zen practitioners may be attributed in part to the failure of contemporary Buddhist teachers to convincingly integrate spiritual awakening with their behavior whether that behavior takes a conventional form or not. Yet this both feeds on and fuels the human resistance to the unknown and the unknowable, which lies at the heart of all religious pursuit, and which has been so successfully suppressed by organized religion. At this time, there is no outstanding public religious voice in the culture at large (no heir, for example, to Thomas Merton) immersed in a view of reality that does not support the socioeconomic political—and religious—establishment.

The United States remains thoroughly attached to proving, validating, and authenticating even mysticism. Humanist psychologists now tell us that Buddhism and psychology are exactly the same; Buddhist physicists applaud scientific proof for the unity of all creation; New Age pundits and stress-reduction experts expound the feel-good effects of meditation; and Zen leaders place ethical norms at the center of their concerns. What all these claims have in common is a reference to what can be known, what can be grasped, to what can be controlled and apprehended by the conventional mind. In these "Americanized" paradigms Zen never strays from the comfort of what is familiar, and is thereby diminished. How radically different this is from Soen Roshi's exhortation to Zen monks to "apply ourselves day after day, year after year, to the study of the 'Unthinkable.'"

In Zen, precept study and the commitment to the Eightfold Path are means of purifying the mind. The more one's mind is cleansed of defilements, the greater the possibility that one's behavior will be liberated from greed, anger, and ignorance. To concentrate on behavior without penetrating the mind-source risks replicating the narrow interpretation of scripture embraced by Christian fundamentalists. According to Zen teachings, getting attached to ethics is no better or worse than getting attached to enlightenment. But the United States has no shortage of blueprints for ethical behavior while enlightenment is too important to be sabotaged by the misdeeds of a handful of teachers.

The importance of maintaining an enlightenment tradition extends far beyond the parameters of Zen and into the quality of American culture. Zen has no monopoly on understanding emptiness. World literature, East and West, is filled with expressions not of "Zen," but of unity and nonduality, which attest to the universality of this insight. What is unique about the Zen tradition is the explicit focus on a rigorous methodology designed to prime this realization.

Only by employing both ideology and method can the authority of the Zen tradition affirm an awakened sensibility for any society in which it is allowed to flourish. The abandonment of religious virtue has left this culture aggressively antagonistic to the pursuit of the unknown, the unknowable, and the mystical realms of reality. The original enthusiasm for Zen in the United States was not just for personal discovery, but for the possibility of developing an appreciation for the unknown in an excessively cluttered society—it was an effort to break ground for new possibilities. What we need to know cannot arise from what we know now. Our liberation from personal and collective suffering must derive from what we cannot envision, what is beyond our imagination, even beyond our dreams of what is possible.

One day an American student asked a Japanese Zen master, "Is enlightenment really possible?"

He answered, "If you're willing to allow for it."

INDEX OF NAMES

Parentheses indicate dharma names

ABOUT THE AUTHOR

Helen Tworkov is a trained anthropologist and a long time student of Zen. She is the founder and editor-in-chief of *Tricycle: The Buddhist Review*, a quarterly publication focusing on Buddhism in America. She currently divides her time between New York City and Nova Scotia.

KODANSHA GLOBE

International in scope, this series offers distinguished books that explore the lives, customs, and mindsets of peoples and cultures around the world.

For information on future titles, please contact the Kodansha Editorial Department at Kodansha America, Inc., 114 Fifth Avenue, New York, NY 10011. To order, contact your local bookseller or call 1-800-788-6262 (mention code G1).